CENTRAL ASIA
through writers' eyes

KATHLEEN HOPKIRK

ELAND
London

First published by John Murray (Publishers) Ltd in 1993

This edition published by Eland Publishing Ltd
61 Exmouth Market, London EC1R 4QL in 2013

Copyright © Kathleen Hopkirk 1993

ISBN 978 1 906011 84 0

Cover image: *A Horseman waiting for a game of* kupkari *in the ruins
of Afrasiab* by Hugues Krafft, from his *A Travers le Turkestan Russe*
by kind permission of the Central Asian Collection of Pip Rau

Inside photographs by kind permission of the Central Asian Collection
of Pip Rau, specifically the very rare photograph study
A Travers le Turkestan Russe by Hugues Krafft

Text set in Great Britain by James Morris

Printed in Spain by GraphyCems, Navarra

Contents

A NOTE ON SPELLINGS

Place names in Central Asia are notoriously difficult to render into English. There are often several different names for the same place, arising from the various languages used by merchants who travelled there. There are also variant spellings caused by transliteration into the Western alphabet from the original Turki, Persian, Arabic, Mongolian or Chinese. On the whole I have used the version current at the end of the nineteenth and beginning of the twentieth centuries, which would have been familiar to most of the travellers I have quoted from.

However, for Chinese names there is the additional problem of the new Pinyin spellings: for example Xinjiang instead of Sinkiang, Xuan Zang rather than Hsuan-tsang. Unpronounceable though some of these may seem, the modern visitor to China cannot avoid encountering them. I have stuck to the traditional spellings, but both are given in the index.

PREFACE TO THE 1993 EDITION

Central Asia covers a vast swathe of territory, two thousand miles from east to west, and I have had to restrict the scope of this book in order to keep it to a manageable size. The fifteen towns and cities which I have included all lay astride the Silk Road, one of the great trade routes of the ancient world. All have witnessed extraordinary events over the centuries. For reasons of space I have left out cities like Xian and Lanzhou which, although once on the Silk Road, are in China proper, as well as the whole of Afghanistan and Tibet, which were never on the main trade routes. Tibet has in any case been thoroughly covered in numerous recent books, while Afghanistan is currently so unstable – not to mention strewn with literally millions of anti-personnel mines – as to be virtually unvisitable.

In gathering material for this book I owe a particular debt to the works of Sir Fitzroy Maclean, the father of modern writing on Central Asia, and John Keay, the master historian of Himalayan exploration. But most of all I am indebted to my husband Peter Hopkirk, who shared with me his knowledge of the region and its travellers, and his extensive library.

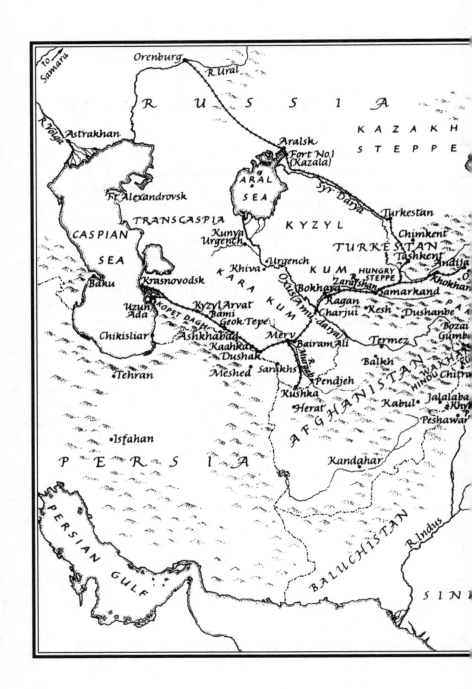

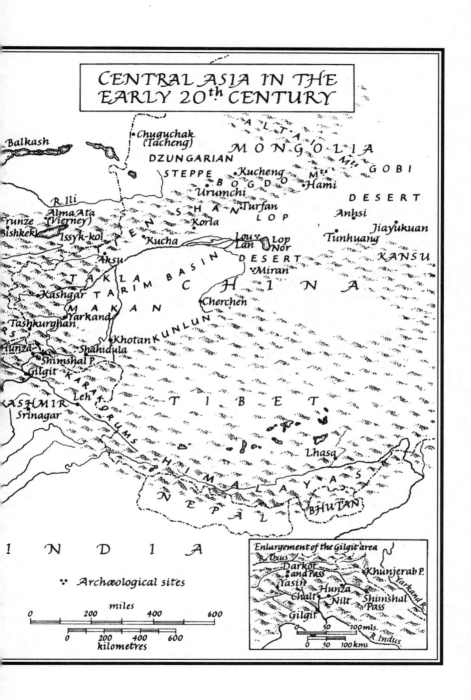

CENTRAL ASIA IN THE EARLY 20th CENTURY

Balkash

Chuguchak (Tacheng)

ALTA'I

MONGOLIA

DZUNGARIAN

STEPPE

BOGDO Mts

GOBI

Kucheng

Urumchi

Hami

DESERT

R. Ili

Alma Ata (Vierney)

Frunze

Bishkek

Issyk-kol

T EN SHAN

Turfan

Korla

LOP

Anhsi

Jiayukuan

Tunhuang

KANSU

Kucha

Lou-Lan

Lop Nor

Aksu

DESERT

TAKLA

TARIM BASIN

CHINA

Miran

Kashgar

MAKAN

Cherchen

Tashkurghan

Yarkand

KUNLUN

Hunza

Khotan

Shimshal P.

Shahidula

Gilgit

KARAKORUMS

TIBET

KASHMIR

Srinagar

Leh

Lhasa

HIMALAYAS

NEPAL

BHUTAN

INDIA

❀ *Archæological sites*

miles

| 0 | 200 | 400 | 600 |

| 0 | 200 | 400 | 600 |
kilometres

Enlargement of the Gilgit area

R. Oxus

Darkot and Pass

Yasin

Khunjerab P.

Hunza

Chalt

Nilt

Shimshal Pass

Yarkand R.

Gilgit

R. Indus

| 0 | 50 | 100 mls. |

| 0 | 50 | 100 kms |

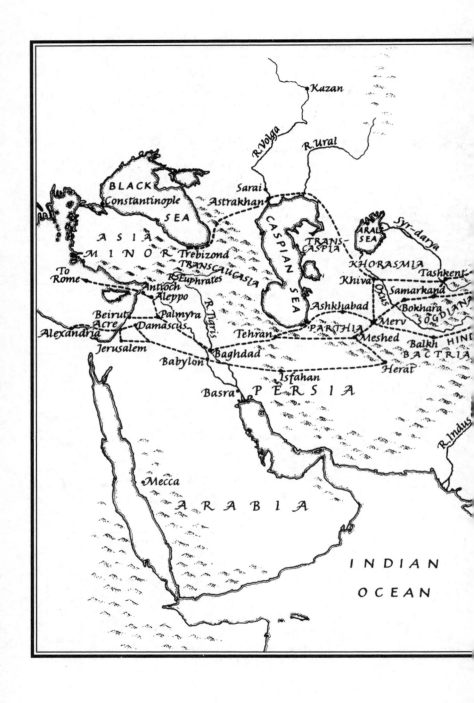

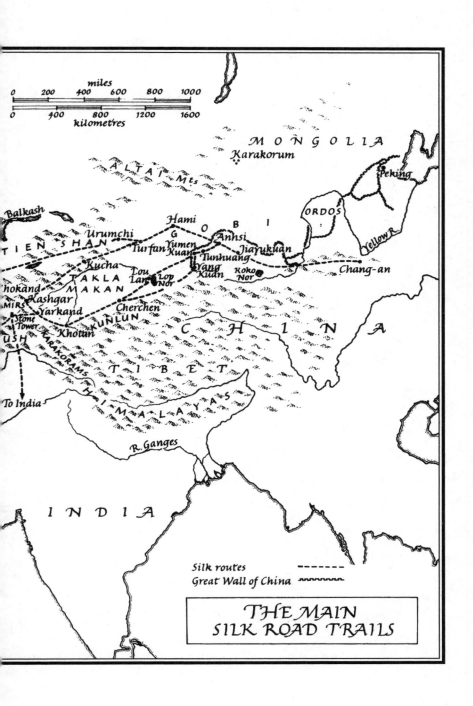

miles
0   200   400   600   800   1000
0   400   800   1200   1600
kilometres

M O N G O L I A
Karakorum

Peking

A L T A I - Mts

Balkash
TIEN SHAN
Urumchi
Hami
G   O   B   I
Anhsi
ORDOS
Yellow R.

Turfan
Yumen
Kuan
Jiayukuan

Kucha
TAKLA
MAKAN
Lou
Lan
Lop
Nor
Tunhuang
Yang
Kuan
Koko
Nor
Chang-an

hokand
MIRS
Kashgar
Yarkand
Cherchen
KUNLUN
C   H   I   N   A

Stone
Tower
Khotan
KARAKORAMS
T   I   B   E   T

USH
H I M A L A Y A S

To India

R. Ganges

I   N   D   I   A

Silk routes   - - - - - - -
Great Wall of China   ~~~~~~~

THE MAIN
SILK ROAD TRAILS

INTRODUCTION
The Rise, Fall and Rise Again of Central Asia

AFTER YEARS OF almost total obscurity, Central Asia suddenly finds itself caught up in events that have changed the world for ever. Following the collapse of Soviet power there, five entirely new countries exist where stagnation had ruled for seventy years. At the same time, the political whirlwind which swept Communism aside in Russian Central Asia has cast doubts on the other half of the region, today still ruled by China.

Three of the new countries have borders with China's vast Sinkiang-Uighur autonomous region, where some six million Muslims have far closer ethnic and religious affinities with their kinsmen across the Pamirs than with their Han Chinese rulers. For throughout Central Asia the forces of religion and nationalism have proved immune to political indoctrination and are now reasserting themselves with an alarming vigour. Anxious to maintain a political grip on the region and to forestall the spread of ethnic unrest across its own borders, Peking was quick to recognise Kazakhstan, Tajikistan, Uzbekistan, Kirghizstan and Turkmenistan, and to sign trade agreements with them. Other powerful neighbours – Iran, Pakistan and Turkey – have also rushed to fill the vacuum left by Moscow's hasty retreat, while representatives of Western consumer society have opened fast-food and fast-clothes emporia in the unlikeliest of places. Central Asia's new leaders, meantime, have suddenly to grapple with the complexities of modern capitalism on the one hand, while being assailed on the other by the conflicting doctrine of Islamic fundamentalism.

For the businessman, diplomat, technical adviser or tourist travelling there today, events are moving so swiftly that no book can attempt to provide up-to-the-minute political or economic information. What I have tried to do in this volume is to set the scene for Central Asia's volatile present by drawing on the experiences of some of those who were there during its equally turbulent past. I have quoted from the diaries and memoirs of travellers from the first century BC to the present day, but the majority date from the nineteenth and early twentieth centuries. These are people with whom we can easily identify, and the events they witnessed or took part in are still highly relevant to the situation today.

But before setting out for this region which was for so long regarded as the back-of-beyond, it is worth taking a brief look at its history. For many people the words 'Central Asia' conjure up a hazy vision of slant-eyed Mongol horsemen sweeping westwards in the Middle Ages, pillaging and destroying everything in their path. And yet religion, art and commerce had flourished there for a thousand years before Genghis Khan and his hordes burst upon the scene in the thirteenth century, and the region had seen the rise and fall of many other conquerors.

Central Asia is a vast region of steppe, desert, mountain and high plateau stretching from the Caspian Sea in the west to Mongolia in the east. Bounded to the north by the endless swamps and forests of Siberia, its southern limits are the long bastion of mountain ranges passing across Iran, Afghanistan, Pakistan, India and Tibet. Contained within this huge oval, 2,000 miles wide, are the world's highest mountains and no fewer than five deserts: the Gobi, Taklamakan, Lop, Kyzyl Kum and Kara Kum. In much of Central Asia man scrapes a living with difficulty, for the climate is as extreme as the terrain, yet wherever there is water flowers blossom and fruit grows in profusion. For at least 5,000 years there have been oasis settlements alongside the steppe culture of nomadic herdsmen and hunters, and the antagonism between these two ways of life overshadowed the region right up to the nineteenth century, when Chinese and Russian expansion curtailed the migrations of the nomads.

Water – the gold of the desert – was the single most crucial factor for all the peoples living in Central Asia. If there was drought, the grass withered, the wells dried up and the herdsmen moved *en masse* to new grazing grounds. Irrigation was essential for the farmers' crops, and if their ditches were neglected, or destroyed by marauders, the entire settlement could be rapidly reclaimed by nature, leaving little trace behind.

But in spite of all the difficulties, civilisation somehow survived. Sometimes the settled peoples tamed their primitive conquerors, sometimes they ran away and hid until the danger had passed, sometimes they were driven out to a completely new area where they had to start all over again. But in times of peace and stability enormous progress was made. City-states grew up, embellished with fine buildings, artists and craftsmen developed their skills, scholars argued and merchants traded. For despite the daunting barriers of desert and mountain, there were always men enterprising enough to load up their donkeys or camels and try their luck in a new market. In time these caravan trails became established trade routes, criss-crossing the whole of Central Asia and extending – wars and marauders permitting – as far as China in the east and Antioch in the west. And along with trade came ideas and influences which often had a profound effect on the lives of people eager for knowledge, or simply curious, or glad of a diversion from the ceaseless toil of subsistence farming. Much later, this network of trade and endeavour, art and religion, became known collectively as the Silk Road.

Sir Aurel Stein, the archaeologist, once said of Central Asia: 'On looking at the map it might well seem as if this vast region had been intended by Nature far more to serve as a barrier between the lands which have given our globe its great civilisations than to facilitate the exchange of their cultural influences.' But in fact, as his own excavations were to show, the cultures of ancient Greece, Rome, India and China met and merged in Central Asia, giving rise to a form of art which Stein called Serindian. And influences closer to home, from Persia and the Arab Near East, and indeed from some of the steppe nomads who went on to found civilisations of their own, all left a lasting imprint on the region. All the great religions of the world left their mark there, too: indeed the two most powerful forces behind the interchange of ideas in Central Asia were religion and trade. But how did it all begin?

Probably the earliest inhabitants of northern Central Asia were tent-dwelling nomads, who about 2,000 BC began to move westwards and southwards, some groups settling, others moving on with their flocks and herds, until they had taken over the whole of southern Central Asia and had spilled over on to the Iranian plateau. They were an Aryan or 'white' race, with no written language, but by the ninth century BC they were being referred to in Assyrian records, and were probably the forerunners of the Medes and Persians. The northern steppes then became the territory of the Scythians and Sarmatians (also 'white' men), who likewise were hunters and herdsmen with no written culture but who were nevertheless skilled craftsmen, and who seem to have had links with the eastern extremities of Greek civilisation. At some point in pre-history the Scythians and Sarmatians made one of those periodic leaps forward in man's development: they learned to ride horses. An offshoot of this was the invention of trousers, when the rest of humanity was clad in skins, robes or kilts – if indeed it wore anything at all.

The art of horsemanship turned the Central Asian herdsmen into formidable warriors, and the Scythians were soon developing a form of armour while the Sarmatians seem to have invented the stirrup. Both perfected the technique of firing arrows from the saddle, and the famous 'Parthian shot' which later helped to rout the Romans was almost certainly learned from the Scythians – who may, in fact, have been the Parthians' ancestors. Herodotus, writing in the fifth century BC described how the Scythian chiefs distributed booty according to the number of enemy heads each warrior produced after a battle. The more successful warriors had entire cloaks made of scalped heads. But despite their ferocity, the Scythians were themselves the victims of the next great migration. Their sister-race, the Sarmatians, who lived to the east of them, had over the centuries become their bitter enemies, and around the third century BC they invaded the Scythian lands. Most probably this was because of an irresistible pressure on their own eastern borders, for the peoples of Manchuria and the Mongolian plateau had nowhere to go but west as they expanded. To the east was the sea (once the Korean peninsula had been populated); to the north the impenetrable *taiga* of Siberia was quite unsuited to horse-borne nomads. And to the south lay the advanced and powerful land of China, which had erected 1,400 miles of wall along its northern boundaries expressly to keep the barbarians out.

Whatever the reason, the Scythians were moved on – many of them to southern Russia and the Caucasus – killing, displacing or absorbing any intervening peoples. Perhaps the Huns were to blame, for soon after this the Chinese Annals, or historical records, began to refer to a race of barbarians whom they called the Hsiung-nu. These people seem to have been neighbours of the Sarmatians and to have picked up horsemanship from them. In time-honoured fashion they then proceeded to drive their neighbours out, and themselves took control of a vast area stretching from western Manchuria, through Mongolia and southern Siberia, into the Tarim Basin and right up to the Pamirs. The Hsiung-nu, later to be called the Huns and become the scourge of Europe in the Dark Ages, were a Turanian or Turkic people, with a language quite different from the Iranian tongue of the Scythians and Sarmatians. They were nevertheless a 'white' race, with prominent noses and deep-set eyes; according to the Chinese they were also 'very hairy'. The Chinese hated and despised the unlettered and uncultured Hsiung-nu, but they had good reason to fear their raids, and during the second century BC they determined to crush them.

The story of how China subdued the Huns and made contact with the West is told in the ninth chapter (THE SILK ROAD). Briefly, after a war of attrition which cost the lives of thousands of Chinese soldiers, the Hsiung-nu submitted to the Han Emperor in 52 BC. This enabled regular trade routes to be established between China and ultimately Rome, where there was great demand for Chinese silk, via the various territories of Central Asia and the Middle East. Naturally, no caravan travelled the entire distance: the route divided itself into numerous segments, and the merchandise changed hands many times. This in turn necessitated a regular string of staging-posts and entrepôts, where goods could be stored and bartered, and caravans equipped. Of course the Huns were not permanently eliminated in 52 BC. They continued to be a nuisance, and raided caravans whenever they thought they could get away with it, but while China was strong they had to keep a respectful distance. Forever after, the power of the Han dynasty and the submission by the barbarians in 52 BC were celebrated by the Chinese as a glorious chapter in their history. Six hundred years later a poet of the Tang dynasty was inspired to write the following poem:

> Beyond the frontiers lie the hard winters and the raging winds;
> The waters of Chiao Ho are frozen over with huge icebergs.
> On the Han Lake come the hundred layers of waves,
> Over the Yin mountains lie thousands of *li* of snow.

The garrisons live hard, gazing out for beacon-fires.
On the highest peaks, the banners of the commander are
    unfurled,
But the soldiers fold theirs: the hunt begins.
They water their horses at the foot of the Great Wall.
Interminable the footprints of horses over endless cold sands.
Hear on the frontier the howling of the north-wind.
We entered the land of the Huns and subdued them in their
    desert strongholds.
To the west were the natives of Chiang, who played on flutes
    and cymbals to welcome us,
Here the Huns themselves laid down their arms and
    surrendered.
The soldiers of Han returned in triumph.
High in the air flew the banner of victory.
A tablet was engraved with their names, for the sake of
    posterity.
In battle with barbarians peace was assured,
And on the altar of Heaven we sang our victory.

Li Shih-ming, AD 597–649
(translated by Wang Sheng-chih)

Having for the time being subdued the Huns, the Chinese were pleased to discover that there were civilised countries to the west, or at any rate semi-settled peoples who had more interest in trade and friendly relations than in war and raiding. The 'natives of Chiang' mentioned in the poem seem to have been the Tibetans, many of whom were in fact rather fierce in this period and more given to banditry than playing on flutes and cymbals. But beyond them, in what is now Afghanistan, were the Bactrians, a peaceable trading people who lived next to a vast territory ruled by the Yueh-chih, former nomads forced westwards by some earlier population migration. Similar but distinct former steppe-dwellers were to be found in the Ferghana valley and in Khorasmia, south of the Aral Sea – tribes or peoples for whom the horse was still pre-eminent but who were in the process of transforming themselves into what the Chinese regarded as civilised. Already they lived mainly in houses rather than tents, they had shops and farms, and they were taking an interest in religion and art. Beyond them in the west lay the powerful kingdoms of Persia and Parthia, which had by now thrown off the Greek yoke, and to the south lay Gandhara and the land of India. For the first time, envoys of China began to hear on their travels of another empire as large as their own – Rome, with whom the Parthians bartered Chinese silk for gold.

Around the beginning of our era China extended its Great Wall and set up garrisons with beacon towers to protect the flow of trade along the routes to the west. Gradually, the fusion of ideas and culture which had already occurred when Alexander the Great encouraged his generals to take Asian wives in the fourth century BC (he himself had married a Bactrian princess) was enriched by the introduction of Chinese influences. China already had a very advanced culture and civil structure, which allowed philosophy as well as art and poetry to flourish, and Chinese scholars were interested in the new religions of Buddhism, Zoroastrianism, Manichaeism and later Christianity which began to come to their notice. All of these, and especially Buddhism, had their converts both in Central Asia and in China, where they joined the existing creeds of Taoism and Confucianism.

During the first century AD trade prospered, for much of Central Asia was ruled by the Kushans, a Buddhist people descended from the Yueh-chih, whose empire stretched from northern India, through Afghanistan and much of what was to become Russian Central Asia, to the shores of the Aral Sea. Caravans were allowed to travel freely through their territories, unlike those of the Parthians to the west. Parthia was another great power of the day, and an unavoidable middleman in the trade with Rome, but the exchange of goods had to take place on the frontier, for its borders were closed to all foreigners. The whole of southern Turkmenistan was included in Parthia at this time, and the remains of the Parthian city of Nissa can be visited near Ashkhabad. East of the Kushan empire lay a third great power, China, approached via the various trails of the Silk Road which skirted the Taklamakan desert or passed through the northern foothills of the Tien-shan. These routes were particularly vulnerable to marauders, for the oasis staging-posts were many miles apart, and the Chinese garrisons often needed to summon reinforcements by means of beacon fires. When the Han dynasty was temporarily ousted by a usurper in AD 8, the Huns were quick to take advantage of the ensuing disorder. Oases were raided, caravans plundered, and in AD 23 the

Huns were even bold enough to invade northern China and sack the capital. They were soon driven out and after AD 25 a restored Han dynasty gradually regained control of the trade routes.

For some of the oasis kingdoms of the Tarim Basin, though, China seemed very far away. Khotan, Yarkand and Kashgar, in particular, often found it more expedient to be on good terms with the Huns or the Kushans. The Huns simply exacted tribute, offering nothing in return, but the more civilised Kushans converted their neighbours to Buddhism, and shrines and temples began to appear along the Silk Road. But in AD 220 the Han dynasty collapsed, and China was too preoccupied with internal power struggles to devote much time to keeping the peace in the frontier lands to its west. The Kushan empire also began to break up, and in the lonely outposts of the Chinese in the Tarim Basin and the Kushans in Khorasmia the soldiers of the garrisons felt cut off and abandoned. Scanning the horizon anxiously from their watchtowers, they listened for the drum of hoof-beats which meant the barbarians were once more on the offensive, and waited for reinforcements which rarely came. Central Asia went through one of its periodic times of trouble and, with no strong overlord to keep the peace, relapsed into a mass of petty oasis kingdoms. Far to the west Rome itself declined, to be superseded later by Byzantium, and even the fierce Parthians were supplanted by an equally aggressive Persian dynasty – the Sassanids.

The Chinese Annals, or historical records, were interrupted for two hundred years in the third and fourth centuries, for China was once again devastated by the Huns and north China became, in the words of one scholar, 'a mere appendage of the Mongolian steppe'. Yet somehow or other trade continued, even if on a reduced scale, for East and West had by now developed an appetite for each other's products, and this was an important factor in foreign relations. Silk still reached the West, sometimes by sea from south China, and the more intrepid merchants still conducted their caravans through steppe and mountain whenever there seemed a chance of getting through. Buddhism remained strong, with a flow of pilgrim traffic between China and India in spite of all the difficulties, and there were evidently local centres of civilisation and wealth even in the darkest of times. Certainly by the end of the fourth century there were flourishing Buddhist townships along the southern arm of the Silk Road, especially in the kingdom of Khotan, which was visited by the Chinese traveller Fa-hsien. There was no sign of devastation here, and the monasteries were richly decorated with gold, silver and precious stones.

In the fourth and fifth centuries the Hunnish clans began to split up, some settling down in northern China, others migrating to the north of India, while some of the most ferocious invaded eastern Europe and the Balkans, displacing the Goths who in turn menaced Byzantium. Then, in about AD 550, a new confederation of nomad tribes known as the Western Turks moved into Central Asia from the Mongolian plateau. To the Chinese they must have seemed like yet another wave of barbarians from a seemingly inexhaustible source in the north, but the Turks were not mere marauders and despoilers. They settled all over Central Asia, giving the region stability and thus encouraging both trade and craftsmanship. They were helped enormously in their endeavours by a very ancient Central Asian people, the Sogdians.

The mysterious Sogdians, a people destined to disappear completely from Western knowledge for about a thousand years, were at their peak in the sixth and seventh centuries AD, but they had been known to the Greeks in the fourth century BC. At that time they controlled a powerful empire from their capital of Maracanda – later the site of Samarkand – and were fierce warriors. After their defeat by Alexander the Great in 329 BC they were never again a warlike power, and saw many other overlords, including the Kushans. But they became the master traders of Central Asia and their language – related to Aramaic – became the *lingua franca* of the region. Over the centuries they adopted a number of different religions through their contacts with other peoples: Zoroastrianism and Manichaeism were picked up from the Persians and Buddhism probably from the Kushans. Some may even have been Nestorian Christians, for after the Council of Ephesus in AD 431 had declared them heretics, many Nestorians fled to Central Asia and eventually to China. Because of their extensive travels the Sogdians played an important part in spreading religion.

The ruins of a Sogdian city can still be seen at Penjakent in Tajikistan, about fifty miles across the border from Samarkand. There Soviet archaeologists uncovered wall-paintings which portray the Sogdians as having long thin faces, prominent noses, deep-set eyes and luxuriant beards. The building excavated seems to have been a prince's residence, and the frescos depict banqueting scenes and either jousting or fighting. But Hsuan-tsang, the seventh-century Chinese pilgrim who left a record of his travels in search of Buddhist scriptures, described the ordinary Sogdians more prosaically. He found them peaceable and industrious, their activities divided between farming and trading. They were also noted for their wood-carving, glass-making (which they seem to have learned through their commercial links with the eastern Mediterranean), carpet-weaving and metal-work, and had introduced both the vine and the cherry tree to China.

By the end of the sixth century China was again a strong and united country, with the new Tang dynasty also controlling Tibet and challenging Turkish supremacy in the Tarim Basin. But a fresh threat to the eastern world was brewing: not this time from the nomads of the north, but from a new religion born in the deserts of Arabia. Syria fell to the sword of Islam in 636, Alexandria in 641. In 674 the King of Persia fled to China, having surrendered his mighty kingdom. A power struggle now developed for mastery of Central Asia, in which both the Western Turks and the Tibetans somewhat short-sightedly decided to back the incoming Arabs rather than their traditional rivals, the Chinese. In 749 a Chinese army was routed near Tashkent by a joint force of Arabs and Western Turks, and a year later the Tibetans captured Tunhuang and cut off the Tarim Basin from direct communication with China. Some of the beleaguered Chinese garrisons of Central Asia managed to hold out for another forty years, unaware that in the meantime the Tibetans had invaded China and sacked the capital in 763. Tibetan domination was not destined to last, however, and in 822 they made peace with China, for their erstwhile friends the Arabs had proved an implacable enemy to Buddhism and the Tibetan way of life.

The Western Turks, too, must have regretted their alliance with the Arabs, who simply brushed them aside once the Chinese had been driven out of Central Asia, and took over instead. It seems likely that some of the Turks moved west, and their allies the Sogdians perhaps moved with them, for Penjakent was abandoned at this time. Certainly, anyone who remained was forcibly converted to Islam. During these violent upheavals many Buddhist, Manichaean and Christian shrines were desecrated or destroyed, for they were invariably adorned with figurative wall-paintings and sculptures, and these were anathema to the Muslims. Many entire monastery settlements in the Tarim Basin were now suddenly abandoned, their monks having been put to the sword, and were gradually engulfed by the desert sands. Thanks to the extreme dryness of the climate, many wall-paintings, sculptures and documents were perfectly preserved by their blanket of sand, and lay hidden for the next thousand years – to the joy of Sir Aurel Stein, Albert von Le Coq and other early twentieth-century archaeologists. Although the Arab Caliphate soon fell into schism and internal wrangling between Shias and Sunnis, allowing Central Asia to succumb to a succession of other conquerors, the region remained overwhelmingly Muslim ever after.

The next great empire to emerge was another Turkic one, that of the Seljuks under their two renowned leaders, Alp Arslan and his grandson Sultan Sanjar, who ruled vast areas of western Central Asia and the Middle East in the eleventh century. Their magnificent capital of Merv was known as 'the Queen of the World', and their territories stretched from the Mediterranean to the Oxus. At the Chinese end of Central Asia, however, the Eastern Turks or Uighurs were now in control. Driven from their traditional grazing grounds in the Altai mountains by the Kirghiz (another Turkic people) in the ninth century, they swept south and west into Kansu and the Tarim Basin, and established kingdoms at Tunhuang and Turfan. Their religious beliefs (like those of their Siberian and Mongolian neighbours) were based on a primitive spirit-worship, but they were evidently impressionable, for as they migrated south the Uighurs adopted first Manichaeism, then Buddhism and finally Islam. Their territories became known as Eastern Turkestan, while those on the other side of the Pamirs were known as Western Turkestan.

The beginning of the thirteenth century saw sweeping changes in Central Asia – not to mention Russia – for this was the time of the great Mongol migration. Unlike the Scythians, Sarmatians, Huns and Turks who had preceded them, these barbarians who erupted from the far-off borders of Manchuria were of an entirely different race. Round-headed, yellow-skinned, with slanting eyes and high cheek-bones, they were related to the peoples of northern China and Korea, although they spoke a Turkic language. They were also indescribably dirty and malodorous, for water was something they regarded as too precious to be wasted on personal hygiene. They were not a hirsute people, but so infested were they with lice that their chests appeared to be thickly covered in hair.

The astonishing conquests of Genghis Khan swept aside several empires and innumerable petty kingdoms, and brought all countries from the Black Sea to the Yellow River under direct Mongol control by the end of the first quarter of the thirteenth century. The unstoppable Mongol tide continued under his successors. Baghdad fell in 1258, the Sung capital of Hangchow in 1276. In Europe the Mongol empire – the largest in history – extended as far as Poland and Hungary, taking in most of Russia on the way. After all this carnage and destruction no one dared challenge the Mongols for a long time. Peace reigned throughout the empire – of distinct benefit to trade and travel – and the conquerors themselves began to acquire at least a veneer of civilisation. The Mongols had been entirely unlettered but now, with the help of the astute Eastern Turks, they set about writing their language down, using the Uighur script. This fruitful collaboration, accompanied by inter-marriage, was in time to produce a new hybrid master-race and a new world leader, Tamerlane, but in the meantime a Mongol emperor sat on the illustrious throne of China and entertained curious visitors from distant Europe.

Kublai Khan, grandson of Genghis, had become Great Khan, or Chief of all the Mongol clans, in 1260. Karakoram, in Mongolia, was the headquarters of the huge empire, to which all the clan leaders were summoned periodically, but in time Kublai came to prefer the splendour of the Chinese court and made Peking his capital. The Chinese aristocracy disdained this upstart dynasty of Yuan and kept their distance, but Europeans flocked to the new emperor's court. Foremost were the monks, for Kublai Khan had a Nestorian mother and was reputedly interested in Christianity. Hot on their heels came the merchants, among them the Polo family from Venice. Marco Polo is said to have served Kublai for seventeen years, between 1275 and 1292, although some scholars wonder whether he ever got as far as China, there being no mention of this 'foreign devil' in the Chinese Annals. Others, like Sir Aurel Stein, were excited at following in his footsteps. As he tramped along the southern arm of the Silk Road on the fringes of the Taklamakan desert, Stein re-read his Marco

Polo and found that the descriptions of Kashgar, Yarkand, Khotan, Cherchen and Tunhuang tallied very well. Whatever the truth of the matter, the thirteenth century was something of a golden age for trade, and eastern Central Asia in particular flourished. For the Yuan dynasty, shunned by the Chinese, depended heavily on the Uighurs, whose capital was at Turfan, both to maintain law and order and to organise trade.

But the mighty Mongols, like all the conquerors before them, had their moment of glory and then declined. In little more than a century the Yuan dynasty came to an end, and in 1368 was replaced by the Chinese house of Ming. The Mongols, weakened by internal power struggles and faced in China by famine, floods and peasant uprisings, were driven back to the steppes, and their collaborators the Uighurs were expelled in their wake. The Ming dynasty concerned itself with reunifying China and consolidating its power: contacts with the West were severely restricted.

Further west the Mongols had fared better. The Golden Horde had established themselves in Russia during the thirteenth century under Genghis Khan's grandson Batu, and became known as the Tatars. Their despoliation of Poland and Hungary so alarmed the Pope and other Western leaders that a succession of plucky friars were dispatched with messages of friendship to the Tatars' tented capital at Sarai, on the Volga. From there, some were induced to attend the Mongol grand capital at Karakoram, 3,000 miles and four months' hard travelling further east. Unfortunately these missions were taken by the Mongols as a sign of submission by the West, and their modest gifts were haughtily cast aside as quite insufficient as 'tribute'. Two of the friars who managed to return safely from their arduous journeys were John of Carpine, sent by the Pope in 1245, and William of Rubruck who was dispatched by the King of France in 1252. Both brought back valuable intelligence on Mongol manners, customs and organisation, together with arrogant and insulting messages for their masters. Nobody in the West felt able to take on the Mongols, and it would be three hundred years before Russia succeeded in casting off the Tatar yoke.

Meanwhile, in 1336, Tamerlane was born in Kesh (modern Shakhrisabz), south of Samarkand. Within thirty years he established a new empire in Central Asia. He first made himself master of Turkestan, and then proceeded to conquer Persia, parts of southern Russia (weakening the power of the Golden Horde), and northern India as far as Delhi. Towards the end of his life, in 1402, he defeated the Ottoman Turks – who had succeeded the Seljuks in Asia Minor – at Ankara, and even took Sultan Beyazit captive. Notorious for his savagery, it has been estimated that he caused the deaths of seventeen million people. Some of these were the slave-labourers used for his extravagant building projects, for paradoxically there was a creative side to his nature. In the course of his conquests he commandeered the best local artists and craftsmen, and sent them back to embellish his capital of Samarkand, which became renowned throughout the world. He died in 1405, on the eve of a campaign against China, and the seeds of decay were planted when his empire was divided among his sons and grandsons. The Timurid princes were a strange mixture of the warrior, the aesthete and the barbarian: they built beautiful mosques and palaces in Herat, Balkh and Meshed, but fought savagely among themselves and had anyone who displeased them skinned alive. The exception was Ulugh Beg, a scholarly man and Tamerlane's favourite grandson, under whom Samarkand continued to flourish for a while as a centre of civilisation. He was assassinated, however, by his own son.

The sixteenth century brought with it a new invader of Central Asia, the Uzbek Turks from the north, who gave their name to a large territory in western Turkestan which has recently become a new country: Uzbekistan. Turks and Mongols were by now thoroughly intermixed, and the Uzbek leader Shaybani Khan could count Genghis Khan as a collateral ancestor. So too could Prince Babur, Timurid ruler of Khokhand and a distant cousin of Ulugh Beg's, but after a fierce fight he was ousted from the Ferghana valley and made his way south to find a new territory. A man of artistic tastes as well as military prowess, he conquered northern India in 1526 and founded the Mogul dynasty. India blossomed, but Central Asia declined. Ming China had long since shut its gates on the West, fearing the power of the Uighurs, and this had dramatically reduced trade. The whole of western Asia was in the hands of the Ottoman Turks, now recovered from Tamerlane's invasion, and they looked west rather than east for both trade and foreign relations, having, for example, particularly close ties with France. So Central Asia, marooned in the middle, became a backwater, a nest of suspicion and fanaticism, subject to the whims and quarrels of rival petty despots.

When Anthony Jenkinson, a merchant from the City of London, arrived in Bokhara at the end of 1558 he had already suffered enough misfortunes to send a less resourceful man running for home. After sailing down the Volga and leaving his boat on the eastern shore of the Caspian Sea, he set out on 14 September across the notorious sandy wilderness of Transcaspia. At various times stricken by fever, attacked by bandits, cheated by his guides, his merchandise rifled by packs of Turcomans, he and his loyal caravan men were forced to fight a pitched battle at one point with 'a banished prince with fortie men' east of Khiva. Jenkinson formed a very low opinion of the petty princes of Transcaspia, for not only were they constantly fighting among themselves – to the impoverishment of their people – but they all 'lived viciously', surrounded by catamites and concubines. 'Arte or Science they have none,' he wrote in his diary, 'but live most idly, sitting round in great companies in the fields, devising and talking most vainely.'

It must have been a relief to arrive in Bokhara which was still an important market town for the region, although none of the merchants showed much interest in the Englishman's woollen cloth. Jenkinson evidently had a talent for making friends, and was soon on familiar terms with the King, Abdullah Khan, who particularly enjoyed firing his guest's arquebur. Like most Central Asian towns, Bokhara was built mainly of baked mud bricks, with a high defensive wall and a bazaar where every trade had its own quarter. Although speaking a Persian language, the Bokharans were usually at war with Persia – and, indeed, with most of their neighbours. Jenkinson had planned to take his goods on to Cathay, or China, but his hopes were soon dashed. No caravans had emerged from Cathay for at least three years, he was informed, and it was impossible to travel even as far as Samarkand because a local war was in progress. After an interesting three months' stay, he retraced his steps to the Caspian, taking with him twenty-five Russian slaves whom he had rescued from Bokhara's notorious slave market. He found his boat still on the beach, but totally stripped of equipment and fittings. (In view of the reputation the Turcomans had for thieving, perhaps he was lucky to find even the boat still there.) Undaunted, he set about spinning ropes from hemp and weaving a new sail. The former slaves joined in cheerfully, and made him a temporary anchor out of an old cartwheel. At last all was ready, and the party gladly turned their backs on Central Asia, the Russians rowing with a will as they approached their native land.

Jenkinson had come to Turkestan by way of Russia and returned the same way, sailing up the mighty Volga and being entertained by the Tsar in Moscow, for while Central Asia stagnated its great northern neighbour had awoken from a long hibernation. The descendants of the Golden Horde, though weakened by Tamerlane's incursions, had remained in control of much of Russia and were divided into three khanates at Kazan, Astrakhan and the Crimea. Every year the Russian princes had the humiliation of paying tribute to these Tatar overlords, until in 1552 Ivan the Terrible, Prince of Muscovy, attacked and defeated Kazan. Four years later, the heady scent of freedom in their nostrils, he and his boyars crushed Astrakhan, and the Tatars were overlords no more. But Russia had been cut off for the best part of three centuries from intellectual and artistic developments in the outside world, including the phenomenon of the Renaissance in Europe. It had become a poor and primarily agricultural land, for its wooden-built towns had been regularly sacked and burnt by the Golden Horde. Tsar Ivan set about modernising his country, and by the time of Anthony Jenkinson's visit the population of Moscow had already risen to 100,000, greater than that of London. It was a thriving city, moreover, unlike the Tatar capitals of Kazan and Astrakhan, which Jenkinson found to be pitifully poor and ravaged by the plague. So desperate were the Tatars of Astrakhan that Jenkinson could have purchased 'many goodly Tatars' Children … from their owne Fathers and Mothers' for a sixpenny loaf. (He did, in fact, buy a little girl on his way back, and presented her to Queen Elizabeth on his return to England.) Nevertheless, despite Russia's newly won freedom it would be a slow and painful process before the huge, unwieldy country became a unified nation, and it would continue to be regarded by the rest of the world as a land of backward savages for many years to come.

In India, meanwhile, Babur's grandson – the Emperor Akbar – was bringing Mogul rule to its zenith. By the end of the sixteenth century he had established a sound administrative framework, while peerless cities like Agra and Fatepur Sikri proclaimed the artistic glories of his reign. Far away in London, however, the East India Company was founded in 1600, with profound implications for the future of the sub-continent.

In China the Ming dynasty was beginning to crumble, and a new race of Central Asian nomads – a Tungusic people who came to be known as the Manchus – was gathering strength in Manchuria, Korea, Mongolia and parts of northern China. Its headquarters were at Mukden, dangerously close to the Great Wall. But in an extraordinary sequence of events, the Manchu armies were actually invited into China in 1644 by a Ming general, to help him put down a rebellion. Unfortunately the Manchus showed no sign of leaving again afterwards, and gradually took control of the whole country. In the event they were to rule China for the next three hundred years, calling themselves the Ching dynasty. By the end of the seventeenth century the Manchus had absorbed the Gobi and Altai districts into the Chinese empire, and by the middle of the eighteenth they had taken over the Tarim Basin. Large numbers of nomads were wiped out by the Manchus between the Altai and Pamir mountains at this time, and colonists from metropolitan China were introduced instead. The days of the freebooting nomad, and even of the migrating pastoralist, were drawing to a close, as both Russia and China expanded.

During the sixteenth and seventeenth centuries Russian Cossacks colonised Siberia, and in the eighteenth it was the turn of the mountain stronghold of the Caucasus, then part of the Shah of Persia's domains. That century also saw Russia's first, disastrous, expedition to Central Asia. In August 1717 Prince Alexander Bekovich, envoy of Peter the Great, was slaughtered with most of his companions outside Khiva after the rascally Khan had pretended to welcome them. Peter was too busy in the Caucasus and elsewhere to exact vengeance at the time, but Russia never forgot this treachery and western Turkestan would later pay dearly for it. Peter the Great was the first of the Tsars to be taken seriously in the West. His tour of Europe in the 1690s opened his eyes to education and technology, which he energetically applied to his own country with the help of foreign advisers, while his victory over the Swedes at Poltava in 1709 gained Russia international status. European architects helped to build his splendid new capital of St Petersburg, and his uncouth boyars were forced to shave off their beards and adopt Western dress instead of the loose robes inherited from Tatar culture. His successors, especially the German-born Catherine the Great, continued the process, but it was the Napoleonic Wars which catapulted Russia into the heart of Europe – and brought it into contact with the rationalist movement known as the Enlightenment.

After Alexander I's triumphal entry into Paris in 1814 nothing could be quite the same again. This mysterious Tsar, whose mainly illiterate people regarded him as a god, and whose entire peasant population was held in a form of slavery, had now to be treated on equal terms by Western leaders. The Russians, for their part, were dazzled by everything Western, and especially French, and carried home with them French chefs, Parisian dressmakers and tutors – and a collection of half-digested liberal ideas which would shortly get them into a lot of trouble. Alarmed at the destabilising effect of liberalism, Alexander tried to back-pedal, and after the abortive Decembrist Revolt of 1825 the new Tsar, Nicholas I, instituted a repressive era. Travel abroad was drastically curtailed, trouble-makers were banished, crippling censorship was imposed, and the dreaded Third Section – or secret police – was set up. The age of the 'superfluous man' had begun, and in view of the universal muzzling of expression it was perhaps not surprising that to an outsider like the Scottish writer Thomas Carlyle Russia seemed to be 'a great dumb monster', lacking any voice of genius. He was mistaken, and the nineteenth century was to produce some Russian writers and thinkers of considerable stature, but to many young men the army seemed the only road to glory, or indeed to activity. At all events, Russia's expansionist campaigns in the Caucasus and in the steppeland of the wandering Kazakhs took on a new impetus at this time. And beyond the Kazakh steppe lay another no-man's land: the deserts and oases of western Turkestan.

Russia's activities in Central Asia were watched with disquiet by the British in India. For by the beginning of the nineteenth century most of India was under the control of the East India Company, which had its own Governor-General, administration and army, the better to protect its trade monopolies. While Russia annexed Kazakhstan and sent 'trade delegations' to the Khans of Turkestan, the British sent 'friendly missions' to Sind, the Punjab and Afghanistan. It went without saying that a great deal of valuable strategic information was gathered in the course of these unsolicited visits, and the native states were filled with foreboding, having seen their neighbours engulfed by the colonial tide. The Khan of Khiva kept the Tsar's envoy, Nikolai Muraviev, under house arrest for seven nerve-racking weeks in

1819, but did not dare kill him for fear of Russian retribution. And the following year the Emir of Bokhara had little choice but to co-operate with a Russian trade delegation when he noticed that it was accompanied by a couple of artillery pieces. In India a holy man lamented: 'Alas, Sind is now gone,' as he watched a British mission sail past him up the Indus in 1831. 'The English have seen the river which is the road to our conquest.'

To the British the prospect of an expansionist Russia seemed very alarming indeed, for if Central Asia were to become another province of the already vast Russian empire, the armies of the Tsar would be literally on India's doorstep. And India was so vital to Britain's economic interests that after the Mutiny in 1857 control of the country was transferred from the East India Company to the Crown. On the face of it, India was impregnable from the north, protected by the massive bastions of the Himalayas, Pamirs and Karakorams. But all the invaders of the past had come that way, from Alexander the Great onwards. The question was, could a modern army encumbered with artillery do the same thing? Military experts could not agree, for the area had never been systematically surveyed and the position of the various mountain passes could only be guessed at.

From the 1860s both Britain and Russia began to map as much of Central Asia as they could, using any means available: officers on 'shooting leave', explorers sponsored by their geographical societies, scientists and naturalists, would-be tea traders – they could all be shown how to use basic surveying equipment. There was no lack of daring young men on both sides to volunteer for such assignments in what became known as the 'Great Game', though it was a hazardous business and not all of them returned. If you escaped death from exposure in the mountain passes or from thirst in the deserts, you were quite likely to die of fever, be murdered by brigands or be imprisoned in loathsome conditions by some brutal petty despot. For there was an extreme distrust of strangers – not to mention Islamic fanaticism – among the backward tribesmen, most of whom had never seen a white man. In fact, some areas were so dangerous that the Survey of India would only send native 'pundits' there, usually in the guise of holy men or pilgrims but with secret surveying equipment hidden in their prayer-wheels or staffs. Even these men took their lives in their hands.

In retrospect it seems doubtful whether Russia seriously intended to wrest India from Britain's grasp, although this was clearly the desire of many Tsarist frontier officers, who thought of little else. Nevertheless, the contradictions between St Petersburg's soothing assurances and military action on the spot did nothing to allay British fears. Tashkent was annexed in 1865 and immediately became the forward base for further Russian incursions into Central Asia, although the Tsar insisted that his aim was not conquest but simply the securing of his southern borders. There was some justification for such a policy, as the nomadic Turcomans in particular were highly unsatisfactory neighbours: unwary Russian subjects from the border settlements were continually being kidnapped and sold into slavery in the markets of Khiva and Bokhara. At all events, the Central Asian khanates began to fall to the Russian army in a dismaying progression: Samarkand and Bokhara both fell in 1868, Khiva in 1873, and the Turcoman fortress of Geok-Tepe in 1881. When the Tsar turned his attention to Merv in 1882 a new word – 'Mervousness' – was coined in Britain, for Merv was a staging-post on the way to Herat in Afghanistan, the traditional 'gateway to India'. And yet in 1879 the Russian Foreign Ministry had assured the British ambassador to St Petersburg that the Tsar had positively no intention of annexing Merv.

This Russian ambivalence to the literal truth has always been inexplicable to Westerners, and sometimes even to the Russians themselves. 'In no other State', sighed the nineteenth-century statesman Speransky, 'do political words stand in such contrast to reality as in Russia.' Turgenev remarked: 'It is a well-known fact, though not very easy to understand, that Russians are the greatest liars on the face of the earth, yet there is nothing they respect more than the truth, nothing they sympathize with more.' In the 20th century Alexander Solzhenitsyn warned the West in one of his Delphic utterances: 'Never forget that the Russians are an Asiatic people.' This element of fantasy in the national make-up infuriated the Germans and pained the British. The French simply shrugged and remarked: '*Grattez un Russe et vous trouverez un Tatare*' ('Scratch a Russian and you will find a Tatar'). Certainly, in the realms of diplomacy it was a hugely complicating factor.

While complaining of Russian duplicity over Turkestan and Transcaspia, the British were not idle themselves during the nineteenth century. But their incursions into Central Asia were far less single-minded than those of the Russians, for the British were subject to the checks and balances of democracy and uncensored public opinion. A hawkish government which supported the 'forward policies' of the military would be succeeded by one advocating a policy of 'masterly inactivity', relying on distance and natural hazards to protect India from invaders. A British officer who exceeded his instructions and negotiated an agreement with a local potentate would probably be severely reprimanded by the government, even if he was applauded in the popular papers. His Russian equivalent, on the other hand, would almost certainly be promoted. Regardless of the avowed policy of the moment, the Tsars were never averse to a territorial *fait accompli*.

Both sides had their tragedies and disasters in the Great Game. Apart from the massacre of the Bekovich expedition to Khiva in 1717, the Russians lost 1,000 men and 8,000 camels when General Perovsky led another expedition to the same isolated khanate in 1840. Alexander Burnes was torn apart by a frenzied mob in Kabul in 1841 and a year later Colonel Stoddart and Captain Conolly were beheaded in Bokhara after spending months in a verminous pit. Yet neither side gave up, and by the end of the nineteenth century the rivalry between Britain and Russia in Central Asia had reached such a fever pitch that Lord Curzon dedicated his magisterial work *Russia in Central Asia*, published in 1889, to 'the great army of Russophobes who mislead others and Russophiles whom others mislead', noting that his book would be found 'equally disrespectful to the ignoble terrors of the one and the perverse complacency of the others'. There was certainly little comfort in Curzon's statistics: in 1725, when Peter the Great died, Russia's empire in Asia had covered four million square miles, whereas it now extended to six and a half million. At the start of the nineteenth century the British and Russian empires had been 2,000 miles apart. By the end of it the gap had shrunk to a few hundred, and in the Wakhan – the pan-handle of Afghanistan – to a mere twenty.

After centuries of oblivion Central Asia had become headline news, and the Victorians regarded this far-off region, peopled by primitive heathens, with a mixture of horror and fascination. Certainly anyone who ventured there could be sure of a wide readership for the book, pamphlet or newspaper article which resulted. Many of these books are long forgotten and hard to find today, but they make wonderful reading, for in the course of all the surveying and colonising, the fabled caravan cities of the old Silk Road had been revealed to Western eyes. And as the Russians built railways through their new territories it gradually became possible for quite ordinary people to travel the iron road to Samarkand. Western travellers began, too, to penetrate the eastern parts of Central Asia, still nominally under Chinese control, where a backward Muslim society existed side by side with the corrupt officials of the declining Manchu dynasty. Persistent rumours of 'buried cities' in the Taklamakan desert brought explorers and archaeologists to the region around the turn of the century, and they found to their astonishment that much of the lost Buddhist civilisation which had flourished before the Muslim conquest in the eighth century was still preserved under the dry sands. Undaunted by the stupendous difficulties posed in transporting their finds, they proceeded to remove wall-paintings and sculptures by the ton and manuscripts by the sackful, and send them to the museums of England, France, Germany, Russia, India, America and Japan.

Most of the travellers left accounts of their triumphs and disasters, as did many of the soldiers, diplomats and administrators whose duties brought them to Central Asia, before the Communists seized control of first Russia and then China, and they became forbidden lands. Some of the writers were caught up in those cataclysmic events and had harrowing stories to tell of their escape. It is from this wide variety of eyewitness accounts that I have drawn in the following pages, in the belief that anyone interested in Central Asia – and especially anyone going there – will want to know what it was like before the dead hand of totalitarianism did its best to destroy its special character.

The centuries have witnessed the rise and fall of countless civilisations in Central Asia, and now the collapse of Communism in Russia has seen the downfall of yet another empire there. Rather as Russia shook off the yoke of the Tatars in the sixteenth century, so the Central Asian republics have broken free from Russia at the end of the twentieth. Today they stand once more on the brink of a new era. Will their newly won freedom and vast natural resources bring them stability and prosperity, or will disunity, backwardness and corruption drag them back into darkness and oppression? At the time of writing the answer is very far from clear. Indeed, to watch the future as it gradually – and painfully – takes shape, one must turn to the newspapers, whose correspondents are the modern eyewitnesses to the momentous events now unfolding in Central Asia.

ASHKHABAD
Heat, Dust and Pestilence

The reception began at nine, and we were all very punctual.
Madame Kuropatkin makes a charming hostess, and quite
won the hearts of the gentlemen by her grace of manner and
sweet smile. The scene soon became a brilliant one as officer
after officer came in, each covered with decorations.

> J.T. Woolrych Perowne, of a party given by the
> Governor-General in Ashkhabad, 1898

Unrest and disturbances in the Transcaspian provinces have
led to the gradual transformation of this area, especially
Ashkhabad, into a major, unquestionably dangerous centre of
revolutionary activity.

> Memo from the Governor-General of Turkestan to the
> War Minister in St Petersburg, 1905

ASHKHABAD, WHICH MEANS in Arabic 'lovely settlement', is situated
where the Kopet Dagh mountains meet the Kara Kum desert,
thirty miles from the Iranian border. Four-fifths of Turkmenistan,
of which Ashkhabad is the capital, is covered by the Kara Kum, or
Black Sands, where temperatures of 78 degrees centigrade (172
degrees Fahrenheit) have been recorded, and the city has a reputation
for heat and dust. However, the clever use of water enabled wheat,
cotton, grapes and melons to be grown there even in antiquity. For
the inhabitants had adopted a system of irrigation called *kyariz*,
probably invented in ancient Persia, whereby a chain of wells is
linked by underground canals, and melt-water from the mountains
transported over long distances with the minimum of evaporation.

The construction work was very skilled, and it has been estimated that one man would only complete two of these subterranean systems in his lifetime. Some are still in use today.

The strategic position of Ashkhabad at the western end of Central Asia, where caravan routes from Merv, Khiva, Bokhara and Samarkand converged before crossing the mountains into either Persia or Afghanistan, meant that it changed hands many times. Prosperous in times of stability, it was also regularly despoiled by invaders. At one time part of the empire of Alexander the Great, it later belonged to the Parthians, whose ruined city of Nissa can be visited nearby. After being a Persian-speaking city for hundreds of years, Ashkhabad became Turkic in the eleventh century when the Seljuks conquered much of Central Asia, as well as the area covered by present-day Anatolia, Iran, Iraq, Syria and parts of the Caucasus. But even this mighty empire fell eventually, and the beginning of the thirteenth century saw the arrival of a terrifying new invader, the most destructive and cruel the world had ever seen. Genghis Khan and his Mongol hordes sacked all the rich and flourishing oases of the region, raping, pillaging and slaughtering as they went. By the time they had finished with Ashkhabad there was not a living creature left, and the city had disappeared into a rubble of earthen bricks.

When the Tsar of Russia ordered his troops to colonise Transcaspia in the last quarter of the nineteenth century, they found nothing in this vicinity but a ramshackle native village next to a large hillock. The Turcomans said their settlement was called 'Ashkhabad'. The soldiers built a fort on the mound in 1881 and then continued with their expansion into the desert and steppe, followed by military engineers who were laying a railway (see THE TRANSCASPIAN RAILWAY). It was not until the 1960s that Soviet archaeologists discovered that 'Fortress Hill', behind the Turkmenistan Hotel, was in fact the remains of an ancient city, going back at least 2,500 years.

The British watched with disquiet as the settlement of Ashkhabad was fortified by Russia. Their worries were not so much commercial as strategic, however, for Russia's rapid annexation of first Turkestan and now Transcaspia had brought the Tsar's huge empire a thousand miles closer to the jewel in Britain's imperial crown – India. The prodigious rate of Russia's expansion into Central Asia made some observers in London and Calcutta wonder whether India itself was not the Tsar's ultimate goal, and the construction of the new railway line through Ashkhabad from the Caspian seemed an ominous confirmation of this fear. For a glance at the map showed that it was heading straight for the Afghan frontier. Afghanistan had always been regarded as the key to India, the gateway through which every conqueror had passed, and Britain had done her best to keep it within her 'sphere of influence'. In this jittery atmosphere a sudden crisis erupted on the river Kushk in the wilds of northern Afghanistan in April 1885, when the British caught the Russians wresting a slice of the Pamirs from the Afghan army.

The Penjdeh Incident, when Britain and Russia very nearly came to blows after the Russian commander deliberately provoked the Afghans into a fight in order to justify snatching some more territory, caused a sensation around the world. Newspaper headlines were soon predicting: ENGLAND AND RUSSIA TO FIGHT, and IT IS WAR. In the event war was averted and a compromise arranged, but Russia was soon pressing on hastily with the building of the railway while Britain was preoccupied with a general election, and the first train steamed into Ashkhabad in December of the same year. Only eighteen months later the line had been completed all the way to Samarkand – an amazing technical feat, but also a political *fait accompli*. In London and Calcutta a host of commentators assailed the public with their often conflicting views on the nefariousness or otherwise of Russian intentions. One man who was determined to see for himself was the Honourable George Curzon, MP, the future Viceroy of India. With great persistence he managed to get a permit to travel the 900-mile length of the new military railway, and set out from London in September 1888. The 477-page book which resulted, in which he assessed the threat to India, contains a wealth of eyewitness information on Central Asia and remains a classic to this day.

Ashkhabad, Curzon found, was 'a large and flourishing place', although it was barely nine years old, with a railway station of European proportions. He was courteously received by the Governor-General, General Komarov, and had 'an interesting conversation' with this gentleman who only three years before had brought their countries to the brink of war. For it was Komarov who at Penjdeh had goaded the Afghans into attacking his Cossacks. He struck Curzon as an unlikely figure for a Commander-in-Chief: bald, stout and bespectacled, his passions were archaeology and beetles, and he reminded the Englishman 'of a university professor dressed up in uniform'. Although politically opposed to Russia, Curzon always got on famously with individual Russians, whose 'frank and amiable manners' he found disarming. Indeed, he felt that Englishmen and Russians had a good deal in common: 'a unity of qualities that make for greatness, viz. self-reliance, pride, a desperate resolve, adventurousness, and a genius for discipline'.

Nonetheless, Curzon had no illusions over Ashkhabad's strategic significance nor over Komarov's role there. But although primarily a garrison town, Ashkhabad had begun to attract people from all over the Russian empire who hoped to make a better living in the New South:

> Ashkhabad has a printing-press, a photographic establishment, and European shops and hotels. The houses are for the most part of one storey, and are freely bedaubed with white. A small fortified *enceinte* supplies a reminder of the days, not yet ten years gone by, when the Russians were strangers and suspects in the land. In the centre of the town is an obelisk erected in memory of the artillerymen who were killed in the siege and capture of Geok-Tepe, and at its base are planted the Afghan guns which were captured in the skirmish on the Kushk. The town is a purely Russian settlement, though the business quarter has attracted a large number of Armenians, Persians and Jews. City life is avoided by the Turcomans, who prefer the tented liberty of the steppe.
>
> Curzon, *Russia in Central Asia*, 1889

However, the appointment – two years after Curzon's visit – of General Kuropatkin to succeed Komarov brought Ashkhabad's cosmopolitan days to a swift end. Kuropatkin, who as Skobelev's Chief-of-Staff had masterminded the defeat of the Turcomans at Geok-Tepe, was determined to keep Transcaspia 'Russian'. In an otherwise favourable profile of him in January 1898, after he had been promoted to War Minister, *The Times* said: 'One of his least commendable actions was to turn out all the Polish railway engineers, Persians, Armenians and other unorthodox Russian subjects engaged on the line, and introduce real Russians in their places.' If Kuropatkin believed that a Russian Ashkhabad would be more loyal to the Tsar than a cosmopolitan one, he was in for a rude shock, but this still lay in the future.

As Curzon had pointed out, Ashkhabad had no 'old town', the local population being nomadic, but by the 1890s it had two distinct districts. The smart end of town was around the fortress, in front of which a spacious esplanade had been laid out for military parades (later renamed Karl Marx Square). The broad streets were bordered by small canals and planted with plane trees, maples and cypresses. The Officers' Assembly Hall was surrounded by pleasant gardens and fountains, and a band played there on Sundays. The select Bicycle Club was the hub of civilian social life. Further north, however, the main east–west thoroughfare was the old caravan road, and here the air was choked with dust from the carts, camel-trains and droshkies, or horse-drawn cabs. Beyond this main road lay the impressive railway station, the centre of the commercial district. In 1898 an American businessman named John Bookwalter, who spent three months on an extensive fact-finding tour of Russia, described Ashkhabad as 'a beautiful town of considerable size'.

> Like all new Russian towns in these regions, it has wide, well-paved streets, and beautiful avenues of trees, with a stream of running water on either side of the streets. Having an abundance of water, supplied by a stream descending from the adjacent mountains, most of which is used for irrigation, Ashkhabad has become the centre of a large and highly productive agricultural region. Fruits of all kinds grow here in the greatest profusion, grapes especially being of the most extraordinary size and quality. Besides all the cereals that grow and develop here, cotton is being grown in considerable quantities. The quality is fairly good and the yield very heavy.
>
> Bookwalter, *Siberia and Central Asia*, 1899

An Englishman who travelled to Ashkhabad in considerable style at about the same time was Mr J.T. Woolrych Perowne, who arrived with his wife and twenty-three companions on the first Cook's Tour of Transcaspia. The Russians rose magnificently to the occasion: a telegram of welcome from the Governor-General of the province (the redoubtable Kuropatkin) was awaiting them in Krasnovodsk, together with a special train for their exclusive use, and two charming young officers to act as their guides. When the train arrived in Ashkhabad, via Geok-Tepe where the Turcomans had made their last stand, one of Kuropatkin's aides-de-camp was waiting on the platform, and the gentlemen of the party were whisked off in droshkies for an immediate audience with the Governor-General. 'As we tore through the streets, wide and planted with avenues of trees,' wrote Perowne later, 'I wondered what sort of a man we should find in General Kuropatkin. Fresh as we were from Geok-Tepe, we could not forget that we were about to call on Skobolev's Chief-of-Staff ...' But Perowne, like Curzon before him, was won over by the innate friendliness of the Russian character. After a cordial exchange of courtesies, and an invitation to a reception in their honour that evening, the English party was taken on a conducted tour of Ashkhabad.

In his book *Russian Hosts and English Guests in Central Asia* Perowne describes the town and its surroundings:

Ashkhabad is situated on the level plain at the foot of the Kopet Dagh, which is distant about eight miles away. This range, running north-east and south-west, rises from eight to eleven thousand feet above the sea level and forms a most picturesque background to the town. Those of us who had been in India at once saw the resemblance of the place to an ordinary Indian cantonment ... Quite a large European town has sprung up since the fall of Geok-Tepe.

After visiting the cathedral and various schools, they were taken outside the town to see the Botanical Gardens, a journey which gave them their first taste of the desert:

Our route lay over the wide plain, and four of our droshkies raced abreast over the hard even ground. On our left near us were the Steppes, a swelling of the ground before the mountains proper beyond rise sheer out of the plain. On our right stretched the limitless plain, dotted here and there with trees and *kibitkas* – a wonderful scene for those who now gazed upon it for the first time ... We halted to examine an encampment of Tekkes, now serving as militia in the Russian army. We entered one of the *kibitkas* or tents; they are circular dome-roofed structures, with a hole in the top for the smoke.

The walls are about six feet high, and the circumference about twenty yards. The walls are of lattice-work inside, covered with reed matting on the outside. The roof, supported by bent sticks, is covered with felt, which the Turcoman women make.

In the evening they attended a glittering reception *chez* the Kuropatkins, and then went on to a ball at the Bicycle Club, where several of the Englishmen became 'hopelessly entangled in the mysteries of a mazurka'. Perowne wisely remained a spectator. Next day a mock battle was staged for their entertainment outside the town, between Cossacks and Turcoman Militia. The *pièce de résistance* was a double cavalry charge, when the Cossacks and Turcomans, their sabres flashing in the sunlight, galloped at full speed at each other's lines, passed through, wheeled and charged again. 'The effect of these double charges was most thrilling,' wrote Perowne. The Russians certainly made sure their guests had a memorable day. Luncheon, served in a large tent, was the occasion for considerable conviviality:

> A royal repast was waiting for us, the courses were seemingly interminable, and included two sheep roasted whole close by in trenches. Nothing seemed to be too good for us, the officers in their courtesy waiting on us. Imagine an English Brigadier waiting on Russian tourists! General Kuropatkin proposed in a few words of French the health of our Queen, and the band played our National Anthem, which was received with loud cheers and drinking of our health. But when I proposed in few and halting phrases the health of the Tsar, the enthusiasm was immense, and all the crowd joined in the magnificently sonorous Russian hymn … An atmosphere of good fellowship rapidly spread between English and Russian.

Quite why the Russians took so much trouble over this group of wealthy but not very important travellers remains a mystery. Perhaps if you were condemned to living in a remote backwater like Ashkhabad, the arrival of twenty-five congenial foreigners was simply a good excuse for a few parties. At any rate, Perowne and his friends parted from the jolly Russians 'much impressed by the nature of our reception – for had we been minor Royalties, to say nothing of a political mission, the authorities could hardly have done more for us'.

A later visitor, Michael Shoemaker, provides a grim postscript to this era. Writing about Ashkhabad in his book *The Heart of the Orient*, he relates:

> Around the place will forever hang the memory of that dreadful visitation of cholera, years since. Some of the scenes, though terrible, were romantic, and one could have been taken as the original of Poe's *Mask of the Red Death*. The pestilence was supposed to have passed on its way, after leaving its five thousand dead. General Kuropatkin, in very desperation at the gloom, concluded on the Emperor's birthday to give a banquet. Gay was the event, but before another sun had set, nearly every soul who had attended was dead. The cholera had returned, and each and all, from the highest guest to the most humble musician, had bowed before its awful presence. Six hundred soldiers perished with the pestilence.

There must have been many more victims in the dust and heat of downtown Ashkhabad, where life was very different from the glittering round of balls and banquets centred on the Governor-General's residence and the Club. Still, the townsfolk had by the turn of the century a cinema, two newspapers and a thriving commercial life. A number of workshops and small factories began to appear, and trade was much easier now there were roads and the railway. In 1904 a municipal coat-of-arms was drawn up for the town incorporating, appropriately enough, a camel caravan and a railway train. But Ashkhabad also had its share of the alienated who, throughout Russia, were forming covert republican – if not downright revolutionary – groups. By the time of the abortive revolution in St Petersburg in 1905, the revolutionary socialists had an underground organisation in Ashkhabad which had succeeded in fomenting sufficient unrest in the area to cause the authorities serious concern.

The hard core of disaffection was to be found among the railway workers imported from central Russia after Kuropatkin's russification edict. This considerable body of men, whose unenviable task was the constant maintenance of remote railway tracks in the blistering desert, lived together as a tightly knit group. Their rough manners and appearance made them feared and shunned by the bourgeoisie and peasants alike, and not just in Central Asia. Chekhov describes in several of his stories how these 'ragged fellows' would come into the towns or villages on feast-days, drinking, swearing, stealing and harassing the women. In Ashkhabad, as elsewhere, they were fertile ground for propaganda. But this dangerous undercurrent, so soon to erupt, was not apparent to the casual visitor. The writer Stephen Graham, who passed through Ashkhabad in May 1914, had already spent many years in Russia learning the language and mixing with students, peasants and pilgrims, yet his description of the town on a summer night is purely lyrical:

> We reached Ashkhabad, the first great city of Turkestan, about eleven o'clock at night, and its platform presented an extraordinary scene. The whole forty-five minutes of our stay it was crowded with all the peoples of Central Asia – Persians, Russians, Afghans, Tekkes, Bokharans, Khivites, Turcomans – and every one had in his hand, or on his dress, or in his turban roses. The whole long pavement was fragrant with rose odours. Gay Russian girls, all in white and in summer hats, were chattering to young officers, with whom they paraded up and down, and they had roses in their hands. Persian hawkers, with capacious baskets of pink and white roses, moved hither and thither; immense and magnificent Turcomans lounged against pillars or walked about … they too held roses in their fingers. I walked out into the umbrageous streets, where triple lines of densely foliaged trees cast shadow between you and the beautiful night sky; in depths of dark greenery lay the houses of the city, with grass growing on their far-projecting roofs, with verandahs on which the people sleep, even in May. But they were not asleep in Ashkhabad. I stopped under a poplar and listened to the sad music of the Persian pipes. In these warm, throbbing, yet melancholy strains the night of north Persia was vocal – the night of my May Day.
>
> I returned to the station and bought a large bunch of pink and white roses and, as the second bell had rung, got back to my carriage, laid my plaid and my pillow, and as the train went out I slipped away from the wonderful city – to a happy dream.
>
> Graham, *Through Russian Central Asia*, 1916

Shortly after this the First World War broke out and Britain and Russia, no doubt to the bemusement of their soldiers, found themselves fighting on the same side. Ashkhabad was to take on an unexpected importance during the war, for Turkey joined in on Germany's side and proclaimed a Muslim Holy War against the Allies. German agents were soon stirring up trouble in Persia and Afghanistan – uncomfortably close to Transcaspia, where a European war was already unpopular with the local Muslims. If this were not enough, revolution broke out in Russia in 1917, and the Allies' eastern front began to waver as Russia's peasant-soldiers slipped back to their villages so as not to miss out on any land distribution. After the Bolshevik *coup d'état* and the signature in Brest-Litovsk of a peace treaty with the enemy, the ragged remnants of the once proud army of the Tsar streamed home to European Russia, leaving the Allies with a colossal hole in their defences.

Chaos now reigned in the Caucasus and Central Asia, some parts of which were in the hands of the Bolsheviks, others in those of rival socialist groups, while yet others had set up anti-revolutionary governments which appeared to be still loyal to the Allies. Large numbers of Austro-Hungarian prisoners who had been interned in Central Asia were now abandoned by their Russian captors (see TASHKENT) and were free to re-form themselves into a fighting force. The Allies feared that they might join up with the Turks, who were now moving east towards the Caspian to fill the vacuum left by the departing Russians, and thus become a serious threat to India. All the towns along the Transcaspian railway had been taken over by the truculent navvies, who belonged to various revolutionary groupings. Ashkhabad was in the hands of the Social Revolutionary (SR) Party, although there were plenty of traditional (White) Russians around, keeping a low profile. To them, no doubt, one revolutionary seemed much like another, but in fact the Bolsheviks were gradually consolidating their power. Although they had been glad to make use of any assorted socialists and republicans in forcing through their coup, by 1918 they felt strong enough to start the systematic extermination of all rival factions.

Tashkent had a particularly ruthless Bolshevik government, who had no compunction in recruiting murderers and other criminals as their hit-men, and who forced large numbers of Austro-Hungarian ex-prisoners to join the Red Army. The Commissars of Tashkent decided to 'deal with' Ashkhabad in the summer of 1918, and dispatched there a Lettish ex-convict named Fralov, together with a bodyguard of one hundred armed Hungarians. On arrival he summarily shot a number of the railwaymen leading the town's SR government, and the others went into hiding as a reign of terror was unleashed. Fralov dispensed 'justice' all day and drank most of the night, often driving round Ashkhabad with a party of shrieking, drunken women, firing his revolver at random. His bodyguard, it seems, were no better and entered into all his excesses with the greatest enthusiasm. But in the end Fralov got his come-uppance. Becoming bored with killing the citizens of Ashkhabad, he travelled down the line to Kyzyl Arvat, incautiously taking his entire bodyguard with him, and leaving a hastily appointed Bolshevik government behind.

As it happened, a British intelligence officer disguised as a Persian trader was passing through Ashkhabad at that moment, on his way to Krasnovodsk. Captain Reginald Teague-Jones got off the train for a breath of fresh air and realised that something was afoot. He wrote in his diary: 'There seemed to be a certain amount of excitement going on in the town and we saw detachments of mounted men moving along the streets. One detachment appeared to be entraining for somewhere and we were told that they were en route to Kyzyl Arvat to impress the population there ...'

As soon as Fralov arrived at Kyzyl Arvat he shot dead three of the railway workers' leaders, and his bodyguard shot indiscriminately into the angry crowd which gathered. A message was quickly passed up the line to Ashkhabad, where the incensed railwaymen marched on their new 'Soviet' and hanged nine Commissars forthwith. Proclaiming a new SR government, they then raided the military stores and distributed several thousand rifles to the populace (including the Turcomans), most of whom had never handled a gun before. Having cut the telegraph line to Kyzyl Arvat, they sent a train loaded with armed men and hidden machine guns down the line to the aid of their comrades. Arriving early in the morning of 12 July, they had the good fortune to find Fralov and his merry men lolling around the station, clearly suffering the after-effects of one of their drunken orgies. In steamed the innocent-looking train: minutes later there was not a single Bolshevik left alive. When word got round, the remaining Bolsheviks along the

Transcaspian railway hastily surrendered, from Krasnovodsk to Merv, and the jails were filled to overflowing.

Captain Teague-Jones arrived back in Ashkhabad at this interesting moment, having accomplished a satisfactory piece of anti-German sabotage on the shores of the Caspian. (German agents had arranged for Transcaspia's entire cotton stocks to be diverted to their munitions industry, but the British agent had the ship unloaded and sent off empty.) Teague-Jones, fluent in Russian, German and Persian, adept at disguises and with nerves of steel, might have stepped from the pages of spy fiction, and anyone who wants to know more of his astonishing story should read his memoirs *The Spy Who Disappeared*. Based in Meshed, in Persia, where the British had hurriedly sent a small military mission when Russia left the war, he spent most of 1918 commuting along the Transcaspian – which he was quite prepared to blow up if necessary – and across the sea to Baku where General Dunsterville and a small British force were helping the populace to hold out against the Turks.

In Ashkhabad Teague-Jones now found himself being introduced to some 'very shady-looking individuals', who turned out to be the leading lights of the new SR government. Hearing that Teague-Jones belonged to the staff in Meshed – for he felt it was now safe to reveal his true identity – the comrades immediately asked if the British could send them some troops to help fend off the Tashkent Bolsheviks, who would be sure to send a revenge force against them. The young officer explained that the task of the Allies was to win the war, and that meant – in this part of the world – blocking any enemy advance into Transcaspia. If the comrades were to help in this, he hinted, the Allies might well help them in return in their struggle against the Bolsheviks. But it was agreed that they should apply formally to General Malleson in Meshed, and Teague-Jones moved on again to Krasnovodsk. What he did not disclose to the Russians was how very few men Malleson and Dunsterville had at their command, in this far-flung corner of the war zone. The Second Battle of the Marne was raging on the Western Front in July 1918, it must be remembered, and the death toll in Europe could already be reckoned in millions.

At Krasnovodsk Teague-Jones jumped on the ferry for Baku, for he desperately needed a map of the harbour and coastal defences. It would be bad enough if the enemy were to gain control of Baku's valuable oilfields, but the British would still do their best to stop them getting across to Transcaspia. On the ferry he met 'rather an attractive little Russian girl, Miss Valya Alexeeva', whose parents lived in Krasnovodsk and who was going to visit her uncle in Baku. Amid all the turmoil and danger, Teague-Jones found time to fall in love, and Valya was later to become his wife. However, having obtained his map, Teague-Jones had to dash back to Transcaspia, leaving Valya behind, for he had heard that the Tashkent Bolsheviks were already sending a revenge force along the railway.

The Ashkhabad government was terror-stricken, for its forces were very few, whereas Tashkent had a seemingly unending supply of well-trained Austro-Hungarians. The Turcoman tribes were an uncertain ally, for although they hated the Bolsheviks, they had been unsettled by Turkish propaganda stressing their common origins, and they were now inclined to hate all Europeans. Still, the Ashkhabad government was in no position to pick and choose, and money and rifles had been handed over to the Turcoman cavalry units. Malleson reluctantly sent a company of the 19th Punjabis along to help, guessing that he would come in for criticism whatever he did. Meanwhile the Transcaspian forces had been attacked by a much larger force of Bolsheviks, and were being steadily beaten back along the railway towards Ashkhabad. Stiffened by the arrival of the Indian machine-gunners and their British officers, they made a stand at a place called Dushakh. The action there was little more than a skirmish, but it was the first time British and Russian troops had actually exchanged fire in Central Asia. When the news got back to Tashkent it was regarded very seriously indeed.

Teague-Jones was wounded in the thigh at Dushakh, possibly by the trigger-happy Turcomans whose shooting from the rear was almost more of a hazard than that of the enemy in front. In Ashkhabad he was nursed back to health by a devoted – and very determined – White Russian girl, Lyubov Mikhailovna, who carried a Colt .32 in her handbag, and kept lists of suspected enemy spies in a notebook.

A formal agreement had by now been entered into by Malleson and the SR government of Ashkhabad, led by Comrade Funtikov, and Teague-Jones was appointed Political Representative. The general aims of the 'protocol' were the establishment of peace and order in Transcaspia and resistance to Turko-German plans to seize control.

It was not an easy assignment for the young Englishman. Funtikov, a former engine driver, was illiterate and rarely sober, and the only member of his government who had any education at all was the 'Foreign Minister', a taciturn ex-schoolmaster called Zimin. In the middle of September Baku finally fell to the Turks, and Transcaspia was virtually cut off from the rest of the world. Food and fuel shortages became acute in Ashkhabad, adding to Teague-Jones's already difficult task, but at least there was one consolation. Valya Alexeeva, after a narrow escape from Baku, made her way to Ashkhabad to give her future husband – now hobbling about on crutches – some clerical assistance. How Valya and Lyubov hit it off together Teague-Jones does not disclose in his memoirs, but Valya was clearly a lot less intimidating than her gun-toting rival.

With the end of the First World War in November 1918 the British in Transcaspia began to plan an orderly withdrawal. This was depressing news for the SR government, and for the Turcoman tribes, who knew that they would never be able to hold off the Bolsheviks without British help. After the Armistice, General Malleson came to Ashkhabad on a visit and, to Teague-Jones's joy, brought with him some jolly young staff officers. Although he admitted that to anyone with a sense of humour, the Ashkhabad Mission was 'one big joke', his isolation and constant difficulties had of late been getting Teague-Jones down. Now, with the arrival of 'these cheery lads', his load was lightened and he could once again see the funny side of things.

One of the staff officers, Captain Ellis, later wrote a book, *The Transcaspian Episode*, in which he recalled the electric atmosphere in Ashkhabad in those days. He was particularly struck by the defiant 'eat, drink and be merry' attitude of the middle classes, whose lives, prosperity and prospects were now in ruins:

> Restaurants and cafés were full, and a number of establishments of the *café chantant* type did a roaring business. Ashkhabad possessed no theatre, but several cinemas continued to show old films, many of them American slap-stick comedies and French bedroom farces of the old Max Linder type. Many officials spent long hours in cafés engaged in interminable discussion over glasses of tea or a bottle of cheap Caucasian

wine. Russian hospitality needs no special occasion to express itself, being limited solely by means. In Ashkhabad at this time there was no end to private parties; dinners, teas or simply informal gatherings to drink and gossip.

It was difficult to make out what the native community thought of the situation. According to Ellis they spent most of their time wandering about the bazaars on the outskirts of the town, or sipping green tea in the *chai-khanas*. Although superficially there was nothing abnormal about day-to-day life in Ashkhabad, he noted that 'the atmosphere of the town was tense', and that the various different communities eyed each other with suspicion, if not dislike.

Teague-Jones missed the cheerful presence of Ellis and his companions when they returned to Meshed – 'in ample time to be back home for Christmas and New Year', as he tartly noted – but his own lonely days were drawing to a close. When he left Ashkhabad in the spring of 1919, he was given a rousing send-off by the government and by representatives of the town, the railway workers and even the Turcomans, in appreciation of his untiring efforts to help them. Within a year Ashkhabad was re-captured by the Bolsheviks, and Funtikov, Zimin and the rest were shot.

The Bolsheviks decided to rename the town Poltoratsk, after the Chief Commissar appointed by Fralov who had been hanged by the SR railwaymen when they seized control. But this was a sensitive area, for anyone associated with Fralov was linked in the people's memory with the reign of terror he had perpetrated, and they found it hard to look upon Poltoratsky as a martyr. At all events, in 1927 the town reverted to its ancient name of Ashkhabad. Gradually the proud nomadic Turcomans were collectivised, and their traditional crafts turned into industries. Rugs had been woven by their women since time immemorial, without any need for formalised patterns, for the tribal motifs were simply passed down from mother to daughter. Marco Polo had admired them in the thirteenth century, and they were evidently exported to Europe by the sixteenth for they appear in Italian Renaissance paintings. Now the Communists did away with the traditional mobile looms, along with the tents of their owners, and the Ashkhabad Carpet Factory was set up instead. There used to be a Turcoman saying: Unroll your carpet and I shall see what is written in your heart. Now the women workers were encouraged to draw up politically correct designs in advance. Lenin's face became a particular favourite.

The fur we know as 'astrakhan' – named after the town from which it was traditionally marketed – comes from the *karakul* sheep of Turkmenistan. The Turcoman word means 'black rose', and every tribesman used to wear a tall black sheepskin hat, or *papakha*, winter and summer alike. Soviet technology enabled the new Ashkhabad fur industry to produce astrakhan in every shade of grey and brown as well as black. Cotton had always been grown in irrigated areas around the city, and in 1898 Mr Woolrych Perowne had noticed experiments at the Botanical Gardens on various strains of the plant. Now this, too, became a major industry, for the Soviet Union was determined to become self-sufficient in cotton. The first textile factory was begun in 1926, but this – like so much else in Ashkhabad – was destroyed by a severe earthquake which rocked the city in October 1948. The splendid colonnaded station collapsed, along with schools, hospitals, theatres, shops and all the municipal buildings. Over 100,000 people are believed to have perished in what is still known locally as 'The Catastrophe'. By a bitter irony, the architect of one of the few buildings which did not collapse had by then been liquidated by Stalin on the pretext that he was a bad builder.

The construction of the Kara Kum Canal in the early 1960s, diverting water westwards from the Amu-darya – to the progressive detriment of the Aral Sea – solved Ashkhabad's water problems and gave the town an even more verdant appearance, as well as enabling more cotton to be grown. After reservoirs had been built either side of the town, the citizens were introduced to the novel pastimes of bathing and boating in the middle of the Kara Kum desert. But for the Turcoman – still wearing his *papakha* in the blazing heat of summer – the main recreation is, as ever, to sit inscrutably in one of Ashkhabad's *chai-khanas* sipping a glass of pale green tea.

BOKHARA
The Forbidden City

In all other parts of the world light descends upon earth.
From holy Bokhara it ascends.

Central Asian saying

Bokhara, the most shameless sink of iniquity that I know in
the East ...

Arminius Vambery

WHEN GENGHIS KHAN and his Mongol horde swarmed into
Bokhara in 1220, after a desperate siege, their only thoughts
were of rape and plunder. After this the remaining inhabitants were
put to the sword and the city was burnt to the ground, leaving the
brick-built central mosque standing desolate amid the smoking
rubble. This mosque had been built in 712 by a previous invader, the
Arab general Kutayba ibn Muslim, on the site of a Zoroastrian temple,
for Bokhara had already passed through many hands and seen many
religions come and go. Compared to Genghis Khan, Kutayba had been
a benevolent conqueror, encouraging the citizens to continue with
the trade for which they were famous and only stipulating that they
give up fire-worship and convert to Islam. When the Bokharans clung
stubbornly to their old beliefs, he devised a two-pronged strategy:
every man attending Friday prayers would receive two *direms*, a sum
worth having, while a devout Arab was billeted on every household
to keep an eye on their religious progress. Before long Bokhara had
become zealously Muslim, and has remained so ever since.

Surrounded on all sides by desert and salt marshes, but watered
by the muddy Zarafshan river, Bokhara was an important staging-

point on the network of caravan trails which criss-crossed Central Asia and which much later came to be known as the Silk Road. In settled times the trade routes stretched to far-off China in the east and the Mediterranean in the west; in times of trouble trade dwindled to the local – to Merv and Samarkand, and perhaps the Ferghana valley. Business had prospered under the Arabs when they ruled Central Asia, and again in the tenth century when the Persian Samanids had taken control. In fact this was a golden age for Bokhara, and scholars, poets, artists and architects congregated there. Abu Ali ibn Sina, better known in the West as Avicenna, devised his medical canons in Bokhara, and Abubakr Narshakhi wrote a *History of Bokhara* which shows that it already had all the hallmarks of a typical Central Asian fortified town. There was a central *registan* or square, a citadel, and markets divided up according to the various trades, and the city was surrounded by stout walls pierced by eleven gates.

One of Bokhara's glories in the tenth and eleventh centuries was its library, which filled several rooms of the royal palace, and which was rivalled only by the famous library of Shiraz, but this – like everything else of no obvious pecuniary value – was destroyed by the Mongols. However, Bokhara's favourable position as a staging-post led to its reconstruction a hundred years later, when it was part of the empire of Genghis Khan's descendant Tamerlane, who amassed riches from trade as well as from conquest.

> Bokhara was not merely a luxurious city, it was also the principal emporium for the trade between China and Western Asia, in addition to the vast warehouses for silks, brocades and cotton stuffs, for the finest carpets and all kinds of gold and silver-smiths' work; it boasted a great money-market, being the Exchange of all the populations of Eastern and Western Asia; and there is a proverb current to this day: 'As wide awake as a broker of Bokhara'.
>
> Vambery, *History of Bokhara*, 1873

By the time Anthony Jenkinson, agent of the Muscovy Trading Company, visited Bokhara in the winter of 1558, the links with China had been severed, but the city was still a thriving centre of trade. 'There is yearly great resort of merchants to this City,' he reported, 'which travel in great Caravans from the Countries thereabout adjoining, as India, Persia, Balkh, Russia, with divers others, and in times past from Cathay, when there was passage.' The language spoken there was Persian, he found, and its ruler was fanatically Muslim. Religious police were empowered to enter any house, and anyone found in possession of alcohol was 'whipped and beaten most cruelly through the open markets'. Slavery was normal practice, and among the slaves Jenkinson was shocked to find many European Russians. After spending nearly three months in Bokhara assessing the possibilities for trade, Jenkinson had the satisfaction of rescuing twenty-five Russian slaves and delivering them personally to the Tsar of Russia on his way home.

In the middle of the eighteenth century Bokhara was conquered by the Mangits, an Uzbek tribe whose rulers seemed to outdo one another in viciousness. 'Drunkenness, gambling, carousing and lewdness are rampant,' wrote a contemporary scholar, 'and the poor people have nowhere to go ...' This depravity, coupled with the unsavoury practice of snatching unwary Russian nationals – often women and children – from the environs of Orenburg and selling them in the slave market, would later give Tsarist Russia a pretext to annex the Emirate. In the meantime it was a dangerous place for strangers, and when the Russians sent a trade mission to the Emir in 1820, they took the precaution of bringing along a couple of powerful artillery pieces just in case. One of the more daring members of the mission, a Dr Eversmann, slipped into the old town disguised as a native. Sure enough, he found there 'all the horrors and abominations of Sodom and Gomorrah', most of which he felt too 'constrained by shame' to describe.

But the artillery pieces had the desired effect and the Emir saw the wisdom of co-operating with his huge northern neighbour, over trade at least. When William Moorcroft, an employee of the British East India Company, managed to get to Bokhara in 1825, hoping to find a lucrative new market for the Company, he discovered that the bazaars were already full of shoddy but cheap Russian goods. It must have been a bitter moment for Moorcroft, who had for many years been warning anyone who cared to listen of Russian designs on Central Asia. He died in mysterious circumstances on his way back to India, along with his two European companions and their interpreter. However, seven years later another emissary from 'John Company' turned up in the oasis, this time with a happier outcome.

Lieutenant Alexander Burnes, later knighted and always remembered as 'Bokhara Burnes', had already, at the age of 26, been entrusted with a number of delicate missions. A brilliant linguist, and possessing a thorough understanding of the flowery hyperbole so necessary when dealing with eastern potentates, he sent a flattering message to the Emir's chief minister, the Koosh Begee, requesting permission to visit the holy city. His letter clearly struck the right note, for he was speedily invited to be the Emir's guest, and granted an immediate audience with the Koosh Begee. On the two-mile walk to the royal palace Burnes says he was 'lost in amazement' at the novel scene before him:

The circumference of Bokhara exceeds eight English miles; its shape is triangular, and it is surrounded by a wall of earth, about twenty feet high, which is pierced by twelve gates. Few great buildings are to be seen from the exterior, but when the traveller passes its gates he winds his way among lofty and arched bazaars of brick, and sees each trade in its separate quarter of the city. Everywhere he meets with ponderous and massy buildings, colleges, mosques and lofty minarets. About twenty caravanserais contain the merchants of different nations ...

Burnes, *Travels into Bokhara*, 1834

Having received the favour of the Koosh Begee, Burnes was able to walk freely about the city and converse with its inhabitants, who came from the four corners of Asia:

My usual resort in the evening was the *Registan*, which is the name given to a spacious area in the city, near the palace, which opens upon it. On two other sides there are massive buildings, colleges of the learned, and on the fourth side is a fountain shaded by lofty trees. A stranger has only to seat himself on a bench of the *Registan*, to know the Uzbeks and the people of Bokhara. He may here converse with the natives of Persia, Turkey, Russia, Tartary, China, India and Cabool. He will meet with Toorkmans, Calmuks and Cossacks from the surrounding deserts, as well as the natives of more favoured lands.

Burnes was, like Jenkinson before him, appalled by his visit to the slave market. In his book he wrote that 'the feelings of an European revolt at this most odious traffic', but etiquette prevented him from making his feelings too obvious. One night he was secretly visited in his lodgings by a Russian who had spent twenty-five years as a slave in Bokhara. Grigory Pulakov told Burnes how he had been abducted as a small boy by a band of Turcoman raiders. He could still speak Russian, however, and confided with tears that he had remained a Christian although he had to keep up an outward semblance of being a Muslim. His dearest wish was to see his native land once more before he died. Burnes was deeply moved, but could only mumble a few comforting platitudes. He was powerless to help.

Alexander Burnes never met the Emir in person, but perhaps that was just as well. Nasrullah Khan had seized the throne in 1826, having secured his accession by beheading his three brothers and, for good measure, twenty-eight other close relatives. He was to become one of the most feared and hated men in Central Asia, and was already paranoid about his personal security. Any food or drink intended for him was first tasted by several officials. After an hour, providing there were no ill-effects, it was sealed in a container and sent to the royal table. 'We shall hardly suppose', commented Burnes, 'that the good king of the Uzbeks ever enjoys a hot meal or a fresh cooked dinner.'

'English imagination has for centuries been stirred by the romantic associations of Bokhara,' wrote the Honourable George Curzon in 1899, 'but English visitors have rarely penetrated to the spot.' In view of what happened to the next visitors to venture there after Burnes this was hardly surprising. The names of the ill-fated Stoddart and Conolly, went on the future Viceroy of India, would be forever inscribed 'in the martyrology of English pioneers in the East'. Their story is too well-known to need repeating in detail here, but briefly Lieutenant-Colonel Charles Stoddart had been hastily dispatched as an emissary of peace in 1838, as a counterbalance to Britain's warlike activities in nearby Afghanistan. A brave and capable army officer, Stoddart was unfortunately not trained in oriental diplomacy. He got off to a bad start when he failed to dismount when he first encountered the Emir outside the Ark, or palace.

Things went from bad to worse when he was granted an official audience. Required by the court usher to make a symbolic act of submission, Stoddart thought he was being manhandled and, knocking the man down, he strode alone and unannounced into the presence of the Emir. Mortally offended, Nasrullah ordered him to be seized and bound, and he was flung into a subterranean prison. 'This horrid dungeon,' wrote a later visitor, 'in which he was confined with two thieves and a murderer, swarmed with innumerable ticks and every disgusting species of vermin, which are especially reared to annoy the wretched prisoners; and should this prison by any extraordinary chance be without inmates, that the vermin might not perish they are supplied with rations of raw meat.'

Sometimes allowed out of prison and kept under house arrest, and then for no apparent reason thrown back into the stinking pit, poor Stoddart began to feel abandoned as the months dragged by. A letter dated 26 June 1841, which he managed to smuggle out to Kabul, in Afghanistan, says poignantly: 'A painful three years have passed away without my being able to hear and give any news, and I venture to inquire of my kind friends what they are doing, and to beg a line in reply ...' His friends had in fact protested loudly and indignantly at the British government's failure to rescue its messenger, but with a storm brewing in Afghanistan there was no way a military expedition could be sent to Bokhara. The wily Emir was aware of this, and also felt he could snub diplomatic efforts by the Russians to free Stoddart since they had just suffered a disastrous reverse in the course of an expedition to his fellow despot and arch-enemy, the Khan of Khiva.

But also travelling in Central Asia at this time was an officer of the Indian Cavalry, Captain Arthur Conolly, who in October 1841 decided on a do-or-die rescue attempt. The Khans of both Khiva and Khokand, whom he had just visited, tried to dissuade him from this foolhardy venture, but Conolly was adamant. A devout Christian, he had been particularly shocked at a report that poor Stoddart had been forcibly converted to Islam. A recent disappointment in love may also have contributed to his mood of reckless courage. He arrived in Bokhara on 9 November, to find Stoddart almost wasted away from fever and ill-treatment but overjoyed to see him. Conolly was a man of considerable charm and at first got on well with the Emir, who allowed the two men to live in decent lodgings. But within a few weeks fate was to deal them a cruel blow. The British garrison in Afghanistan was ignominiously defeated, the British puppet Shah Shujah removed from the throne, and most of the departing troops and camp-followers slaughtered in the Hindu

Kush during the long retreat from Kabul. Confident that he need fear no reprisals from the defeated British, the Emir of Bokhara had Stoddart and Conolly flung into prison.

There they remained, in filth and squalor, for about six months, occasionally smuggling brief letters to the outside world. Conolly also managed to scribble tiny notes in the margins of his prayer-book. The last written evidence left by the two men was dated May 1842, and it seems likely they were executed around the middle of June. The following account was given a couple of years later to the Reverend Joseph Wolff by the Emir's Chief of Artillery:

> His Majesty became displeased, and both Captain Conolly and Colonel Stoddart were brought, with their hands tied, behind the Ark, in the presence of Makhram Saadat, when Colonel Stoddart and Captain Conolly kissed each other, and Colonel Stoddart said to Saadat: 'Tell the Ameer that I die a disbeliever in Muhammed, but a believer in Jesus – that I am a Christian, and a Christian I die.' And Conolly said: 'Stoddart, we shall see each other in Paradise, near Jesus.' Then Saadat gave the order to cut off, first the head of Stoddart, which was done; and in the same manner the head of Conolly was cut off.
>
> Wolff, *Narrative of a Mission to Bokhara*, 1845

Dr Wolff, who had courageously travelled to Bokhara in 1844, undergoing innumerable vicissitudes *en route*, in order to ascertain the fate of the two officers, was himself lucky to come back alive. When he asked for the bones of Stoddart and Conolly, so that they could be given a decent burial in England, he was told angrily that his own bones would need to be sent home if he was not careful. At one point he wrote a valedictory letter to his wife, the Lady Georgiana, feeling sure that his last hour had come. But fortunately, his eccentricity – or his faith – saved him, and the Emir decided he was harmless. Wolff returned to his devoted family in one piece, despite having been robbed, beaten and stripped naked in the course of his travels. Much later it transpired that Conolly's little prayer-book, its margins crammed with notes of alternating hope and despair, had been retrieved by a Russian prisoner who preserved it carefully until it could be smuggled to the outside world. Twenty years after her brother's death, Conolly's sister received it through the post in London.

After the tragedy which befell Stoddart and Conolly, few Englishmen felt inclined to venture into the domains of the treacherous Emir, but in 1863 a Hungarian scholar of linguistics, Arminius Vambery, arrived there with a party of Muslim pilgrims, disguised as a mendicant dervish from Turkey. This was not quite as suicidal as it sounds, for Vambery had spent some years in Constantinople studying oriental languages and customs, and was well-versed in the doctrines of Islam. All the same, he was perpetually under surveillance and was frequently cross-examined on religious matters – clearly to test his *bona fides*. He found Bokhara 'a most perilous place' for strangers and 'one of the dirtiest and most unhealthy places in all Asia', where the profligacy and wickedness of the inhabitants were only matched by the viciousness and hypocrisy of its rulers. The evil Nasrullah had died in 1860, but the present Emir shared his late father's depraved tastes and xenophobic tendencies. Three unfortunate Italians were already languishing in the Khana-Khaneh dungeon at the entrance to the Ark, where Stoddart and Conolly had been held during their last period of imprisonment. The Italians' only crime was to have come to Bokhara in search of silkworm eggs.

Vambery thought of the Italians every day, and shuddered as he passed the Ark ('this nest of tyranny') on his way to the *registan*. There he had made friends with a Chinese tea-merchant, who was tolerated by the Bokharans because he pretended to be a Muslim. He had sixteen different varieties of tea in his little shop, and could distinguish between them by touch, though the only tea on sale in the *chai-khanas* was the green type. Vambery soon discovered that there was a strict etiquette to tea drinking. It was indecorous, for instance, to blow on the tea if it was too hot: it must be swirled gently in the cup. 'One must support the right elbow in the left hand and gracefully give a circular movement to the cup,' he wrote in *Sketches of Central Asia*, warning that: 'No drop must be spilt.'

Tea was a very important commodity in Muslim Bokhara, for wine was forbidden and the city's water supply arrived from the Zarafshan river along an open canal. When the river was low, water was only allowed to flow into the canal once a week, or even once a fortnight, whereupon the hot and dusty citizens would precipitate themselves into the muddy water and perform their ablutions. They would be followed by their horses, cows and asses, and finally by the packs of stray dogs which lived on the city's dung-heaps. Not surprisingly, Bokhara was notorious for a parasitic infection, the *rishte* worm, dreaded by all travellers:

> One feels at first on the foot or on some other part of the body, a tickling sensation, then a spot becomes visible whence issues a worm like a thread. This is often an ell long, and it ought some days after to be carefully wound off on a reel. If the worm is broken off, an inflammation ensues, and instead of one, from six to ten make their appearance, which forces the patient to keep his bed for a week, subjecting him to intense suffering. The more courageous have the *rishte* cut out at the very beginning.
>
> Vambery, Travels in Central Asia, 1864

According to Vambery, Dr Wolff had been infected and had 'dragged with him all the way from Bokhara one of these long memorials of his journey'. It had been extracted eastern-fashion by one of the most eminent surgeons of his day, Sir Benjamin Brodie, sergeant-surgeon to George IV, William IV and Queen Victoria, when Wolff got back to London.

Some time after Vambery's departure the Italian prisoners were released after a year's incarceration and made their way back to Milan. One of them, Modesto Gavazzi, published an account there in 1865 in which he told the sad but heroic tale of a compatriot who had been the last European victim of the infamous Emir Nasrullah. Giovanni Orlandi was a clockmaker who had by mischance fallen into the hands of Turcoman slave-raiders near Orenburg. Acquired by the Emir of Bokhara, he had soon incurred his master's displeasure by refusing to embrace Islam, and was sentenced to death. Gavazzi, who heard the full story from a fellow prisoner who had known Orlandi personally, continues the tale:

> Orlandi, knowing that Nasrullah was a great lover of mechanical works, promised to construct for him a machine for measuring time, and thus obtained his pardon. Orlandi then made the clock which is on the tower over the palace gate, the only one which exists in all Bokhara. Nasrullah was so satisfied with it that he appointed Orlandi his artificer,

and gave him at the same time his liberty. Orlandi then lived an endurable life with the fruit of his labours, and as independently as he could under a government as capricious as that of Bokhara. During this time he made a telescope for the Emir, who unfortunately one day let it fall from the top of a minaret. He sent immediately for Orlandi to repair it; but Orlandi that day had been drinking with an Armenian or Hebrew who was allowed to drink wine, and came to the Emir a little intoxicated. The Emir therefore condemned him a second time to death, but repenting shut him up again in prison, enjoining him to embrace Islam if he wished his life to be spared. A Cossack, then a slave in Bokhara, was ordered to persuade Orlandi to be converted. He said that a mere appearance of submission would satisfy the Emir, who wished an act of submission rather than a formal renunciation of his religion, but Orlandi was so firmly opposed to it, saying that he preferred death to shame, that the Emir resolved on a hard trial. He had the executioner cut the skin of his throat, warning him that if on the morrow he should still be obstinate, he would have him killed. The threat did not move him, and the next day he was beheaded.

Gavazzi, *Alcune Notizie raccolte in viaggio a Bucaru*,
Milan, 1865

In 1868 Bokhara was absorbed into the Russian empire after a skilful military campaign by General Kaufmann from the new Russian base in Tashkent. The Emir was allowed to remain on the throne and his domains were officially a 'protectorate', but there was no doubt that the Russians were now in charge. This at least made it possible for Europeans to travel there in safety, and curbed the worst excesses of the ruler. Eugene Schuyler, an American diplomat from St Petersburg, was favourably impressed by Bokhara when he visited it in 1873:

I am not surprised at the high idea Asiatics entertain of Bokhara – it is officially called *al sherif*, the noble, for in spite of all its discomforts, it made upon me a very strong and a very pleasant impression. You cannot walk the streets without seeing at once that it is really a capital; the persons at leisure, well dressed, and riding well groomed and richly caparisoned horses, the crowd of idlers who beset the market place, even the very narrowness of the streets and height of the houses, the numerous bazaars and the great amount of trade which is constantly going on there, every day seeming like a bazaar day, show you that this is a metropolis.

Schuyler, *Turkistan*, 1876

One thing which Schuyler, in common with other Westerners, found abhorrent in Bokhara was the slave trade. Although the Russians had insisted that the slave market be closed down, Schuyler suspected that the trade still went on secretly. He was proved to be right:

We started out, without telling where we were going, and although the Mirzas followed after, they were not in time to prevent us. Entering into a large *sarai* we went upstairs into a gallery, and found a number of slaves – two little girls of about four years old, two or three boys of different ages, and a number of old men – all Persians. There were no women, either young or old, such being bought up immediately. The slaves were shown me by an old Turcoman, who told me that the market was rather dull just then, but that a large caravan would probably arrive in the course of a few days.

Although every sort of difficulty was put in his way, the kindly Schuyler eventually succeeded in purchasing a slave and giving him his freedom:

The boy, Hussein, who displayed remarkable cleverness and intelligence, remained with me for two years at St Petersburg, going to school, where he learned to read and write Russian and a little of German. He was afterwards apprenticed to the Court clockmaker, a worthy Tatar of the Musselman faith.

In 1882 Bokhara saw the arrival – forty years after Wolff – of another English clergyman. Henry Lansdell, rather scathingly dismissed by Curzon as 'the so-called missionary', was a man of determination as well as religious zeal. He somehow persuaded his terrified guide to conduct him to the Zindan, or main prison, where 'looking up a passage as we rode along, I saw outside a lofty building two prisoners chained together by the neck, and who, on my approach, cried most piteously for alms, which I gave them …' The two prisoners, it seemed, had the task of begging for all the inmates of the jail, who were otherwise allowed to starve. Lansdell was told that the Zindan had two compartments, the upper and lower dungeons, 'the latter consisting of a deep pit, at least twenty feet deep, into which the culprits are let down by ropes.' This latter, he continued, in his two-volume work *Russian Central Asia*, 'I suppose to have been the one in which Colonel Stoddart was first placed.'

Lansdell was not, however, permitted to see the Emir's personal dungeon, the Khana-Khaneh at the entrance to the Ark. Not a man to give up easily, he enquired whether it was true that vermin were specially bred there 'to annoy and prey upon the prisoners', but this was indignantly denied. Lansdell elicited the information that most prisoners admitted their guilt after a good beating, and were then speedily dispatched. Colonel A. Le Messurier, who passed through Bokhara in 1887 on his way back to India from home leave, was somewhat taken aback on first entering the *registan* to find himself witnessing a public execution. This was carried out, as in the case of Stoddart and Conolly, with a large knife. However, strangling had in the past been used for certain crimes, while other malefactors had been pushed off the top of the Minari Kalian, or Tower of Death. Curzon was told in 1888 that three criminals had been flung to their death in this way during the preceding three years:

> The execution is fixed for a bazaar day, when the adjoining streets and the square at the base of the tower are crowded with people. The public crier proclaims aloud the guilt of the condemned man and the avenging justice of the sovereign. The culprit is then hurled from the summit and, spinning through the air, is dashed to pieces on the hard ground at the base.
>
> Curzon, *Russia in Central Asia*, 1889

But this was a merciful fate compared to that reserved for a murderer whose victim came from a rich or influential family. Curzon heard of a recent case:

> He was handed over by the Emir to the relatives of the murdered man that they might do with him what they willed. By them he was beaten with sticks and stabbed with knives. Accounts vary

as to the actual amount of torture inflicted upon the miserable wretch, but it is said that his eyelids were cut off or his eyes gouged out. In this agonising condition he was tied to the tail of an ass and dragged through the streets to the market place, where his body was quartered and thrown to the dogs.

'It is consoling to know', commented Curzon, 'that this brutal atrocity was enacted in the absence of the Russian Resident who, it is to be hoped, would have interfered to prevent its accomplishment had he been upon the spot.'

Curzon had arrived in Bokhara via the new military railway built by the Russians from the Caspian Sea to Samarkand, thus linking – as Curzon picturesquely put it – the capital of Peter the Great with the capital of Tamerlane. During the 1860s and 1870s Russia had steadily absorbed large tracts of Central Asia which until then had been ruled by an assortment of despotic khans and roamed by wild tribesmen. Although some Westerners, including Arthur Conolly, had regarded rule by Christian Russians as preferable to that by heathen tyrants, it was nonetheless worrying for those in charge of the defence of India. Where would Russian expansion end? Curzon, then a young Member of Parliament, had hurried off to Central Asia to try and find out, the moment the Russians allowed foreign passengers to travel on the Transcaspian line.

Whatever strategic significance the railway might have, for the locals it had brought unheard-of prosperity, Curzon found. Foreign tourists were all eager to buy carpets, silks and embroideries, while dealers bought up arms, knives and metal-work, and pelts of the famous *karakul* sheep – known in the West as astrakhan. Ukrainian farmers had even carried off live sheep, to improve their flocks, and one way and another prices in Bokhara's markets had soared. At first, though, the local population had regarded the railway as something evil and menacing, and the Emir had insisted that it must not contaminate holy Bokhara by passing too close. This meant that the station, as well as the actual railway line, had to be built some distance away, and a 'new town' gradually grew up there. (As the station was called 'Bokhara' this led to some confusion, and the new town became known as New Bokhara or Russian Bokhara, until eventually it grew big enough to be a place in its own right and in Soviet times was given the name Kagan.) The Emir soon became a railway convert, however, and had a new palace built within easy reach of the station, while his subjects quickly overcame their fears – as Curzon recounts:

> Shaitan's Arba, or the Devil's Wagon, was what they called it. Accordingly it was stipulated that the line should pass at a distance of ten miles from the native city of Bokhara. This suggestion the Russians were not averse to adopting, as it supplied them with an excuse for building a rival Russian town around the station and for establishing a cantonment of troops to protect the latter ... When the first working train steamed into [New] Bokhara with rolling stock and material for the continuation of the line, the natives crowded down to see it, and half in fear, half in surprise, jumped into the empty wagons. Presently apprehension gave way to ecstasy. As soon as the line was in working order they would crowd into the open cars in hundreds, waiting for hours in sunshine, rain or storm, for the engine to puff and the train to move.

Curzon noticed that flowers were highly prized in this desert-girt city, and that 'many of the men wore a sprig of yellow blossom stuck behind the ear'. He was much taken by the appearance of the male population of Bokhara:

> Tajik and Uzbek alike are a handsome race, and a statelier population I never saw than in the streets and bazaars of the town. Every man grows a beard and wears an abundant white turban, and a long *khalat* of striped cotton or radiant silk.

Women, however, were a very different matter:

> I have frequently been asked since my return – it is the question which an Englishman always seems to ask first – what the women of Bokhara were like? I am utterly unable to say. I never saw the features of one between the ages of ten and fifty. The little girls ran about unveiled, in loose silk frocks, and wore their hair in long plaits escaping from a tiny skull-cap. Similarly the old hags were allowed to exhibit their innocuous charms, on the ground, I suppose, that they could excite no dangerous emotions. But the bulk of the female population were veiled in

a manner that defied and even repelled scrutiny. For not only were the features concealed behind a heavy black horsehair veil, falling from the top of the head to the bosom, but their figures were loosely wrapped up in big blue cotton dressing-gowns, the sleeves of which are not used but are pinned together over the shoulders at the back and hang down to the ground, where under this shapeless mass of drapery appear a pair of feet encased in big leather boots.

One of Curzon's favourite haunts was the Tcharsu or Great Bazaar:

It covers a vast extent of ground, and is said to consist of thirty or forty separate bazaars, of twenty-four caravanserais for the storage of goods and accommodation of merchants, and of six *timis*, or circular vaulted spaces, from which radiate the principal alleys, shaded with mats from the sun, and crowded with human beings on donkey-back, on horse-back and on foot. Long lines of splendid camels laden with bales of cotton march superciliously along, attached to each other by a rope bound round the nose …

Moneylending in the town was exclusively in the hands of Hindus from India. 'Living in caravanserais without wives or families,' noted Curzon, 'they lead an unsocial existence and return to their country as soon as they have made their fortune.' He noticed many Persians, who were presumably the descendants of slaves, and also Jews 'who are here a singularly handsome people of mild feature and benign aspect'. Professor O. Olufsen, a Danish geographer who made a number of visits to Bokhara between 1896 and 1899, was also struck by the appearance of the Jewish community:

They are all of distinct race and very handsome; especially their women, who are unveiled, are among the most beautiful in Bokhara. It is not known with certainty when the Jews came to Bokhara. They maintain themselves that their ancestors immigrated into Bokhara in the twelfth or thirteenth century, proceeding both from Persia and from Tunis. They no more speak Hebrew, but are able to read this language, and all their houses are decorated with Hebrew sentences.

Olufsen, *The Emir of Bokhara and his Country*, 1911

Nikolai Khanikoff, who had visited Bokhara in 1842 with a Russian mission, had commented on the unenviable social position of the Jews there:

> Their rights and privileges are exceedingly restricted; thus, for example, they dare not wear a turban, but must cover their heads with small caps of a dark coloured cloth, edged with a narrow strip of sheepskin. Neither are they allowed to wear any other apparel than plain *khalats*, nor to gird their loins with a broad sash, still less with a shawl, but must twist a common rope round their waist. But the most galling and degrading persecution to which they are exposed, and one which cramps their active pursuits in life, is the prohibition to ride within the walls of the town, either on horseback or on asses. This is felt the more severely because the streets of Bokhara, after a copious shower of rain, can with difficulty be traversed, not only by foot-passengers, but even on horseback, on account of the deep mud. Add to this that any Mussulman may strike a Jew in the town without incurring any responsibility, and kill him with the same impunity outside the walls.

> Khanikoff, *Bokhara: Its Amir and its People*, 1845

Indeed, the obligatory rope round the waist was to remind its wearer that he might be hanged at any moment. After the Russian annexation of Bokhara, the position of the Jews improved, and the hated rope was allowed to dwindle to a mere string. Olufsen noted the irony of Russians, associated in Central Europe with the contemptuous ill-treatment of Jews, being in Central Asia their saviours.

When he first visited Bokhara Olufsen was puzzled by the crowds of people swarming around the station, for the surrounding landscape was a sterile and desolate plain, glittering with salt. 'On what do all these people live,' he asked himself, 'who swarm here by hundreds on the arrival of the trains?' He soon realised that these picturesque natives were not residents of the station-town, but merchants from the old city, who had by now completely forgotten their distrust of the 'Devil's Wagon'.

As a guest of the Emir, Olufsen was quickly ushered to a carriage and whisked off to the palace, but things were very different for an ordinary tourist. The American travel writer, Michael Shoemaker, describes his arrival in June 1903:

> We were two very dusty, tired men as we descended last night from the cars at this station – descended from the comparative quiet of our compartment to the midst of such a throng as can only be found at a railway station or river-bank in the Orient: a sea of black faces topped by gigantic white turbans, thousands of glittering eyes and chattering tongues, thousands of hands eager to take possession of one's luggage. No chance of hearing, no chance of progress in such cases, until you lay about you with your stick, utterly regardless of what you hit and utterly forgetful of your early religious training ...
>
> Shoemaker, *The Heart of the Orient*, 1904

About half-way between the station-town and old Bokhara, the dreary plain was transformed into a fertile oasis with cultivated fields and gardens, shaded by elms, willows and an assortment of fruit trees. Olufsen always found this road thronged by picturesque travellers:

> Camels and dromedaries in long caravans solemnly drag along their heavy bales, hundreds of small donkeys loaded with hay or charcoal trip along, two-wheeled *arbas* creaking and groaning in all their joints find their way with difficulty among the numerous riders who in many-coloured caftans and with white turbans always gallop to and fro on this road, veiled women timidly trudge along on the edge of the road or ride on a donkey, generally with husband and child behind them ...

When he reached the city, the professor noticed some large spikes fixed to the entrance gateway. He enquired of the dignitary who had ridden out to welcome him whether these were used for displaying the bodies or severed heads of miscreants. 'Not any more,' was the laconic reply. Those not fortunate enough to be guests of the Emir or the Russian Resident had to choose between the rather primitive Russian hotels at the station, or a bare room in a caravanserai. Michael Shoemaker opted for the station, but some of the more enterprising Western visitors decided to stay in the old town. Ella Christie, a practical middle-aged Scotswoman, came well-prepared when she made two extensive trips round Central Asia just before the First World War. In Bokhara a collapsible bed was a must:

> Having secured a room at a caravanserai kept by an Armenian, I moved in my baggage. My portable bed and suitcases were the furnishing, for nothing was provided but the empty room. Had I ridden there on a camel or donkey, they would have been stabled in the court below. When evening fell the whole establishment was closed in by a huge nail-studded door, strongly barred, with a mouse-hole of an entrance at one side and a peep-hole through which to inspect the would-be entrant, all telling of troublous times …
>
> As to the question of food, the traveller has to make his own arrangements. Nothing is obtainable in the inn unless it be the standard bowl of *pillau* cooked once a day. Restaurants, or their equivalent, are wayside stalls offering bits of mutton broiled on skewers, and certain kinds of fried foods which emit a savoury smell; while drinks are to be had from the sherbet-seller who clinks his brass bowls as he walks along the street, or from the numerous tea-houses which serve as a form of club to the natives.
>
> Christie, *Through Khiva to Golden Samarkand*, 1925

Alexander Polovtsoff, who also travelled around Central Asia in the early years of this century, before being forced to flee as a refugee by the Bolsheviks, chose a caravanserai in Bokhara because of the view:

> The window, an open frame with no glass, encloses a square of deep blue sky with pale blue enamelled domes and minarets boldly towering in outline against the radiant background of azure. The top of each cupola is crowned by a stork's nest, and the clumsy birds stand flapping their black and white wings and clapping their coral-coloured beaks in deep contempt of the busy city down below.

Polovtsoff's memoirs of Central Asia, entitled *The Land of Timur*, were not published until 1932, when he was established in the West. Most visitors to Bokhara commented on the size of the storks' nests, including Stephen Graham, who gave up a conventional life in London to tramp on foot all over the Russian empire until the revolution put a stop to his wanderings. Inspired by Russian literature, he learned the language and then threw in his lot with Russian peasants and pilgrims, returning to London periodically to write his many books. In 1914 he roamed Central Asia – partly by train this time – and the resulting book, *Through Russian Central Asia*, published in 1916, contains this vignette of Bokhara:

> The Bokharans are a gentle people. They wear no weapons. They sit in the grass market and chatter and smile over their basins of tea. The little pink doves of the streets search between their bare feet for crumbs. The wild birds of the desert build in the walls of their houses and bazaars. On the top of the tower of every other mosque is an immense storks' nest, overlapping the turret on all sides. Some of these nests must be eight to ten feet high; they are round, and so look like part of the design of the architecture.

Ella Christie, a keen anthropologist, was delighted one day to receive an invitation to visit the house of a wealthy native family in Bokhara. As a woman, she was allowed to enter the harem:

> I was then led on to the women's quarter by a little son of the house, who showed it off with the airs of a *père de famille*, and with great dignity, in his little flowered coat and turban. Two young wives, fair in complexion, and two old women were the occupants, dressed in Bokhara red and yellow silk trousers, over which was a sort of coloured chemise in silk or muslin, and a profusion of jewellery, among which coral seemed greatly in favour, judging from the many strings of bright red beads around their necks. Their hair was dressed in countless little plaits ending in handsome ornamental and jewelled tassels. On their heads were little silk caps, round the edge of which was tied a high stiff handkerchief. Various children were running about, and even the little girls had two nose-rings apiece, one a button and one a pendent one.

She also spent time studying the various bazaars of the town:

> Bokhara is what may be called a 'sheepy' place. All the furs are sheep in various stages of growth, all the meat is sheep, and most of the cooking is done in sheep fat extracted from the

tail ... The centre of the astrakhan fur trade is in the Kara-Kul bazaar, as that is the name by which the fur is known in Central Asia. It is a two-storey building. On the upper one may be seen the buyers, walking up and down, while trying to effect a deal, and secret offers are made by pressure of the hands beneath the very long sleeves of the *khalats*. Representatives are to be found from all the chief European markets – London, Paris, Berlin, Leipzig, Moscow and Constantinople. The lambs of various ages, from a day old and upwards, are kept on the ground floor or court, and when sold are then slaughtered, the skins roughly cured with salt or alum, and then hung out to dry upon the stone wall balconies of the courtyard. Black is most in demand, though grey and white have a sale.

She was particularly impressed by Bokharan silk:

The silk bazaar, with its wonderful embroideries and velvets in colouring peculiar to Bokhara, also displays silk scarves of a texture unmatched for softness, woven in the natural colour of silk, and dyed in shades unknown to aniline, the secrets being handed down from father to son, chiefly by those of the Jewish community. Under the shade of some mulberry grove one may see these same scarves being woven on primitive looms, so different from the noisome manufactures that so-called civilization may bring.

Stephen Graham also visited the silk bazaar, and bought 'a delicious silk scarf of old-rose colour full of light and loveliness, falling into a voluminous grandeur as the melancholy Eastern showed it me'. He and Ella Christie must have been among the last to acquire such treasures, however, for the second decade of the new century was to see momentous changes throughout Russia. Bokhara in 1914 still had its air of immutability, as if it would be forever marooned in the Middle Ages. But in reality the Emir's days were drawing to a close. Tolerated for fifty years by the Tsars, the Central Asian potentates would receive short shrift from their Bolshevik successors. One by one the ancient caravan towns fell to the Red Army. Bokhara managed to hold out until 1920, but by then the entire Transcaspian rail network was under Communist control, including the station-town of Kagan, and it was only a matter of time before Bokhara itself was seized.

In the autumn of 1919 when a British intelligence officer, Colonel F.M. Bailey, passed through in disguise, the old city was an uneasy temporary home to fleeing White Russians who hoped to get across the desert to northern Persia. It was also infiltrated by Bolshevik secret agents from time to time, but these usually came to a bad end, for Bokhara was still swarming with the Emir's customary spies and informers. Bailey himself arrived there in decidedly peculiar circumstances and with a price on his head. He had been sent to Tashkent in 1918 by the British government, who needed to know what the Bolshevik attitude would be if Germany's allies the Turks made a push towards India through the former Tsarist provinces of Transcaspia and Turkestan. It soon became clear that the Tashkent government was a law unto itself, and extremely hostile to all Westerners (see TASHKENT), and Colonel Bailey was obliged to don a series of disguises and escape from Russia as best he could. After a nerve-racking year on the run, when all his escape routes seemed to be blocked, he had hit on a desperate expedient. Posing as a Serbian ex-soldier, a piece of flotsam from the Great War, he had managed to get himself recruited by the Cheka as a spy and sent to Bokhara. The secret police of Kagan were desperate for new recruits – and there were very few applicants – for the Emir of Bokhara was suspected of employing British officers to train his private army.

Once in Kagan, Bailey evaded the curiosity of his Bolshevik 'colleagues' by declaring that his mission was top secret. 'In the hotel the Bolshevik agents looked on me as a very brave man, who for the Soviet cause, was about to meet an unpleasant death in Bokhara,' he related in his book *Mission to Tashkent*. (For security reasons it was not published until 1946.) At least he now had a chance of escaping to Persia, after being hunted by the Reds for a year in and around Tashkent, far from any friendly border. The final irony occurred as he was about to set off for the old city. A wire had just arrived from Tashkent, he was told; it seemed that a dangerous Englishman might be on his way to Bokhara. Would he watch out for this villain, whose name was Bailey, and if possible arrest him?

Happily, Bailey did manage to get away from Bokhara with a small party of White Russians and two Indian Army NCOs, who had indeed been advising the Emir on military training. After three perilous weeks spent dodging Red Army patrols and contending with blizzards, thirst and near-starvation, they completed their journey across the intervening desert and steppe and crossed the Murghab river into Persia on 6 January 1920. Nine months later the Emirate of Bokhara was overthrown.

The Emir, abandoning his harem but taking with him his favourite dancing boys and as much of his wealth as he could carry, fled from his capital in September and eventually retired to Afghanistan. His precipitate departure left the Red Army with the task of disbanding the 400-strong harem, most of whose inmates were very reluctant to leave. M.N. Roy, an Indian Communist who helped 'liberate' Bokhara, describes the dilemma in his memoirs, published in 1964:

> Evidently some bold measure was called for. I advised the Revolutionary Government to issue a proclamation that the Emir's harem were entitled to go out and marry again. I felt that the proclamation would be a temptation for the soldiers, because the inmates of the harem were all good-looking and mostly young women. It was further declared that any soldier who would take a former inmate for his wife and settle down in peaceful domestic life, would receive a grant of land and some cash to cultivate it.

Still the ladies would not leave, and in the end the soldiers were allowed to go in, on their best behaviour, and choose for themselves. All ended happily, the women leaving dutifully with their new husbands.

Bokhara did not cast off its medieval image overnight, however, as the American Joshua Kunitz found even in the 1930s:

> I rise early and take a stroll through the outskirts of the old city. There are grey streets, grey fences, grey walls, low flat-roofed grey houses, all merged into one monotonous mass of corrugated grey, the same as they have been for centuries, hardened, immutable. As one gropes one's way through the endless labyrinth of Bokhara's narrow alleys, a queer sensation of timelessness creeps over one – millions of days, thousands of months, hundreds of years – as silent, as soft, individually

as indistinguishable as the vague silhouettes of the few veiled
women who glide mutely along the walls.

Kunitz, *Dawn Over Samarkand*, 1936

But this was only an outward impression. In fact the Bolsheviks
had been working hard to turn the feudal kingdom into a socialist
state. As an enthusiastic supporter of the Soviet system, Kunitz
sympathised with the problems encountered by the Commissars
with the local population, who were riddled with the most regrettable
bourgeois and mercantile tendencies:

> Revolutionary daring was needed, bold policy, measures that
> would activize the city workers, the handicraftsmen and the
> poor and middle peasants and draw them closely around
> the Party and the Soviets. But the complex nature of the
> revolution and the lack of any Bolshevik training among the
> local leaders precluded such a course ... In Soviet Bokhara
> people could buy and sell and bequeath to others their lands
> and their other belongings just as unrestrainedly as in any
> bourgeois country!

Indeed the locals displayed a distressing desire to continue their
old hierarchical habits by joining the Party in droves:

> The lack of theoretical clarity accounts also for the
> unwholesomely swollen ranks of the local Communist Party
> – a membership of 14,000 within a few weeks after the fall of
> the Emir. True, in the 1922 purge the membership was rapidly
> reduced from 10,000 to 6,000, then to 3,000, and finally to
> 1,000! But even that scarcely improved matters ...

Kunitz does not disclose the fate of those privilege-seekers who were
purged, but he admits that there was a lot of trouble with the Uzbeks, who
saw the revolution as a splendid opportunity to gain the upper hand over
their rivals, the Tajiks. However, a few years of correct Bolshevik training
suppressed such problems, and in 1924 the Soviet State of Bokhara
had an attack of theoretical clarity and unanimously voted itself out of
existence. Two new Socialist Republics were born instead – Uzbekistan
and Tajikistan – the town of Bokhara being absorbed into the former.
Old Emir Nasrullah must have turned in his grave.

Although the Soviet authorities were delighted to let people like M.N. Roy and Joshua Kunitz wander around their Central Asian dominions, they soon closed the area to foreigners when other visitors took a less uncritical view of the state of affairs there. But to a certain type of traveller such prohibitions simply acted as a challenge. In 1937 a young diplomat from the British Embassy in Moscow decided to see how far he could get in Central Asia before the KGB turned him back. Fitzroy Maclean was shadowed by a couple of morose secret servicemen, whose attentions he periodically eluded but who always managed to catch up with him in the end. They found the ten-mile walk from the station to the old town a sore trial, and Maclean himself was beginning to wonder if he was on the right road, when

> all at once the road took a turn, and topping a slight rise I found myself looking down on the broad white walls and watch towers of Bokhara spread out before me in the light of the rising moon. Immediately in front of me stood one of the city gates, its great arch set in a massive fortified tower which rose high above the lofty crenellated walls. Following a string of dromedaries I passed through it into the city.
>
> Maclean, *Eastern Approaches*, 1949

The moonlight made Bokhara 'an enchanted city, with its pinnacles, domes and crumbling ramparts'. Having no official permit, Maclean had to keep a low profile. He settled down for the night in the garden of a mosque, lulled to sleep by the flapping of the huge red flag which now adorned the top of the Kalian minaret, the former Tower of Death. With an air of martyrdom his escort followed suit. Next day the young diplomat explored the ancient city, resonant with its memories of the Silk Road, of Tamerlane, of 'Bokhara Burnes', Stoddart and Conolly, and Dr Wolff. But by daylight he saw that Bokhara was in a state of near-dereliction. 'The only changes', he wrote, 'are those which have been wrought by neglect, decay and demolition.' Maclean also noted percipiently:

> In Bokhara the process of Sovietization can have been neither rapid nor easy. The population were accustomed to being oppressed and tortured by the Emirs, but they were not accustomed to interference with their age-old customs and

their religion. There were the mullahs to be reckoned with, who possessed great influence over the population, and there were the capitalist class, the Begs, the merchants, both large and small, and the landowners.

The Bolsheviks clearly hoped that the old city would simply crumble to dust, taking all these problems with it. But Bokhara refused to die, and in the end the Soviet authorities began grudgingly to repair and renovate it. Much of the Ark was destroyed by fire, but the entrance has been restored – though not the infamous prison cell. The twin domes of the Mir-i-Arab *medresseh* once again sparkle with blue tiles, made in the traditional manner. Most of the city walls and all of the gates and watchtowers have disappeared, but some crumbling remnants can still be seen next to the sprawling open market. Bokhara no longer boasts the vast warehouses for silks, brocades and carpets, and there are no more bazaars for gold, silver and precious stones, but the market stalls of today are ablaze with fruit, as well as bright embroidered Uzbek caps, and garish modern fabrics.

Since the break-up of the Soviet empire, Islam has re-emerged as a dominant force in this holiest of all the Central Asian cities. Bokhara the Noble, at one time a place of pilgrimage and learning, with 360 mosques and 80 *medressehs*, once more resounds to the call of the muezzin. At weekends hundreds flock to the ancient shrines of saints, and the Koran schools are again full of young boys devoutly learning their scriptures.

GEOK-TEPE
Last Stand of the Turcomans

In war men are nothing; a man is everything.

Napoleon Bonaparte

Skobelev was the god of War personified.

General Kuropatkin

T HE NAME OF Mikhail Dmitrievich Skobelev will always be associated with Geok-Tepe, the mighty fortress of the Tekke Turcomans. His ruthless conquest of it in 1881 avenged earlier Russian humiliations at the hands of these fierce tribesmen and led to their permanent subjugation. It also cleared the way for the Tsar's annexation of the vast desert region between the Caspian Sea and the Amu-darya, or Oxus, river and enabled the Transcaspian railway to be built. The Tekke stronghold at this time was the long, thin Akhal oasis, starting about 100 miles south-east of Krasnovodsk, on the Caspian, and extending 187 miles along the line of the present railway. At its extremities the oasis was only about 20 miles wide, and no more than 45 at the centre, where Geok-Tepe was situated. This was the main settlement and the base from which the Tekke set out on their raids or *alamans*. The ruins of Geok-Tepe can still be glimpsed from the train today.

The nomadic Turcomans, whom scholars believe to have come originally from the Altai mountains to the north of Mongolia, had long been a thorn in everyone's flesh. The struggle for survival in the inhospitable tracts of Transcaspia led to bitter quarrels between the various Turcoman tribes, of whom the Tekke were one of the biggest. Colonel Petrusevich, a Russian scholar and soldier, made a study of the

Turcomans while surveying their lands in the 1870s and was forced to the conclusion that they were all 'rascals and thieves', raiding the Khivans, Bokharans, Persians and each other with equal enthusiasm. Every so often the settled peoples would rise up in fury and try to crush their Turcoman tormentors, but this only led to a sort of musical chairs: the Persians might drive the Salor out of Sarakhs, who would then flee to Merv and oust their kinsmen the Sarik, who would in turn seize Ashkhabad, driving the Yamud to the Akhal oasis, which was already full of Tekke. A new outbreak of raiding and plundering along the Kopet Dagh mountains would then ensue, and Persia would find the problem had simply moved westwards. And whichever tribe of Turcomans was ultimately left homeless would soon turn up at Sarakhs anyway, and the whole process would begin again.

The trouble was, as Petrusevich pointed out, there was just not enough water or grazing to go round, but it had to be admitted that the Turcomans really enjoyed raiding, and every young warrior longed to lead an *alaman*. The peaceable agricultural settlements of northern Persia suffered greatly, and more and more of their inhabitants, as well as their possessions, were abducted. For the Turcomans had found that there was a brisk market for Persian slaves at Khiva and Bokhara. Snatching Turcoman hostages proved to be of no use as a bargaining counter, for they were simply abandoned to their fate by their brethren. The problem was not new: the Persians had been searching desperately for a solution for at least 200 years. In the seventeenth century Shah Abbas the Great, finding himself harried on one side by the Turcomans and on another by the Kurds, had dumped 15,000 Kurds forcibly in the Kopet Dagh mountains on his northern border in the devout hope that these two turbulent peoples would exterminate each other. Needless to say, they did not.

But help was now at hand in the shape of the Russians. As successive Tsars had extended their borders southwards, and begun to trade with Central Asia, so Russian men, women and children became a prey to the 'man-stealing Turcomans'. Early in the eighteenth century it had already been estimated that 3,000 Russian subjects were being held as slaves in Bokhara alone, most of them abducted in Turcoman raids on caravans, or snatched from the isolated fishing communities along the northern shores of the Caspian Sea. Some, mostly unwary children, had even been taken from the outskirts of

Orenburg. In 1840 a British officer was able to persuade the Khan of Khiva to release 416 Russians enslaved in his city (see KHIVA), but as recently as 1875 a Russian caravan had been waylaid as it travelled between Krasnovodsk and Khiva and totally pillaged. The Turcomans were incorrigible, and in 1877 the Tsar decided to teach them a lesson.

General Lomakin was ordered to march on the Akhal oasis and occupy the Tekke fortress of Kyzyl Arvat at its western end. This entailed a 100-mile trek across the Kara Kum desert from Krasnovodsk, with large numbers of baggage animals carrying food and water as well as arms, ammunition and artillery. Lomakin's eight guns filled the Turcomans with terror and they quickly dispersed, but for some reason – presumably a shortage of supplies – Lomakin did not wait to receive their formal surrender but retreated hastily to the Russian fortress at Krasnovodsk. Because of the Russo-Turkish War which intervened in 1877–8, Russia was unable to follow up this action until the autumn of 1879, when Lomakin attacked the Tekke camp at Geok-Tepe. Inside the ramparts were 15,000 warriors, together with several thousand women and children. This time no fugitives were allowed to escape, and the *kibitkas*, or tents, within the clay walls were continually raked by artillery fire. But the Turcomans were driven to such fury that when the Russians tried to storm the stronghold, they were repulsed with heavy losses. 'Describe it as blind fanaticism or something higher,' a Russian eyewitness told the writer Charles Marvin, 'it was impossible not to see in the enemy men calmly contemplating death and meeting it with heroism.' Ignominiously, Lomakin was finally obliged to limp back to base with the remnants of his shattered force, abandoning most of his baggage animals on the way.

The blow to Russian prestige in Central Asia was devastating, and Turcoman insolence knew no bounds. They presented the Khan of Khiva with some captured Russian rifles, boasting that they now had so many they did not know what to do with them. They also began raiding villages along the Amu-darya river, on the edges of Russia's newly annexed province of Turkestan. General Lomakin was disgraced, and the Tsar turned instead to the vigorous, not to say ruthless, General Skobelev. This brilliant soldier, who was said to pursue danger as enthusiastically as he did women, was passionately anti-British, and he saw here an opportunity to spike their guns. The Russian Foreign Ministry had denied any intention of annexing Transcaspia, but they had said the same of Turkestan. Somehow this had not prevented General Kaufmann from quietly adding this territory, which was half the size of the United States, to the Tsar's already vast domains. The British were thus watching anxiously, wondering whether to believe the soothing assurances of the diplomats or to heed the bellicose noises of the generals, who often boasted that they would not stop until they had taken India. Now, Skobelev assured Tsar Alexander, the insufferable behaviour of the Turcomans of Transcaspia would enable him to pacify this lawless region with a clear conscience: it was his duty to confer on it the benefits of Russian suzerainty.

Lomakin had lost over 8,000 camels and Skobelev realised that transport would be one of the main problems, together with water. A light railway track was laid between Mikhailovsk (south of Krasnovodsk) and Kyzyl Arvat, and a water distillery was built near the fort of Krasnovodsk. Skobelev was a firm believer in the power of artillery to demoralise Orientals, and he allowed ten artillery pieces for every 10,000 troops. He also ordered a large supply of petroleum-filled shells, the better to terrify them, for his maxim when fighting natives was 'to astonish is to conquer'. He laid his plans carefully, and appointed as his Chief-of-Staff Colonel Kuropatkin, a man with an impressive record in the field who would soon become a General, and later War Minister.

Skobelev set out in the summer of 1880 from Chikisliar, a Caspian port near the Persian border, and continued to hug the frontier, which was well supplied with water from the Persian mountains, until he reached the edge of the Akhal oasis. Having captured the Turcoman stronghold of Bami, seventy miles from their capital of Geok-Tepe, he went forward with 1,000 men to reconnoitre the enemy positions. There were in fact three camps, each surrounded by enormous clay ramparts: the central one, on a mound, was known as Dengil-Tepe; the fort at the base of the hills was Yangi Kala; and the least significant was known by the general name of the area, Geok-Tepe. Skobelev decided that a full-scale siege was required, and retired to Bami – much harassed by roving bands of Turcomans, who were also attacking the supply lines to his other base at Kyzyl Arvat. Reinforcements of men and guns were summoned from the Caucasus. By the beginning of December all was ready.

This time the Tekke must have realised that they were in for serious trouble, and some 30,000 of them massed behind their crude fortifications, the majority in the central camp of Dengil-Tepe. This covered an area of about a square mile and was enclosed by mud walls eighteen feet thick and ten feet high on the inside, and surrounded by a ditch. Their only piece of artillery was an antiquated smooth-bore which they had captured from the Persians. The main Turcoman arms were Russian rifles seized from General Lomakin's force, and razor-sharp sabres, lethal in hand-to-hand fighting, but they had no effective long-range weapons. On 1 January 1881 Kuropatkin led an assault on Yangi Kala, using fifty-two cannon and eleven Hotchkiss machine-guns. The Tekke were forced to abandon this encampment, despite resisting fiercely, for they were helpless under the murderous artillery barrage, and on 3 January the Russians made Yangi Kala their new base. The following day they began their attack on Dengil-Tepe but the Tekke, now desperate, fought like men possessed. In a frenzied sortie they fell on their besiegers with their sabres, and the ground was soon strewn with severed heads and limbs. Three hundred Russians were left dead, including Colonel Petrusevich, whose study of the Turcomans had been published only a few months before in Tiflis.

The sheer heroic ferocity of the Turcomans gave them many such minor victories, but always the Russians were able to bring up reserves and advance their trenches, under the covering fire of their artillery. And all the time Skobelev was getting the enemy's measure and adjusting his tactics. Observing the slaughter – and terror – wrought by the fanatical Turcomans when they leapt suicidally into the Russian trenches, brandishing their vicious knives, he instructed his troops to creep back after sundown and lurk ten paces in the rear. So the next time the warriors made a sortie and leapt into the trenches, they found them empty, and it was the turn of the Russian soldiers to hack the enemy to pieces from above.

All the same, after three weeks of stubborn resistance by the Tekke, Skobelev was forced to revise his original plan. Clearly a siege was going to take too long, for these Turcomans would hold out to the last man. He would have to storm Dengil-Tepe, but he must not risk being routed like his predecessor. The General had come to respect this primitive foe, who refused even to evacuate the women and children who had to

endure stoically the terrifying hail of petroleum shells among their felt
kibitkas. On the eve of the final assault Skobelev reminded his troops
that they were up against a tribe 'full of courage and honour'. Dressed
in a white uniform, with all his decorations, he was a charismatic figure
and adored by his men. In the recent war in the Balkans the Turks had
called him Akh-Pasha, the White Leader, and the name had stuck.
After a battle, however, he was always covered in mud and dust, for he
was not one to lead from the rear, and his face would be haggard, his
eyes bloodshot and his voice a hoarse whisper. 'Old Bloody Eyes' was
what the Tekke called him.

On Skobelev's instructions, Russian sappers dug tunnels beneath
the walls of Dengil-Tepe and filled them with over a ton of gunpowder.
The Tekke watched uncomprehendingly, calling the Russians pigs,
digging their snouts into the earth. Early in the morning of 24
January two Russian officers blew a preliminary hole in the walls with
gun-cotton, and at first light the artillery battery began firing through
the gap, inflicting severe damage. At 11.20 a.m. the gunpowder-filled
mines were exploded, sending up a plume of smoke and rubble.
The sappers had done their work well, and fifty yards of ramparts
had been blown down. In well-ordered waves the Russians stormed
into Dengil-Tepe, each battalion with its band playing, its colours
flying and its drums beating. They would have been amazed to know
that twelve miles to the south an Irishman was watching the action
through binoculars from a spur of the Kopet Dagh mountains.

Edmond O'Donovan, special correspondent of the *Daily News*,
had persuaded some Turcoman chieftains to invite him to the Akhal
oasis as the Russians had barred him from the area. He arrived at his
vantage point rather late, but he was in time to witness the final victory
of the Russian forces and the panic-stricken flight of the Tekke:

> With my double field-glass I could easily make out the lines of
> the Turcoman fortress, and the general position of its besiegers,
> but I was too far off to be able to make notes of details. I could
> plainly see, by the smoke of the guns and the movements of the
> combatants, that the attack had begun in earnest, and I watched
> its result with intense anxiety. The Russian assault was directed
> against the southerly wall of the fortifications, and after what
> was apparently a desperate conflict there, it was evident that

they had forced their way. A crowd of horsemen began to ride in confusion from the other side of the town, and spread in flight over the plain. Immediately afterwards, a mass of fugitives of every class showed that the town was being abandoned by its inhabitants. The Turcoman fortress had fallen, and all was over with the Akhal Tekkes.

O'Donovan, *The Merv Oasis*, 1882

General Skobelev was later accused by his enemies of allowing his troops to rape and slaughter Turcoman women and children, running them down if necessary in the desert, although Colonel Kuropatkin always strenuously denied this. Certainly, like any good commander, Skobelev sent his dragoons and Cossacks in pursuit of the fleeing enemy, and many of both sexes were killed. His official report concludes: 'The enemy's losses were enormous. After the capture of the fortress 6,500 bodies were buried inside it. During the pursuit 8,000 were killed.' His policy towards an Asian foe was born of experience in the Caucasus and the Balkans, and was brutally straightforward: 'My system is this: to strike hard, and keep on hitting till resistance is completely over; then at once to form ranks, cease slaughter, and be kind and humane to the prostrate enemy.' In his declaration of victory to the Tekke he invited 'the whole remaining population of Akhal-Tekke to place its destiny at the unconditional mercy of the Emperor, in which case I hereby make it known that the lives, families and property of those who declare submission will be in complete security, like those of the other subjects of His Majesty the White Tsar'.

What undoubtedly did happen to some of the Tekke fugitives, however, was that they had the misfortune to fall into the hands of a rival Turcoman tribe – the Yamud – and that many old scores were paid off against the defeated Tekke. 'Private feuds are at all times more powerful among the nomads than even national interests,' wrote O'Donovan in his book, adding that 'any Turcoman will, when an opportunity arises, plunder friend or foe indiscriminately.' Seven years later, however, the Honourable George Curzon was certainly not prepared to give Skobelev the benefit of the doubt, when he visited the remains of Dengil-Tepe in 1888. The future Viceroy of India described the fall of Geok-Tepe sternly as 'not a rout, but a massacre; not a defeat but an extirpation', adding that 'it is not surprising that after this drastic lesson, the Tekkes of the Akhal oasis have never lifted a little finger against their conquerors'. Curzon first caught sight of the 'mouldering ruins' from the newly opened Transcaspian railway, while on a fact-finding tour of Russian Central Asia in 1888. The rammed-earth walls were still clearly scarred by shell holes, and the breach made by the Russian mine could easily be seen. So many thousands of slain were found inside the fortress, he was told, that the Russians had demolished more of the walls immediately after the battle, in order to cover the bodies in a makeshift mass grave. A French engineer, Edgar Boulangier, who saw the ruins briefly from the train at about this time, described the walls as looking from a distance as though they were full of rat holes. 'The shells had sunk into the massive clay walls as if into butter,' he wrote in his book *Voyage à Merv*.

Ten years later an English traveller on the Transcaspian railway felt uncomfortable when some survivors of the siege were wheeled out as a tourist attraction:

At 9.30 in the morning the train stopped close to the enormous mud walls of what was evidently a disused fort. We rightly guessed that this was the famous Geok-Tepe, the last strong-hold of the Tekke-Turkmans, when they were almost annihilated by the Great White General, Skobelev. When the train came to a standstill at the platform we found about forty Turkmans drawn up to receive us, headed by their *starshina* or headman. This latter was apparelled most gorgeously in cloth of gold, while the others wore the usual dress of the Turkmans, namely a long sort of dressing-gown of a dull red with small black stripes, high leather boots and the great sheepskin hat. Some there were present who had been in the fort when it was taken, and were fortunate enough to escape with their lives.

I have no desire to moralize, but who could fail to be struck with the fact that these fierce warriors who had held the power of Russia at bay for three campaigns should be drawn up on a railway platform within a stone's throw of their great ruined stronghold to do honour to a handful of English tourists? And though I was human enough to photograph these men, I was also human enough to be sorry for them, intensely interesting though it was to see them.

Perowne, *Russian Hosts and English Guests in Central Asia*, 1898

But Perowne, like Curzon, had to concede that 'whatever we may think of this wholesale slaughter, it answered in the end, for the Turkmans were thoroughly cowed, and the necessity for further bloodshed ceased from this time forward'. Indeed, so cowed were the Turcomans that at the opening ceremony for the Transcaspian railway they fell on their knees and begged for mercy when the band began to play. The only other time they had heard a military band was when Skobelev's troops stormed their fortress of Dengil-Tepe.

By 1914, when the writer Stephen Graham visited Geok-Tepe, the passage of time had softened some of these painful memories, and removed the starkness of defeat from the scene:

> At the railway station there is a room in which are preserved specimens of all the weapons used in the fight. There are also waxwork representations of a Russian soldier with his gun, and a native soldier cutting the air with his semi-circle of a sword. Many passengers turned out to have a look at these things. It was sunset time, and the west was glowing red behind the train, the evening air was full of health and fragrance, the stars were like magnesium lights in the lambent heaven, the young moon had the most wonderful place in the sky, poised and throned not right overhead, but some degrees from the zenith, as it were on the right shoulder of the night. It was an evening that touched the heart.
>
> Graham, *Through Russian Central Asia*, 1916

As for Skobelev, the victorious White General had died eighteen months after the fall of Geok-Tepe, at the age of only 38. His end was inglorious for he succumbed not on the field of battle but to a heart-attack in a seedy Moscow hotel, in compromising circumstances. Perhaps Nur Verdi Khan, the leader of the Akhal Tekkes, rested more peacefully in his grave at Dengil-Tepe.

GILGIT, HUNZA AND THE GREAT GAME

> The point of Gilgit is strategic. High above the snowline, somewhere midst the peaks and glaciers that wall in the Gilgit valley, the long and jealously guarded frontiers of India, China, Russia, Afghanistan and Pakistan meet. It is the hub, the crow's-nest, the fulcrum of Asia.
>
> John Keay, *The Gilgit Game*, 1979

To the east of Gilgit lie the Karakoram mountains and the glistening white peak of K2, to the south lie one end of the Himalayas and Nanga Parbat. The Hindu Kush range towers to the west, the Pamirs to the north and, completing the circle, the Kunlun rise bastion-like along the edge of Tibet to the north-east. Nowhere else on earth is there such a meeting of mountains. Small wonder that this region is known as the roof of the world.

Gilgit itself is simply a small trading post, once remote but now linked to Islamabad in the south and Kashgar in the north by means of the Karakoram Highway. When John Biddulph became Britain's first Political Agent there in 1877 the 220-mile journey from Srinagar in Kashmir took three weeks, and much of the road was a goat-track too difficult even for baggage ponies. The resourceful Biddulph got round this by attaching his bags to the backs of sheep, which had the additional advantage of not requiring fodder. Indeed, in case of need, they could always be eaten themselves. There was no telegraph in those days, and Gilgit was entirely cut off from the outside world for six months of the year by snow. It was a lonely posting for a young man and Biddulph rarely saw another white face, for the 'Pamir Knot' was a no-go area for foreigners. The ferocity of the local tribesmen – the Dards – was legendary. Remote Hunza was a refuge for caravan-raiders, while Chitral specialised in supplying captives for the slave-trade. The inhabitants of Yasin were a perpetual thorn in the side of Gilgit, which belonged to the Maharaja of Kashmir and which was inhabited by Dogras, enemies of the Dards. They all hated each other, but this was as nothing to their hatred of foreigners, for they were fanatical Muslims.

Yet this area had not always been a wilderness preyed on by bandits. Alexander the Great had crossed the Pamirs and the Hindu Kush in 326 BC and some of his followers settled down in the Indus valley, adopting the local religion of Buddhism and giving birth to the Indo-Greek art known as Gandharan. This rich civilisation spread northwards, for to the south it was opposed by the Hindus of India, and then east towards China, absorbing influences as it travelled. By the first century AD the Gilgit and Hunza region was part of the great Buddhist empire of a Central Asian people called the Kushans, who ruled from northern India to the Aral Sea. The steep track through Gilgit became a branch of the Silk Road, although some merchants preferred to travel through the Karakoram pass to Leh, on their way to India. There was always some looting of caravans, and a constant risk of avalanches or rock-falls in the mountains, but the profits were evidently worth the dangers and the traders never gave up. Equally tenacious were the pilgrims, for once China had been converted to Buddhism in the first century AD a stream of devout Chinese monks began to tramp the long road to Gandhara and India – birth-place of the Buddha – in search of holy places and further enlightenment.

After the fall of the Kushan empire in the fourth century the region was assailed by White Huns in the fifth and militant Hindus in the eighth, and finally fell to Islam in the eleventh when Mahmud of Ghazni led his warriors over the mountains from Afghanistan to conquer the Indus valley. Trade along the Silk Road declined for a while, for banditry flourished in troubled times, until ruthless subjugation by the Mongols in the thirteenth century imposed order throughout their vast domains. The pacification was so complete that even the dedicated raiders of Hunza and Chitral were obliged to retire to their mountain fastnesses, and caravans could pick their laborious way along the precipitous paths with only the natural hazards to contend with. But when Tamerlane died in 1405 the Mongol empire broke up and the Gilgit and Hunza region once again became the fiefdom of petty warlords and bandits.

Britain's interest in the area resulted from the ever-increasing activity of the East India Company from the seventeenth century onwards, and the need to safeguard its commercial operations. Indeed, by the mid-nineteenth century, the riches of India had become so important to the British economy that the government stepped in after the Mutiny and took control of the sub-continent in the name of Queen Victoria. Eastern Turkestan was by then a far-flung – and unruly – province of the Chinese empire, and Russia was beginning to expand southwards into the mass of petty khanates which comprised Kazakhstan and western Central Asia. Although the mighty mountain system to the north of India appeared at first glance to be an impregnable barrier to an invader, particularly one encumbered with all the paraphernalia of a modern army, India had certainly been invaded from the north in the past, and a number of passes through the mountains were evidently known to native traders. Mapping the area became a priority.

Both the Royal Geographical Society in London and the Imperial Geographical Society in St Petersburg began to sponsor travellers who were intrepid enough to venture into the region, and the Survey of India used native 'pundits' trained in covert surveying techniques. By the time Biddulph arrived in Gilgit the general outlines of the Karakorams and Hindu Kush had been mapped, although the Pamirs were still a mystery. Eight or nine passes were now known to lead to India from Central Asia, and no fewer than six of these were only a week's march from Gilgit, hence its strategic importance. The Maharaja of Kashmir, to whom Gilgit belonged, had agreed to Biddulph's appointment with some reluctance, for although he was officially Britain's ally, he was averse to the concept of fixed boundaries. Any territory he could wrest from the neighbouring Dards was, in his view, one of life's natural bonuses, and the last thing he wanted was interfering officials and surveyors telling him where his frontiers lay. Biddulph soon discovered that the Kashmiri Governor of Gilgit was actually in collusion with his supposed enemies, the Dards, and their combined hostility made his position as Agent well-nigh intolerable. His spirits were scarcely raised when he discovered in his garden a fallen headstone inscribed with the name of George Hayward. In an ill-advised surveying expedition to Yasin in 1870, Hayward had been treacherously murdered near the Darkot pass – apparently on the orders of Mir Wali, the ruler of Yasin. His body was later recovered and taken to Gilgit where it was buried beside the fort, and a headstone erected by the Royal Geographical Society. Biddulph had the melancholy memorial re-erected, and it can still be seen today in Gilgit's small Christian cemetery.

At first Biddulph was inclined to trust the good intentions of the ruler of Kashmir and to blame his difficulties on local obstructiveness, but after a while he was forced to the conclusion that 'the Maharajah whom for years I had looked on as a weak fool in the hands of knaves turns out to be as great a scoundrel as any in Asia and disloyal to the core'. It also seems likely that Britain's so-called ally had arranged for poor Hayward to meet his death, rather than Mir Wali who had conveniently become the scapegoat after fleeing from Yasin and dying in mysterious circumstances. Pahlwan, Yasin's equally rascally new ruler, was bold enough to besiege Biddulph in the winter of 1879, when the weather made it impossible for him to be relieved from India, and for a time the British Agent's position looked perilous. Fortunately the Khan of Chitral – Aman-al-Mulk – took advantage of Pahlwan's absence to seize Yasin for himself, and the siege of Gilgit was hastily abandoned while the Dards fought among themselves. After this little drama, though, the cautious new Viceroy of India, Lord Ripon, recalled Biddulph to Simla and closed down the Agency.

However, Russian activities in the Pamirs in the 1880s began to cause alarm in British India, and the 'Penjdeh Incident' in April 1885 – when Russian troops were discovered annexing a slice of Afghanistan – led to the adoption of a far more hawkish attitude by Britain. In fact, the Liberal government fell shortly afterwards, and a new British mission immediately set out for Dardistan under the leadership of Colonel William Lockhart. The native chieftains, now thoroughly scared, were only too eager to have their boundaries mapped if the alternative was having bits of their territory snatched by the Tsar, and they made no objection to Lockhart bringing half a dozen surveyors with him. However, the object of the surveying expeditions was, in John Keay's words, 'not the usual one of finding a way through the mountains and opening it up, but of finding all possible ways through and closing them', for the British authorities were now paranoid about a Russian invasion of India. The predatory policy of Imperial Russia and the fears for its frontiers of the British Raj collided in the high wilderness of the Pamir Knot, and the 'Great Game' began.

By dint of presents – breech-loading rifles were especially popular – Lockhart made himself reasonably welcome in Gilgit, helped in no small part by his medical officer Dr Giles. The standard punishment or reprisal around Gilgit was having your nose slashed, if not cut off completely, and Giles's skill in patching up noses soon brought him a stream of patients. In the course of their surveying expeditions the British mission visited the colourful Kalash people who lived in the mountains and valleys west of Chitral. They were a non-Muslim people, called Kafirs or unbelievers by the Dards, thought by some to be the descendants of the Macedonians left behind by Alexander the Great. Lockhart and his party were greeted by the Kalash as long-lost brothers and entertained with wine, feasting and dancing, although some of the Englishmen found the attentions of the Kalash women a little too cordial. 'To judge from their manners their morals cannot be very high,' wrote Lockhart censoriously. 'To put it in the mildest language they cannot have much modesty.'

The mission established that Chitral was the largest and most important of the Hindu Kush valleys, and also the most vulnerable from the north. Aman-al-Mulk, now a toothless old man, assured Lockhart that the British could rely on him to hold the passes against the Russians, and the Colonel rather naïvely believed he had thus 'secured Chitral'. However, there were others who felt, like Biddulph, that Aman-al-Mulk was 'avaricious, unscrupulous and deceitful to an uncommon degree', not to mention the fact that he was fast becoming senile. A further complication arose from his vast progeny. He was said to have at least sixty sons, any of whom might succeed as ruler, since fratricide was the usual manner of proceeding when one's father expired. Lockhart returned to India after a year of surveying and negotiating, and was shortly afterwards rewarded with a knighthood.

His confidence seemed justified two years later when in May 1888 the French explorer Gabriel Bonvalot arrived in Chitral from Russia. For he was promptly arrested by one of Aman-al-Mulk's sons on suspicion of being a Russian spy, and sent down to Simla. There the British were rather relieved to hear that he had suffered every sort of difficulty in his journey through the Pamirs, losing his baggage train and very nearly his life. Clearly it would be impossible for an entire army to come that way. But another shock was to come, for in 1889 a real Russian agent turned up, this time in Hunza, with a Cossack escort if not an army.

Safdar Ali, who had secured the throne of Hunza three years before by murdering his father, accepted Captain Gromchevsky's gifts of money and arms with unconcealed delight. His main income derived from raiding caravans on the road between Ladakh and Sinkiang, and he was quite willing to accept 'subsidies' from anyone – be it Russia, Britain or China – provided he was not required to cease these business activities. Emboldened by Gromchevsky's friendly overtures, Safdar Ali soon began aggressive moves against Gilgit, and the incompetent Kashmiri defenders were obliged to sue for peace. Britain riposted by reopening the Gilgit Agency, this time under Captain Algernon Durand, whose powerful brother Mortimer was Foreign Secretary of the British government of India. One of his first priorities was to persuade Safdar Ali to desist from his caravan raiding and to stop flirting with the Russians and Chinese.

But Durand found that getting to Gilgit in the first place was just as difficult as it had been in Biddulph's day, and required a good head for heights. Sometimes a circuitous zigzag path wound across the mountains for baggage animals, while foot travellers could take a shorter but dizzying goat-track which clung precariously to the sheer cliff sides, overlooking the boulder-strewn Gilgit river far below. Lockhart had lost practically all his expedition's cash when one of his mules had toppled over the edge, its saddle-bags stuffed with silver. Lord Curzon, who travelled this road a few years later, described it as being of the 'most villainous description, the descent of one very steep place only accomplished by the aid of a sort of fixed pole with projections, very much like the pole in the bear's den in the Zoological Gardens'. In his book *The Making of a Frontier* Captain Durand described the path as

> never more than a foot or so wide. Taking advantage of a ledge in a rock here, supported on pegs driven into its face there, carried across a bad place on a single shaky plank or light bundle of tamarisk, ascending fifty feet up a cleft in the rock

by a series of small tree trunks notched to give a foothold, and polished by years of use, the path is impossible for animals and is exclusively used by men on foot.

While Durand was settling in as British Agent in Gilgit, another young officer was making his way to Hunza on a military intelligence mission. Captain Francis Younghusband was the archetypal Great Game player. Only 26, but already a Fellow of the Royal Geographical Society, a born explorer with a knack for getting along with natives, he had already proved his worth as an intelligence-gatherer. (As he rose to fame, a number of people claimed to have been the first to spot his talents, including Sir William Lockhart who was by then a General and Commander-in-Chief in India.) Younghusband's first task was to identify the pass through which Safdar Ali's bandits crept on their caravan-raiding forays, and the best method seemed to him to make contact with some of their victims. Accordingly, after a gruelling journey of 185 miles – including three 18,000-foot passes – which typically took him only six days, he tracked down the Kirghiz caravan men to their encampment near the village of Shahidulah. Delighted that someone cared about their tribulations, the Kirghiz offered to show Younghusband the secret pass and begged to be regarded as Kashmiris, and therefore under British protection.

Between Shahidulah and the unknown Shimshal pass lay 200 miles of boulder-strewn ravines threaded by icy rivers which had to be forded several times each day. Although it was high summer, Younghusband's ponies emerged from these streams with icicles festooning their shaggy coats. But the pass was mapped by October, and at the far end the British party found themselves confronted by a bleak stone fortress known as 'the Gateway to Hunza'. There was no one to be seen, but a wisp of smoke rose from within, and the great door was wide open. Younghusband decided that any show of fear or indecision might well be fatal, so he boldly approached along the zigzag path, leaving his Gurkha escort behind him to provide covering fire in case he had to retreat in a hurry. As he reached the doors they were slammed shut and immediately 'the whole wall was lined with the wildest-looking men, shouting loudly and pointing their matchlocks at us from only fifty feet above'. Eventually the clamour died down and Younghusband was able to explain that he was on his way to visit their ruler or *mir*, Safdar Ali. His sang-froid paid off, and he was allowed to proceed after courtesies had been exchanged, tea drunk, and goodwill gained by the Gurkhas who handed round tobacco to their new-found friends. But Younghusband had other fish to fry before meeting the Mir: he had heard that Britain's old bugbear Gromchevsky, now a Colonel, was skulking in the vicinity, and he was determined to track him down. This was not difficult, as it turned out, for the Russian sent him a letter in Turki suggesting a meeting place.

So it was that in a remote spot called Khaiam-Aksai, where the Pamirs meet the Kunlun and the Karakorams merge into the Hindu Kush, the agents of the two great imperial powers of the day met over a camp-fire on 23 October 1889. Gromchevsky was a tall, fine-looking man with the usual Russian beard and a 'pleasant, genial manner', dressed in military uniform and accompanied by seven Cossacks. Younghusband, a slight man of middle height, was nevertheless endowed with a personal charisma which attracted a host of devoted followers all his life. The two men got on famously. After the vodka had flowed freely Gromchevsky confided that the Russian army thought of little else but the 'coming invasion of India', and Younghusband could not help noticing that a wedge of territory between Afghanistan and Chinese Turkestan, previously regarded as a no man's land, was marked on Gromchevsky's map as part of Russia. This was alarming, for it brought the Russian empire dangerously close to Kashmir and India, and confirmed the worst suspicions of the 'Forward School', as the British hawks of the day were known.

Gromchevsky, a Pole by birth, later rose to the rank of General under the Tsar, but was incarcerated in a Siberian prison-camp by the Bolsheviks. He eventually escaped, his health broken, and made his painful way back to his native land, where he ended his days in a state of near-destitution. Younghusband was surprised to receive a letter from him in 1925, from Warsaw, where he was lying bedridden, enclosing an account of his Central Asian travels. No one in his own country was interested in his pioneering expeditions of the 1880s and '90s, and he thought his old rival might like a copy. Younghusband hastened to send his thanks and some money, but he heard not long afterwards that Gromchevsky had died a lonely death. Sadly, there seems to be no trace now of his manuscript.

However, despite their friendly relations, Gromchevsky was in 1889 a thorn in Younghusband's flesh, for it transpired that

Safdar Ali had agreed not only to a Russian fort being built on his territory but also to his army being trained by Russian soldiers. Younghusband formed a very low opinion of Hunza's leader when he met him shortly after leaving Gromchevsky. Impressed by a display of the Gurkhas' accurate shooting, Safdar Ali begged them to take a pot-shot at a man on the opposite side of a ravine. It was perfectly all right, he assured the appalled Younghusband, for the man was one of his subjects. Meanwhile back in Gilgit Durand was strengthening the British position, and the freebooting days of the Dards were drawing inexorably to a close. The setting up of the Imperial Service Corps, whereby all the troops belonging to the native states of India were to be trained by British officers, effectively put the Maharaja of Kashmir's army at Durand's disposal. By 1892 there were 23 British officers attached to the Gilgit Agency, together with 200 British Indian troops and a mountain battery. Unlike poor Biddulph, who had been obstructed at every turn by the Kashmiris and had sometimes feared for his life, Durand was in no doubt as to his position of supremacy.

Durand shared Younghusband's judgement of Safdar Ali as a coward and a villain, and was convinced that 'young Saffy' and his mountain perch of Hunza would soon need to be dealt with. But having experienced the tightrope walk which passed for a track up the Hunza valley, Durand recommended that his government pay the Mir a handsome subsidy in return for good behaviour until engineers could build a decent mule-road. Once this was completed from Srinagar as far as Gilgit, the garrison could at least be adequately supplied and if necessary relieved.

In the meantime Younghusband continued to roam the Pamirs on his lone intelligence missions, and Durand surrounded himself at Gilgit with like-minded young officers – all anxious for action, glory and promotion, and who sensed that 'a scrap' was in the offing. Indeed, remote and primitive Gilgit became a most desirable posting for the adventurous and ambitious, although only friends of Algy Durand were accepted. He was himself an acting Lieutenant-Colonel by 1891, and in the next four years no fewer than six British officers were to win the Victoria Cross in Dardistan.

By the summer of 1891, when the journalist E.F. Knight travelled up to Gilgit, the new road already extended for 240 miles, as far as

Astor. Messrs Spedding & Co., led by the energetic Mr Spedding in person, had set to with a will, employing 5,000 navvies and bringing up every single piece of equipment and material – not to mention food and fodder – from Kashmir. It was no easy task to handle so large a work-force, composed as it was of a dozen different nationalities, many of them mutually antagonistic. The Pathans in particular inspired great terror in some of the other, more timorous tribesmen, and usually got the blame for any sort of outrage. But Knight had a soft spot for the Pathans, who were

> for the most part big, handsome men; but some of them looked thorough ruffians, as in fact they were – fugitives from justice, who had been robbers and murderers in their own land. But, with all his bloodthirstiness and general savagery, the jovial, courageous, independent Pathan is a more pleasing and respectable character than the effeminate Kashmiri, mild and harmless merely because he is so complete a coward. The Pathan is brutal, but he is a man.
>
> Knight, *Where Three Empires Meet*, 1895

Allowing himself a little side-trip in the foothills of Nanga Parbat, Knight suddenly found himself on the edge of an icy chasm: he had inadvertently wandered on to a thawing glacier. The surface was so covered in boulders and bushes – debris from the mountain brought down by the sheer weight of the moving ice – that he had assumed he was walking 'on the solid surface of the earth'. Looking down cautiously he saw

> dark caverns opening out under me, with walls of solid ice; while in places the ice had melted away, leaving the crust of moraine above unsupported. The water was fast dripping down from the roofs of these icy caverns, and rocks were continually tumbling in from above as the thaw proceeded. It was curious to see, far down, at the bottom of these dim chasms, uprooted rose-trees, still covered with blossoms, lying among the blocks of ice and fallen boulders.

On this occasion Knight spent only three days in Gilgit, where he was hospitably entertained at Biddulph's now much-extended bungalow by Durand's military secretary Lieutenant Manners Smith, a convivial young man and a keen mountaineer. But there was little time for recreation, for it was reported that Safdar Ali – despite his subsidy from the British – was encouraging Russian activities in the Pamirs and was strengthening his forts as if in preparation for a fight. Knight returned to Srinagar by the new road, staying with the English engineers at their camps along the way. He was filled with admiration when one of these young men stepped coolly between two rival groups of navvies who were on the point of settling their differences with picks and crowbars, and swiftly prevented 'what would no doubt have been a most bloody and Homeric conflict'. Younghusband, at the end of his account of his Central Asian travels, *The Heart of a Continent*, speculates on this mysterious ability of Europeans to sort things out and get things done, even in a foreign language and in the most unpromising circumstances. For him, it was a matter of 'grit', together with high moral standards. In a battle of wits the 'nimble-minded and subtle' Asiatic would win, but 'the European shows his greater moral strength by his tenacity of purpose, his persistence in the object he has before him, his disregard for selfish interests in the advancement of that object, and his sympathy with those about him'.

This was certainly true of Francis Younghusband himself, who felt an instinctive empathy with the sturdy and courageous hillmen among whom he lived and travelled. 'It would be a thousand pities', he wrote, 'to destroy the freedom of these mountain peoples ... to wither their simple customs, as the grass is withered by the frost, by introducing the cold system of British administration, the iron rules and regulations.' And at five o'clock one freezing morning in the Pamirs, while persuading his native guides to lead him across a difficult pass in a blizzard, he reflected: 'How thankful we in England ought to feel that the Oriental does not come raging round our country and insist upon turning us out to climb mountains in the depth of winter, and in the middle of snowstorms, while he rides comfortably along by our sides and tells us that there is no difficulty!'

While Younghusband continued to map the Pamirs, Spedding's cheerful young men and their native legions pressed on steadily with their road-building. Then suddenly, at the end of September 1891, a sensational story was broken by *The Times*: Captain Younghusband was dead, killed in a skirmish with the Russians somewhere in the Pamirs. In the event it was not true, but he had certainly been involved in a most provocative incident, which sent shock-waves round the chancelleries of Europe. At a place known as Bozai Gumbaz, usually regarded as part of Afghanistan, the British officer had come upon a party of thirty Cossacks with six Russian officers who informed him that the Pamirs now belonged to Russia. Younghusband was stunned, knowing that this would give the Russians direct access to all the passes into Yasin and Hunza. The Russian leader, Colonel Yanov, was 'a modest, quiet-mannered man', lacking the easy *bonhomie* of Gromchevsky, but courteous and clearly well-respected by his men. The Russians invited Younghusband to dine with them, and Yanov showed him his maps and the surveys they had just completed – all on the 'Indian' side of the watershed. But worse was to come. A few days later Yanov galloped up to Younghusband's tent at midnight and explained with considerable embarrassment that he had received orders to eject the Englishman from 'Russian territory'. Younghusband had no Gurkha escort on this occasion, and he had little choice but to comply. Yanov tried to make amends by presenting Younghusband with a haunch of *ovis poli* – the huge, curly-horned sheep discovered by Marco Polo – and reiterated that he was the unwilling instrument of the politicians.

There was a furore in England and India, and many people regarded this action as tantamount to a declaration of war. A strong diplomatic protest was sent to St Petersburg and the Russians, alarmed at the hornets' nest they had stirred up, backed down hastily, blaming the hapless Yanov for 'exceeding his orders'. But for Algy Durand, then visiting his chiefs in Simla, the Bozai Gumbaz incident was just what he needed. The moment to deal with 'young Saffy' had come.

Troops, officers, more mountain batteries and a Gatling gun were rushed up to Gilgit, and Durand was given *carte blanche* to go ahead with a campaign against the double-dealing Dards. Winter was coming on apace in the mountains and there was no time to be lost. Captain Fenton Aylmer of the Royal Engineers threw a new bridge across the Astor river, where a lot of supplies were held up, and with the help of a spare roll of telegraph wire managed to rig up a rope ferry across the Indus. Everyone in the area became grist to Durand's mill. The Pathan road navvies were overjoyed to be pressed into military service and issued with rifles. Their English bosses became officers in the Volunteer Reserve, as did two passing sportsmen and the eager Mr Knight, who was delighted to find himself in command of a platoon of Pathans as well as being the war correspondent of *The Times*.

Safdar Ali, confident that his friends the Russians would come to his aid, had of late increased his caravan-raiding, in defiance of British demands, even capturing Kashmiri subjects and selling them into slavery. His replies to Colonel Durand's protests had become ever more boastful and insulting, and in a recent one he had threatened to chop off Durand's head. (Some of his messages were so abusive that Durand declined to pass them on verbatim to Simla.)

Somehow or other, the men, horses, mules, arms, ammunition, stores and fodder were moved up to Gilgit before the snows closed the passes, although some of the latecomers were caught in blizzards and suffered cruelly from frostbite. 'The mule-drivers', wrote Knight, 'had been supplied with warm clothing before leaving India, but in their short-sighted folly had sold much of it on the road.' Several men lost hands and feet, some died later of tetanus or gangrene, and the Borzil pass was said to be 'strewn with corpses' of men and animals. Amazingly, the preparations for the Hunza campaign were kept secret, the Indian papers simply referring to them as the 'strengthening of the Agent's Bodyguard at Gilgit', and Safdar Ali felt he was unassailable in his mountain eyrie.

In November a Hunza spy was caught and brought to Gilgit, where he revealed a plan to take the Kashmiri fort of Chalt – twenty miles to the north – by stratagem. It was time for Durand's forces to move northwards. Preceded by Aylmer, the ubiquitous Knight, Mr Spedding and a party of Pathans, who did their best to create a rough temporary road and bridge system, a thousand men marched slowly up to Chalt. An ultimatum was sent to Safdar Ali and his new ally the Khan of Nagar, who had recently murdered his brothers in the time-honoured manner. While supplies were being brought up, Knight found time to admire the scenery:

> I ascended the heights above Chalt, in order to obtain a view of that magnificent mountain, Rakaposhi, which is well seen from here. Unlike Nanga Parbat, it has one sharp, prominent peak, whose granite crags tower high over the surrounding vast glaciers and snow-fields. Surely no military expedition ever before penetrated into so sublime a mountain region as that which now lay before us.

The indefatigable Captain Aylmer occupied his time in making a temporary winter bridge across the river, and Spedding continued blasting away bits of sheer cliff to make a mule-road. Safdar Ali's reply to the ultimatum being, predictably, a stream of abuse, the British forces prepared to attack the great Dard fortress of Nilt, fifteen miles further up the Hunza river.

On 30 November, Knight records, 'the welcome orders were issued that we should advance across the frontier on the following day', and the medical officer gave them 'an ominous little packet to put in the pocket, labelled First Field Dressing, which recalled to mind the handing round of basins by a Channel-steamer steward before the commencement of an unpleasant voyage'. As well as the regular Imperial Service Corps troops there were Spedding's Pathans and 160 irregulars from Punial – a small precipitous state next to Yasin – who were accompanied by their Rajah in person. After one day's musketry practice at the Gilgit ranges, these tribesmen had been armed with Snider carbines which they now carried proudly, along with their native swords and shields. Baggage had been cut down to the bare necessities, which in Knight's case included a couple of golf clubs, though where on earth he expected to practise his driving or putting in the Hunza mountains is anyone's guess.

Crossing Aylmer's bridge, and preceded as before by Spedding's road-blasters, the British force toiled up the mountains to Nilt, which they hoped to storm easily with their mountain guns. The fortress was hidden by a spur until they were 200 yards away, and there was a deathly silence. 'Not a human being was to be seen,' wrote Knight, 'and even when we were close up to the fort itself, there was nothing to show that it was occupied, save the flags waving on the walls and the smoke rising from the fires within.' Nilt, as Durand soon realised, was a formidable place. The well-built stone walls were fifteen to twenty feet high and twelve feet thick, with only narrow loopholes piercing them. A second wall, about eight feet high and also loopholed, surrounded the main wall, and the ground fell away precipitously on all sides, apart from the narrow approach road which led to the single gate. A sudden rattle of musket fire from the loopholes signalled that the battle had begun.

The 5th Gurkhas advanced quickly towards the fortress and kept up a brisk fire at the loopholes and at any of the enemy who showed themselves on the battlements. They were to bear the brunt of the day's

Batcha boy dancers in a tent of notables in the ruins of Afrasiab, Samarkand

left: A Tajik
merchant from
Bokhara

right: A Tajik from
the region around
Bokhara
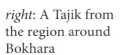

above: A horseman
waiting for a game of *kupkari*
in the ruins of Afrasiab

right: An elder in Samarkand

A young Tajik woman, Samarkand

An Uzbek from
Khujand with his
child

A Jewish lady, Samarkand

above: A silk merchant

left: A melon merchant in Bokhara

left: A tobacco merchant

right: A kneeling beggar

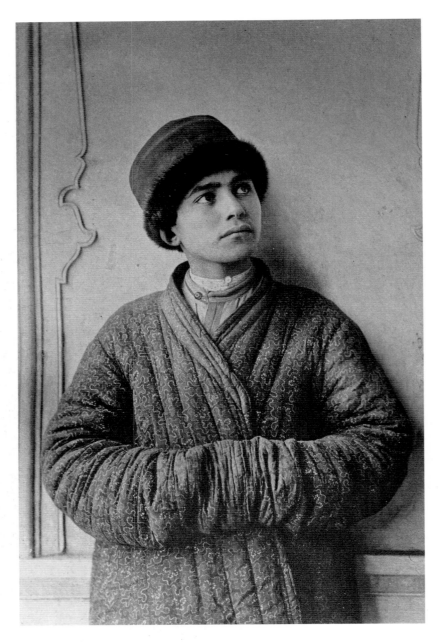

A young Jewish boy in his fur-trimmed hat, Tashkent

fighting, led by two young subalterns – Lieutenants Boisragon and Badcock – for their commanding officer had been struck by frostbite in the blizzards of the Borzil pass. Lieutenant Manners Smith, meanwhile, scrambled up the steep mountainside with the agile Punialis and fired boldly into the loopholes from a few yards' range. The big guns were dragged up a bluff and proceeded to pound the walls, but could make no impression on the heavy stone. To make matters worse, the Gatling machine-gun kept jamming. The Dards, for their part, were hampered by the narrowness of their loopholes, and a sort of stalemate ensued. But the British could not afford a long-drawn-out bombardment, for there was no water on their side of the fort and the soldiers had all but drained their water-bottles on the way up.

Durand decided that the gate of the fortress must be blown open without delay, and sent young Aylmer with fifty Gurkhas to lay the charges. An intense covering fire was opened by the British, and Colonel Durand – who was perhaps unwisely in the thick of the fighting – was severely wounded and had to retire. Having hacked his way through the wooden gates of the outer wall, Captain Aylmer, his Pathan orderly and a handful of Gurkhas rushed forward to the barricaded gate of the main wall, while Boisragon and Badcock fired into the loopholes. 'The enemy', recounts Knight, 'now concentrated their fire upon this gallant little band, and it is marvellous that any escaped death.' He continues:

Captain Aylmer placed his slabs of gun-cotton at the foot of the gate, packed them with stones, and ignited the fuse, all the while being exposed to the fire from the towers which flanked the gate, as well as from some loopholes in the gate itself. He was shot in the leg from so short a distance that his clothes and flesh were burnt by the gunpowder. He and his orderly then followed the wall of the fort to a safe distance, and stood there awaiting the explosion. But there came no explosion, for the fuse was a faulty one, so Captain Aylmer had once more to face an almost certain death. He returned to the gate, readjusted the fuse, cut it with his knife, lit a match after two or three attempts, and re-ignited the fuse. While doing this he received another wound, his hand being terribly crushed by a stone that was thrown from the battlements.

This time a terrific explosion followed, and at once, before even the dust had cleared or the stones had ceased dropping from the crumbling wall, the three British officers, with six men at their back, clambered through the breach and were within Nilt Fort. Enveloped in dense smoke and dust, their comrades could not find the breach; indeed they did not realize that one had been effected and that their officers were within the gates. So for many minutes that little handful of gallant Englishmen and Gurkhas was engaged in a hand-to-hand fight with the garrison in the narrow alley leading from the gate. Having gained this position, they held it resolutely, but soon two were killed and most of them were wounded, and it was obvious that not one of them would be left alive unless they were soon supported. Accordingly Lieutenant Boisragon went outside the gate once more to find his men, and thus exposed himself not only to the fire of the enemy at the loopholes, but to that of our own covering party. In a very short time he was back again, at the head of a number of little Gurkhas eager to avenge the comrades they had lost. The Gurkhas poured into the narrow alleys of the fort and fought as they always do fight …

The Rajah of the Punialis, watching this action from the ridge above, raised his hands in wonder and cried: 'This is the fighting of giants, not of men.' Captain Aylmer and Lieutenant Boisragon were later both awarded the VC and Lieutenant Badcock received the DSO.

However, in the confusion most of the enemy had escaped from the back of the fortress, and had re-formed behind defensive breast-works across the Nilt ravine, having smashed up the road behind them. Spedding and his stalwart Pathans tried to repair the road, but were caught in a hail of fire from the enemy position which was only eighty yards away as the crow flies. The mountain guns were trained on the breastworks, or *sangars*, but once again made no impression on the solid stone. To make themselves even more secure, the Dards diverted streams to pour over their cliff, which soon turned into a sheet of ice, and they amassed piles of rocks to hurl over the edge at anyone foolhardy enough to try the almost impossible ascent. For eighteen frustrating days the British force was held up.

During the stalemate Knight tried the odd swing with his golf clubs, but found the ground 'hopelessly bad'. The Gurkhas amused themselves by playing football with the officers in the afternoons – a practice which seemed to enrage the enemy, who immediately began beating their drums and firing across the gorge. 'It was an original experience', remarked Knight, 'to play football under an artillery fire.' At night the tireless Spedding crept down to the valley bottom and constructed stone *sangars* from which the British could later study the sheer rock-face of the Dard position without being shot to pieces. But even at night the engineers were not safe, for the Dards were a most resourceful enemy. If their suspicions were aroused they would roll blazing balls of resinous wood down the cliff, illuminating the sappers and miners below, who would be forced to flee from the ensuing hail of bullets.

Also under cover of darkness, a number of daring reconnaissances of the cliff-face itself were carried out by small groups of native soldiers, led by a skilled Kashmiri mountaineer called Nagdu. There were many alarms and false starts, but Nagdu persevered and eventually succeeded in climbing undetected to the foot of the enemy's *sangars*. 'Having satisfied himself that the thing could be done,' wrote Knight in his book, 'he returned and promptly thought out the outline of the scheme of attack which was afterwards adopted with success. Nagdu is a quiet, simple-looking young fellow, to whom no-one at first sight would attribute the possession of many brains; but he proved himself to be an excellent soldier, as full of resource as he was brave.' However, it was one thing for Nagdu to scale the cliff silently in pitch darkness, but quite another for an army to do the same thing. There was no help for it, the ascent would have to be made in broad daylight.

Lieutenant Manners Smith, who had earned a reputation at Gilgit as an 'intrepid cragsman', was put in charge of 100 men of the Kashmir Bodyguard Regiment, all of them hillmen accustomed to clambering up precipices. Nagdu had reported that the cliff curved in under the Dard *sangars* and that the scaling party would not be seen provided the enemy did not lean over the breastworks. All the best British marksmen would accordingly be lined up on the ridge above Nilt, and the mountain guns would need to keep up a heavy bombardment. By 19 December everything was ready.

The plans for the assault had been kept completely secret, for the Dards had seemed remarkably well-informed on earlier British moves, and spies were suspected in the camp. At 7 p.m., before the moon rose, Manners Smith and his band crept down into the valley bottom and positioned themselves, some two hours later, in the safety of Spedding's *sangars*. Before daybreak on the 20th the covering party – including Knight – ascended the ridge and trained their weapons on the four Dard *sangars* which were to be stormed. While the mountaineers began their 1,200-foot climb, a steady fire was commenced at the *sangars*, and so accurate were the British sharpshooters that the return fire soon slackened and then stopped altogether. As it grew lighter Knight and his companions were spotted by some Dards in another of their emplacements and a frantic beating of drums began. The enemy realised that something out of the ordinary was afoot, although as yet they could not tell what. 'It was certainly an extraordinary scene for a fight,' wrote Knight, continuing:

> From our ridge we looked down the crags on the far-stretching landscape of the Kanjut valley, with its winding, rushing river, its belts of terraced cultivation and its numerous fortified villages that lay beneath the stupendous cliffs; while high above the lesser mountains that enclose the valley, the snowy summits of the Hindoo Koosh rose into the cloudless sky.

But there was little time to admire the scenery. All along the enemy's line of defences the tribesmen were looking on in their hundreds, waiting to see what happened, and the British watched with bated breath as Manners Smith, 'active as a cat', managed to scramble unseen 800 feet up the cliff. To their consternation, however, the observers realised that he had taken a wrong turn and was heading for a stretch of unscalable precipice. Manners Smith himself soon saw his mistake, but it meant leading his men laboriously down again and making a fresh start. The officers on the ridge redoubled their fire, hoping to create such pandemonium that the activities of the climbers would continue to go unnoticed. After a nail-biting two hours, Manners Smith hit on Nagdu's route and managed to clamber up with his Gurkhas and Kashmiris to within sixty yards of the first *sangar*.

At this moment there was a commotion from one of the enemy's lower positions: they had at last spotted the scaling party and were shouting warnings from post to post, until the news reached the four *sangars* under attack. At once rocks and stones were hurled over the edge in a deadly avalanche, but by a miracle very few of the men were hit. 'It was a fearful thing to watch from our side,' admitted Knight. 'A little lack of caution or an unlucky accident might have so easily led to scores of our men being swept off the face of the cliff during this perilous ascent.' He was filled with admiration as Manners Smith and another British subaltern, Lieutenant Taylor, coolly steered their men from point to point, between the repeated showers of stones, working their way steadily up the mountainside:

At last – and it was a moment of intense suspense for the onlookers – we saw Lieutenant Manners Smith make a sudden dash forward, reach the foot of the first *sangar*, clamber round to the right of it, and step on to the flat ground beside it. A few *sepoys* were close at his heels, and then the men, having got to the back of the *sangar*, the rifles of the storming party were for the first time brought into play. A few shots in rapid succession, a rush through the opening behind with bayonets and *kukris*, Lieutenant Manners Smith himself pistolling the first man, and the *sangar* was ours ...

As the Dards fled, they were picked off by the British marksmen opposite. The three adjoining *sangars* were quickly taken, and the sepoys fanned out and systematically carried all the fortified positions with which the mountainside was studded.

And now the tom-toms that had been beating in the distance became silent, and suddenly we saw a strange sight beneath us, which made our men raise cheer upon cheer. The garrisons of the enemy's fortresses, realizing that we had effectively turned this position, on whose impregnability they had relied, that we had outflanked them, and that their retreat would be speedily cut off did they remain where they were, were seized with panic, and we looked down upon long streams of men hurrying up the valley on both sides of the river, racing up to Hunza and Nagar for their lives, and abandoning to us all the country within sight.

101

John Manners Smith was rewarded with a VC, the third to be won in three weeks.

Twenty miles further up the valley, Safdar Ali was faced with the bitter truth that Gromchevsky's promises of Russian support were worthless. His Chinese friends were also conspicuous by their absence in his hour of need. Never a courageous man, he now fled ignominiously – but not without first packing the treasures he had accumulated from a lifetime of caravan-raiding. When the British arrived in Baltit his palace was deserted and contained little of material value. However, among his bulky correspondence with the Russians and Chinese were most of Younghusband's letters to Gilgit, evidently intercepted by Safdar Ali's agents. The Mir himself spent the rest of his days in exile in Chinese Turkestan.

Thus ended the Hunza campaign. Durand wrote from his sick-bed in Gilgit: 'If you only knew how happy and relieved I am,' and appointed one of his gallant band of subalterns – Lieutenant Charlie Townshend – as military governor. The great cannon of the Mir's castle was carried to Gilgit as a trophy for the Agency, and a proclamation was issued declaring that Hunza now belonged to the British. Spedding and his young engineers went back to peaceful road-building, having done sterling service for Queen and country. As Knight acknowledged in his book: 'It would be difficult, I imagine, to mention an instance since Mutiny days, of such splendid service rendered by civilians in time of war.'

The door had now been slammed in the face of the Russians in Hunza, but it would take a few more years before the same could be said of Chitral. A small British force under Surgeon-Major Robertson would be besieged there, and heroically relieved, before the British in India could in 1895 heave a sigh of relief: the Russian threat to India had been contained, and there was a formal Pamir Settlement. In fact, in 1907 a Convention was drawn up between Britain and Russia which set out their various spheres of influence in Asia, and it seemed that the Great Game was over. Both countries had other things to worry about.

During the first half of the twentieth century, feelings of Muslim solidarity would gradually develop until they became stronger than tribal alignments, or loyalty to particular *mirs*, culminating in the creation of the separate Islamic state of Pakistan. But in the meantime

Gilgit and Hunza remained part of British India, and the writer Raleigh Trevelyan, whose father was military adviser to the Gilgit Agency between 1929 and 1933, remembers being one of nineteen Europeans there. He was only 6 when he arrived, but his happy and vivid memories came crowding back when he revisited Gilgit in 1977. In his delightful book *The Golden Oriole*, published in 1987, he recalls the Jhalsa, or ceremonial durbar, which took place each spring:

> Every Mir and Rajah came in turns to pay calls on the sahibs, usually with a retinue of about twelve followers. They arrived in order of seniority, the most important (and the most popular) being the Mir of Hunza. Then would come the Mir of Nagar, followed by the Rajahs of Punial, Yasin, etc. The Mir of Hunza, Sir Mohammed Nazim Khan KBE, was well fleshed and jolly, very fond of jokes and a contrast in character to his hereditary rival, the more serious and thinner Mir of Nagar, Sir Shah Sikhander Khan KBE. The difference between the temperaments of the people of Hunza and Nagar was put down to the fact that Hunza was on the sunny side and Nagar on the shady side of a valley. Also at Hunza they made and drank wine, which at Nagar they didn't.

Throughout the Jhalsa week there would be polo matches of terrifying ferocity – especially when Hunza played Nagar – and European-style parties when the *mirs* had to join in uproarious parlour games. 'I think they thought we were a bit dotty,' one of the ex-sahibs later told Trevelyan.

His parents and devoted nanny tried to shield young Raleigh from the more unpleasant side of life, but one day in 1931 he was startled to find a strange ragged man with glaring eyes skulking in the garden. He was a Ukrainian who had somehow managed to escape from Stalinist Russia. Raleigh was surprised to notice the man was trembling: 'When I asked Nanny why he was shaking so much, she told me that he didn't want to be sent back to Russia.' A couple of years later White Russians were camping out on the lawn in tents, and it was only when he was grown up that Raleigh understood why. Many Whites had taken refuge in western China after the Reds had won the Civil War in Russia but had been forced to flee when a violent uprising by the Muslims of Sinkiang plunged the region into turmoil (see URUMCHI). It was the task of Raleigh's father, Colonel Walter Trevelyan, to debrief the refugees and weed out any Soviet agents. With the utmost reluctance, little Raleigh was uprooted from his beloved home, his best friend Amin (son of the Mir of Hunza), and the Gilgit Wolf Cubs, of which he was the sole white member, and sent home to boarding school.

After the Second World War the international scene changed radically. When India became independent in 1947, Gilgit found itself at the centre of a tug-of-war. While Hunza and Chitral immediately became part of the new state of Pakistan, Gilgit had traditionally been regarded as part of Kashmir and the Maharaja – a Hindu – had opted to join India. The situation in Muslim Gilgit was explosive, but a bloodbath was averted by the cool, if highly irregular, initiative of a young Scotsman. When a Kashmiri governor was appointed to Gilgit to take over from the British, the 24-year-old Major Willie Brown decided to act swiftly to preempt the riot brewing in the town. He and his Gilgit Scouts took the new governor and his Hindu entourage into 'protective custody' and Brown sent a telegram to the Pakistani Prime Minister of the North West Frontier Province announcing that a coup had taken place in Gilgit, which now regarded itself as part of Pakistan. When the turbulent tribesmen saw the Pakistani flag flying from the Gilgit flagpole there was rejoicing instead of rioting, but in London the civil servants were thoroughly bemused. 'The fate of Gilgit appears to rest with Major William Brown,' the Foreign Office noted. 'Who is Major William Brown?'

Unfortunately the division of Kashmir between India and Pakistan did not pass off as smoothly elsewhere as it had in Gilgit, and a bitter war was fought with much loss of life. Eventually the United Nations arranged a ceasefire and in January 1949 the province was apportioned between the two countries, Gilgit remaining with Pakistan. The proximity of so many national frontiers has made this an uneasy, volatile region, but the *rapprochement* between Pakistan and China in 1964 allowed plans to be made for the construction of the Karakoram Highway. The 1,200-kilometre road was officially opened in August 1982, and the Northern Areas opened to tourism. Further east, the undeclared war between Muslims and Hindus has, at the time of writing, virtually destroyed tourism in Kashmir.

In Gilgit the most important day of the year is 1 November, Uprising Day, which commemorates the demand of the town – abetted by Willie Brown – to join Pakistan in 1947. It is the occasion for much merrymaking, dancing and loud music, followed by a week-long polo tournament. (It is claimed by some that polo was invented here.) After this the winter sets in rapidly and tourists hurry away before the passes are blocked by snow. There is no more gossiping in the bazaars, for no one goes outside unless he has to, and social life is forced indoors. A young British anthropologist describes winter in Gilgit:

> And then, gradually, the season of 'long nights' gives way to 'extreme cold', the ground freezes, and building and polo stop. Snow falls in many villages, isolating the highest ones for months. Even in the lower villages, where snow does not lie and where the winter is shorter, the nights become bitterly cold. By eight o'clock on a December evening Gilgit bazaar, instead of the familiar, relaxed, slightly torpid place of exchange of goods and news, has become bleak and anonymous, with every shop closed and every light hidden. I remember walking through the bazaar on such a night. The cold was intense but so insidious, and the air so still, that I had no sensation of it and felt no shiver to give me warning. For a few moments the physical world seemed to recede, leaving me somehow disembodied in remote Central Asian emptiness. Then I remembered that one does not linger outside on winter nights, whatever the altitude.
>
> John Staley, *Words for my Brother*, 1982

The Spring Festival on 21 March signals the end of winter and is celebrated, as in Raleigh Trevelyan's day, by music, dancing and the visiting of friends. There is often a polo match on the *maidan* at Gilgit, and the stall-holders in the bazaar prepare their wares. Crocuses and gentians carpet the fields, soon there will be clouds of apricot blossom, and on 1 May the Khunjerab pass opens once more to those travelling to Kashgar and the other Silk Road oases beyond.

KASHGAR
Great Game Listening-Post

The people of Kashgar have an astonishing acquaintance with the devilries of enchantment, inasmuch as they make their idols to speak. They can also by their sorceries bring about changes in the weather, and produce darkness, and do a number of things so extraordinary that no one without seeing them would believe them.

Marco Polo

One's first impression on arrival at the Consulate-General is of greenery and shade; of limes and acacias, willows and planes and fruit trees of all kinds; of tall bushy poplars rising like a wall against the sun, and slender poplars with little white-backed leaves which flutter silently in the faintest breeze like the waving of fairies' hands; of confused gardens on three different levels, with an orchard and a vine-pergola and a little meadow and a dense thicket of Babylonian willow and a pond with lotuses in it and a carved Chinese summer-house, all mixed up with trees and an amazing riot of flowers and vegetables.

Sir Clarmont Skrine, *Chinese Central Asia*, 1926

MARCO POLO WAS able to visit Kashgar in 1265 with little fear of being robbed, murdered or sold into slavery – the usual hazards of travel in Central Asia before the twentieth century – thanks to the temporary subjugation of the region by the Mongols. The town had seen many conquerors in its time, for it was a strategic centre for anyone wanting to control Kashgaria, or what is now western Sinkiang, and it was also an important staging-post on the Silk Road which linked China with India and the eastern ports of the Mediterranean.

Caravans from China, their camels laden with bales of raw silk, would unload thankfully in the caravanserais of Kashgar, for one of the worst stretches of the long trade route was over: the 800 miles skirting the Taklamakan and Lop deserts. Whether one took the northern route via Turfan, Kucha and Aksu or the southern route via Cherchen, Khotan and Yarkand, the dangers were the same. Fierce winds blew across the area from the north-east at all seasons, freezing in winter, blistering in summer, covering the track and confusing the guides. Many a caravan wandered off course, never to be seen again, and indeed the name Taklamakan means in Turki 'Go in and you won't come out'. From Kashgar fresh caravans, using pack-horses and then yaks, would transport the silk over the icy passes of the Pamirs to Balkh, Bokhara, Merv and Damascus, or southwards through the Karakorams to Kashmir. But sometimes Kashgaria was so plagued with wars and invasions that international trade came to a standstill and only local journeys could be undertaken.

Kashgar has existed as a settlement for at least 2,000 years. Watered by streams from the Tien-shan (Celestial) mountains to the north, it was always easy to irrigate the surrounding land by canals and ditches and grow abundant produce, for the sand is composed of wind-eroded clay and is perfectly fertile. Sir Aurel Stein, the archaeologist, who spent so much time excavating in and around the Taklamakan in the early years of this century that he calculated he had walked or ridden 25,000 miles all told, found that all the oases, including Kashgar, had much in common:

The aridity of the climate accounts for the striking uniformity in physical conditions which prevails throughout these oases. Whatever their position or size, the traveller sees everywhere the same fields of wheat, maize or cotton slightly terraced for irrigation, the same winding lanes lined with white poplars and willows; the same little arbours or orchards inviting him with their shade and their plentiful produce of European fruits.

Stein, *On Central Asian Tracks*, 1964

The oases must have looked particularly tempting to marauding nomads from the steppe north of the Tien-shan, and Kashgar was overrun many times, by Scythians, Huns, Turks and Mongols. But the Chinese did their best to keep the barbarians at bay, for by the first century AD they had established valuable trade links with the West. At this time the Han emperors extended the Great Wall westwards and set up garrisons at strategic points to protect the caravan traffic, with beacon-towers to signal impending attacks from nomad horsemen. However, the Han dynasty collapsed in the third century and Kashgar was sacked and plundered by the Huns. But as Stein has pointed out, the narrow belts of cultivation around the Taklamakan could never provide adequate grazing for horse-borne nomads with flocks and herds, who were not usually attracted to the laborious life of a cultivator anyway. So the freebooting nomads either passed on in search of new pastures, or withdrew north of the Tien-shan after their raids, exacting tribute from the hard-pressed peasants.

Kashgar came under Chinese protection again in the seventh and eighth centuries when the Tang dynasty was strong, but a confederation of tribes known as the Western Turks took the town in 752. Allying themselves with the Arabs, who had just fought their way into Central Asia through Persia, they succeeded in driving the Chinese out of the Tarim Basin. But the Turks themselves soon became subject to the Arabs, and were forced to adopt the new religion of Islam. The earlier religions of Buddhism, Manichaeism and Nestorian Christianity lingered on for several centuries, however, and Marco Polo found Nestorians still worshipping in Kashgar when he was there.

In 1219 Kashgar fell to perhaps the most terrifying invader of all, Genghis Khan, who swept down from the Mongolian plateau to establish a vast empire in Asia and eastern Europe. Such fear did the Mongols engender that peace reigned in Central Asia for nearly 200 years, and as a result trade prospered, allowing Westerners to visit the region for the first time. But the *pax mongolica* was under threat as soon as their power declined, and Kashgar was razed to the ground by Tamerlane – a Turk of part-Mongol extraction – towards the end of the fourteenth century. His death in 1405 signalled the collapse of yet another empire and Kashgar, like the rest of Central Asia, reverted to a prolonged time of troubles. Trade with China came abruptly to an end in the fifteenth century, when the Ming dynasty slammed the door on the West. But the Chinese returned to the Tarim Basin in the mid-eighteenth century, under the Manchu dynasty of the Ching, causing much local resentment. The whole region had remained Islamic – indeed its Buddhist past had been totally obliterated – and a series of Muslim uprisings led by local warlords occurred which the Chinese found it increasingly difficult to suppress.

In 1865 a Turkic leader called Yakub Beg crossed the Pamirs from Khokhand, seized control of Kashgaria and declared it an independent state. He made tentative diplomatic contacts with both Russia and Britain, boldly defied the hated Chinese and set about improving the moral standards of his new country. Having come from Khokhand in what was to become Russian Turkestan, and where Islamic practice was very strict, he was shocked by the more easy-going standards of Kashgar. One of his laws, designed to preserve 'the sanctity of the family', made it obligatory for any male visitor to marry within three days of arriving, if he had come without a wife. He was not obliged to take the new wife away with him afterwards, however, and if the marriage was agreed to be a temporary one the mullah would usually oblige by reading the words of divorce in advance – often directly after the wedding feast – to make matters easier. There was no problem in finding a bride in the first place, for the available girls would parade, unveiled, in the bazaar every morning, ostensibly selling milk.

But while native traders following the caravan routes from all over Asia were accustomed to visiting Kashgar, it was not a place for a lone European. One who did venture there, a scientific traveller from Kashmir named Adolf Schlagintweit, was seized and tortured in 1857 and finally beheaded in the Horse Market. The first Englishman to see Kashgar was Robert Shaw, a tea planter, who had hoped to interest Yakub Beg in importing tea from India, now that his Chinese supplies were cut off. In the event Shaw spent an uneasy three months under house arrest and saw very little of the town. However, he must have made a good impression, for an invitation was afterwards sent from Yakub Beg to British India, and as a result a delegation led by Sir Douglas Forsyth visited his court at Kashgar in 1873. Among the English party was the young Central Asian traveller, naturalist and Great Game player, John Biddulph, who a few years later was to become Britain's first Political Agent at Gilgit. At about the same time Russian explorers began to penetrate the region from the north, one of the first being a Captain Kuropatkin who would later find fame and promotion in crushing the Turcomans at Geok-Tepe, and then became Governor-General of the new Russian province of Transcaspia (see GEOK-TEPE and ASHKHABAD).

In 1877 a Ching army put an end to Yakub Beg's rebellious state, and after a few years eastern Turkestan became the Sinkiang (New Frontier) province of China. By 1882 the Russians had been allowed to open a consulate in Kashgar, but the British – as a punishment for flirting with Yakub Beg – were not permitted a presence there until 1890, and then only a 'representative' and not a diplomatically recognized consul. Little did the 24-year-old George Macartney suspect, when he took up this posting, that he would spend the next twenty-eight years of his life in this remote and lonely listening-post. A fluent Chinese speaker – his mother had been Chinese – he set out from Simla at the end of June 1890 in company with Captain Francis Younghusband, who had recently been playing the Great Game in Hunza (see GILGIT). Both men were members of the Political Department of the Government of India, and their task was to establish good relations with the Chinese authorities in this sensitive corner of Central Asia where the empires of Britain, Russia and China met.

They arrived in Kashgar on 1 November, having done some more surveying of the Pamirs *en route*, and in his book *The Heart of a Continent* Younghusband recalls their first impressions:

> We were to make Kashgar our winter quarters, and we found a native house prepared for us on the north side of the old city. It was pleasantly situated on some rising ground, and looked out to the north over the cultivated and tree-covered plain round Kashgar to the snowy peaks of the Tien-shan. From far away on the west, round to the north, and then away again on the east, these snowy mountains extended; and from the roof of our house we could see that magnificent peak, the Mustagh-ata, rising twenty-one thousand feet above the plain. About the house was a garden, which gave us seclusion, and in this garden I had pitched a Kirghiz *yurt*, which I had bought on the Pamirs.
>
> It was curious to note the changes from the lonely mountains to this populous town. On the Pamirs at night all had been as still as death, but here we felt the town beside us; the great gongs of the Chinese guard-houses beat the hours through the night, and at nine o'clock a gun was fired and trumpets were blown. The deep booming of the gongs through the stillness of the night, the blaring of the trumpets, and the noise of the cannon,

nightly remind the inhabitants of the towns of Turkestan that the conquerors, who have returned again and again to the country, are still among them and still on the watch.

The house – known as Chini-bagh, or Chinese Garden – became for many travellers a haven of tranquillity and an unlikely home-from-home in this inhospitable desert land. For not far away lies the awesome Taklamakan desert, swallower of caravans, its yellow dunes like 'the giant waves of a petrified ocean'. Younghusband, who spent a year at Kashgar, thought the sand-laden atmosphere was to blame for the 'Central Asian listlessness' of the people. Even the 'wild and fanatical Pathan from the Indian frontier allowed his ardour to cool down here till he became almost as mild as the comfortable merchant from Bokhara'. When he left, it was with few regrets:

Chinese Turkestan is an interesting country to visit, but a dreary place to live in. Even the air is oppressive; it is always 'murky'. For a few days one does not notice it particularly. There are no clouds; but when week after week goes by and the clear sky is never seen, then a feeling of oppression comes on. The air is always filled with this impalpable dust from the desert, and Chinese Turkestan is for ever shrouded in sand.

Macartney, of course, simply had to make the best of it. He was not the only European in Kashgar. The Russian Consul, Nikolai Petrovsky, together with his wife and son, a secretary and a Cossack officer in charge of the escort, made up what Younghusband called 'a very pleasant little Russian colony'. Petrovsky was a notoriously touchy man, however, and refused to say goodbye to Younghusband when he left, as he had called at 'the wrong time of day'. After his wife and son returned to Russia he became ever more eccentric, and Macartney was to find him a difficult and devious colleague in the years to come. More sympathetic was a Dutch priest, Father Hendricks, who had arrived in Kashgar in 1885 on a lone mission to the natives, and who lived in a mud-built hovel in a state of near-destitution. Macartney began to share his meals with him, and found Hendricks to be intelligent, an excellent linguist and very well-informed on local affairs. He soon invited the priest to move into Chini-bagh, where he remained until 1898 when Macartney returned from home leave with a young bride.

It was just as well that Catherine Theodora Borland had been friends with George Macartney from childhood and that they shared a sense of humour, for the long journey to Kashgar was very far from being a conventional honeymoon. 'If two people can go through the test of such a journey without quarrelling seriously,' she wrote in her memoirs, 'they can get on under any circumstances. We just survived it, and it promised well for the long journey through life.' She cheerfully admitted in her book *An English Lady in Chinese Turkestan* that she was not cut out for an adventurous life:

> I was the most timid, unenterprising girl in the world. I had hardly been beyond the limits of my own sheltered home, and big family of brothers and sisters, had never had any desire whatever to see the world, and certainly had no qualifications for a pioneer's life, beyond being able to make a cake.

She had never ridden a horse before, but at Osh – after a long and uncomfortable journey through European Russia, across the Caspian, along the Transcaspian railway to Andijan and thence by cart – there was nothing for it but to ride through the Tien-shan mountains. Her first problem was to mount the pony. A sidesaddle would have been unsuitable for the rough tracks ahead, even if such a thing had existed in Osh, and after a few unsuccessful attempts she was given 'a great heave-up behind' by their servant and began her journey helpless with laughter. Her good spirits deserted her temporarily that night, when she was so stiff after the day's riding that she had to be 'almost carried in, and laid down gently on some bedding, feeling the most miserably homesick creature in existence'. There were sixteen more days of riding still to be faced, but after a few days she got used to it and began to enjoy the scenery.

The Russian District Officer of Osh and his wife had taken a great fancy to Catherine, who was only 21, and discovering that she was musical, insisted on giving her their harmonium which was duly dragged over the mountains on the back of a yak. She mentions modestly in her memoirs that she 'sang a bit', but she was in fact quite an accomplished musician and later had a portable piano sent out to Kashgar from London. Her new home, she soon discovered, contained precious few luxuries:

To my English idea, the house was very quaint. It was built all on one floor on account of the frequent earthquakes, on three sides of a courtyard. Like all native houses it had no windows, the rooms being lit by skylights. The walls were about two feet thick and were of sun-baked brick, covered outside with mud, and inside they were plastered with gypsum to make them smooth and white. I soon found the comfort of thick walls, for they kept the house warm in winter and cool in summer.

Glass was almost unknown in Kashgar, but windows were being introduced, generally covered in oiled paper. Petrovsky had managed to obtain proper glass windows for his Consulate, however, to the general wonderment and admiration of the local population, and as a great mark of friendship he now presented one to the Macartneys. Unfortunately, he took offence at something shortly afterwards and demanded the glass back again. But not long after, a Russian merchant arrived in Kashgar with a caravan-load of window panes, and the situation was saved. The glass was of very poor quality, and Catherine was often convulsed with laughter at the distorted figures who passed, but 'it was glass, and it let in the sunlight'.

Most of the furniture was very primitive, having been knocked together by George and Father Hendricks, neither of whom, Catherine noted, had a vocation as a cabinet-maker. Paint and varnish were unknown in Kashgar, but Catherine had brought her sewing basket with her and she set to work to brighten the place up with cushions and silk shades for the paraffin lamps. Both she and George were keen gardeners:

> We had a large picturesque garden, laid out on two levels, with a flight of steps leading from one to the other. The upper garden was the orchard and kitchen garden, and it was full of the most wonderful peaches, apricots, figs, pomegranates and black and white mulberries. Later my husband grafted on to the native stocks English apples, pears, plums, greengages, cherries etc, from cuttings sent from home. I think there is hardly a place in the world for fruit-growing like Kashgar.
>
> The lower garden was shady with willows, elms, poplars and a native tree called Jigda. The most fascinating part of the whole garden was the terrace that ran the entire length of it.

Gardening was not an easy matter, however, owing to the extremes of the climate: vines, figs and pomegranates all had to be buried in the earth in winter to protect them from the frost, and Catherine found that only the hardiest of English flowers could survive. But in spring and early summer the air would be heavy with the scent of the Jigda blossom, and the Macartneys would sit in the garden and watch the sunset:

> I shall never forget some of the wonderful summer evenings in Kashgar, which began with indescribably lovely sunsets, when the world was just a golden haze that deepened in colour until the sun went down behind the mountains, leaving a sky of orange and red, to fade almost at once into night, fragrant with flowers and filled with music of the frogs and crickets; while away in the distance could be heard the singing of the people and the droning of their instruments in the bazaar. It was then that the real spirit of the country was felt, and once experienced, never forgotten.

May was the month when the roses burst into bloom, filling the air with their intoxicating scent. Modern visitors to Sinkiang will still find it a feast for rose-lovers. There is a beautiful yellow bush rose (possibly a Rose des Turcs) in the garden of Kashgar's great mosque, with grey-green foliage and an exquisite scent. Further south, at Khotan (Hotan), the entire town turns out in May to harvest the blooms of a deep pink Rugosa-type rose. The blossoms lie about in huge fragrant heaps, waiting to be made into rose-petal wine. Of the Macartneys' garden at Chini-bagh almost nothing now remains, apart from a wonderful old Zelkova tree which was still there in 1991, and the town of Kashgar has, of course, changed out of all recognition.

In the 1890s Kashgar comprised two separate cities: the old native town and the Chinese new town six miles to the south. (The latter is now closed to foreigners.) Both were surrounded by high crenellated walls of mud-brick, pierced by four massive iron gates which were shut at sunset and opened at daybreak to the blowing of horns and firing of guns. Catherine Macartney has left a vivid description of the old town in her memoirs:

> The streets of the Mohammedan City were very narrow and dirty, with the ground all ups and downs, and mostly muddy

from the water slopped over from the pails of the donkeys and water carriers. Dark little shops lined the streets, in some places made darker by the covering or awning of reed mats that was erected right across the road for shade. The shopkeepers squatted in the midst of their goods, and never seemed particularly anxious for customers.

Just inside the gates, and along the street leading to the central bazaar, the beggars congregated, and most horrible sights many of them were, with their faces and limbs eaten away and distorted with the most frightful diseases.

The narrow bazaars seemed to be always crowded, and especially so on Thursdays, the Bazaar-Kun, or Market Day. Then it was a slow business to push one's way through the throng of people, some on foot, others mounted on donkeys and horses, animals so loaded with fodder that only a nose and four hoofs could be seen, and caravans of camels and horses, carrying great hard bales of cotton.

The main streets seemed mostly to run into the big Market Square known as the Id-ga, in the centre of which stood the Chief Mosque. I wish I could adequately describe the beauty and picturesqueness of the Id-ga bazaar, as seen from the steps of the Mosque. In the centre of the great square were the fruit stalls; in summer piled high with fruit, crimson peaches, apricots, mulberries, enormous bunches of black and white grapes and purple and yellow figs. Enormous water melons, almost too heavy to lift, with their red flesh and black seeds; melons green all through and intensely sweet; melons with pink insides, and others pure white, or apricot-coloured when cut open. Fruit in Kashgar was too cheap to be appreciated.

Then the Cap stalls gave a wonderfully pretty touch of colour. They looked like flowers on their stands. Bright coloured velvet caps of every hue, some lined and trimmed with fur for winter, others gaily embroidered for summer wear, and round which a turban could be wound for full dress; and some decorated with patterns of silver beaten thin and sewn on: these were for the women to wear on high days and holidays.

The people, too, were dressed in brilliant colours, and many of the women went unveiled. Some of the younger women would tuck a scarlet pomegranate flower or a marigold behind their ears, to set off the sheen of their long black plaits. Men and boys always had their heads shaved, however, and were never seen without a cap. Every sort of colouring and feature could be met with in the crowds, and Catherine noted that 'one could hardly say what the real Kashgar type was, for it has become so mixed by the invasion of other peoples in the past'. Like all Central Asian towns, Kashgar was well supplied with tea-houses, or *chai khanas*, where 'people sat and drank tea while they listened to dreamy native music played by a band consisting of perhaps one or two long-necked mandoline-shaped instruments that produced very soft fairy-like music, accompanied by a small drum'. Or on another occasion they might listen with rapt attention to a professional story-teller.

Although most Chinese, including the garrison, lived in the less interesting new town, the Taotai or Governor had his official residence in the old town. He was a man of considerable local importance, as the representative of the colonial power, and when he went out his sedan chair was preceded by men with gongs and trumpets, and a salute was fired as he left and returned to his residence. Younghusband recalled a conversation with the elderly and dignified Taotai of his day in which the old man criticised Western civilisation. Europeans, he pointed out, were always fighting one another:

> We were not bad at inventing machines and guns, but we had none of that calm, lofty spirit which the Chinese possessed, and which enabled them to look at the petty squabbles between nations with equanimity and dignity. We spent all our time in matters which should only concern mechanics and low-class people of that sort, and gave ourselves no opportunity for contemplating higher things.

This Olympian detachment was all very well, but it was the task of Younghusband, and later Macartney, to focus Chinese attention on the need for extreme vigilance *vis-à-vis* the Russians. The Tsar had already swallowed up vast tracts of Central Asia on the other side of the Pamirs and the Tien-shan: if the Chinese were not careful, their remote province of Sinkiang might also find itself part of the burgeoning Russian empire. George Macartney's mixed parentage, something of an embarrassment in Victorian England, was a distinct advantage here. Having spent the first ten years of his life in Nanking, he was bilingual and thoroughly at home with the intricacies of Chinese etiquette. During his time in Kashgar he made many friends among the Chinese community – for whom a posting to barbarous Sinkiang was a sore trial – and this did nothing to endear him to his diplomatic opponent, Petrovsky. The latter's tactics were simply to browbeat and intimidate the Chinese and, for that matter, everybody else. From November 1899 until June 1902 he actually refused to speak to Macartney at all, and for a while forbade other Europeans to call at Chini-bagh. (The pretext was a less-than-flattering cartoon of the Tsar in an old copy of *Punch* which the British representative had passed on to the Russian Consulate in an exchange of magazines.) In a place like Kashgar, with its tiny European community all clustered together outside the walls of the old town, Petrovsky's two-and-a-half-year sulk must have caused no end of inconvenience.

Fortunately, not all the Russians were so rebarbative, and Catherine Macartney became firm friends with the wife and children of the Secretary of the Consulate, with whom she conversed in her schoolgirl French. (With the help of Father Hendricks her French soon improved.) She was also delighted to find that the two charming families of Swedish missionaries, the Högbergs and the Raquettes, spoke excellent English. While her husband performed the monumental diplomatic task of blocking Tsarist designs on Chinese Turkestan, Catherine wrestled with the problems of housekeeping – and in due course child-rearing – in this back-of-beyond. It was lucky that she liked cooking, for her homesick Indian cook soon left and there was nobody in Kashgar who had the slightest notion how to prepare European food. Undaunted, Catherine decided to do it herself. The resourceful Mr Högberg made her a stove out of old oil-cans, and Catherine trained up a local boy, Isa, as her assistant, using 'a wonderful language of our own, made out of Turki, Hindustani and English'. Everything had to be done from scratch: they even had to make their own yeast, as well as butter. Soon they decided to keep a cow, as the milk on sale in the bazaar was a mixture of cow's and sheep's milk and made tea and coffee taste revolting.

Combining the jobs of memsahib and cook during official dinner parties was a nerve-racking business for Catherine, who had 'to sit at the head of the table and try to appear as though I had not a worry in the world, when all the time my mind was on what dreadful things might be happening in the kitchen'. And sometimes dreadful things were indeed happening in the kitchen. Once while she was sitting at table waiting for the joint to be brought in, the boy came in and announced in a stage whisper that the meat smelled.

> I rushed out to the kitchen, and sure enough the meat did smell horribly. It was intensely hot weather, and the heat of the oven had just finished the turning process. What was to be done, for there was a table full of hungry people waiting? I flew to the store cupboard and got out some tins, which we feverishly opened, heated the contents and put them in a dish with a border of mashed potatoes round, and sent them in. And our guests never knew what a shock to my nervous system I had just had.

Catherine's first Christmas pudding was also a kitchen casualty:

> The first big plum pudding I made for our Chinese entertainment at the New Year came to a sad end. As we were settling down to a cosy evening, Isa came in, looking very scared and said: 'I don't think the big pudding is quite well, will the Memsahib come and see?' I rushed out to the kitchen, and there was my beautiful pudding a shapeless mass on the floor, looking very unwell indeed. I will not enlarge on my feelings, but it was a very real tragedy to me when I knew I could not easily replace the ingredients it had been made of. One does not mind these things so much when one can send to a shop and get just what one wants, but it is rather heartbreaking to see stores wasted that one will have to wait months to replace.

Informal entertaining was more relaxed and much more fun, especially when the guests brought news and gossip from the outside world. Though remote, Chini-bagh saw many such visitors after 1900, for Chinese Turkestan had been discovered by the archaeologists. Manuscripts and antiquities found by the local people in the

Taklamakan desert had been eagerly bought by both Petrovsky and Macartney and sent home for study, where they were found to pre-date the Islamic culture of the region. The Swedish explorer Sven Hedin also reported seeing, in the course of his daring forays into the Taklamakan, what appeared to be the remains of houses – possibly whole towns – half-buried in the sand. The lure of a lost Buddhist civilisation soon had archaeologists from half a dozen countries converging on Kashgar, and many of them stayed at Chini-bagh.

Dr, later Sir, Aurel Stein made his first expedition to the area in 1900, following meticulous preparation. After studying Sven Hedin's book *Through Asia*, in which the explorer described how two of his men and most of his camels had died of heat and thirst in the Taklamakan, Stein decided that the only time of year for an archaeological expedition would be winter, when ample water could be carried in the form of ice. Arriving in Kashgar from India in August, he stayed at Chini-bagh until the worst of the summer heat had passed, making firm friends with the Macartneys and Father Hendricks, and putting together his small caravan.

> Chini-bagh had been a simple walled-in orchard with a little garden house, such as every respectable Kashgari loves to own outside the city walls, when Mr Macartney, more than ten years before my visit, took up the appointment of the Indian Government's Political Representative at Kashgar. Continuous improvements effected with much ingenuity and trouble had gradually changed this tumbledown mud-built garden house into a residence which in its cosy, well-furnished rooms now offered all the comforts of an English home.
>
> Stein, *Sand-Buried Ruins of Khotan*, 1903

The 'cheerful impressions' of that stay under the Macartneys' hospitable roof were to be repeated many times during the next fifteen years. Stein's first expedition lasted eight months, during which time he did not speak to another white man, for unlike the French, German, Japanese and American archaeologists who followed him, Stein travelled alone and very simply, with only native servants and caravan men for company. Back in Chini-bagh he was a little nervous lest a 'pent-up torrent of talk' would make him a colossal bore, but he was soon reassured by the Macartneys' eager interest in all he had discovered.

Stein next saw George and Catherine in London in 1903, where they took advantage of their long leave to produce their first child, Eric. By the time they all met up again at Chini-bagh in 1906, Eric had a baby sister. Stein wrote:

> After five years' absence Chini-bagh still showed all the attractions which had so often made me look back with longing regret to my previous stays there … But little had I foreseen how greatly the brightness of Chini-bagh, with the old setting faithfully preserved, would be added to by the advent of a new master, the British Baby. Eric, the Macartneys' little son, who when barely six months old had proved himself a born traveller by doing the long journey from London to Kashgar at a tryingly early season without a day's illness, had long ago discarded the quaint conveyance, half perambulator, half sledge, in which I had seen him last in London preparing for his travels. It was a joy to see the lively little boy running about in the garden, climbing its mud-built parapets whenever the protecting eyes of mother or nurse were turned … But Master Eric, the happy possessor of this Kashgar kingdom, had for a few months enjoyed the additional good fortune of a baby sister to admire and to play with – the first British Baby which had made bold to see the light in innermost Asia. Ever smiling and cheerful, the little ruddy-cheeked maid was a constant visitor to the garden, imbibing robust health and good spirits with its fresh air.
>
> Stein, *Ruins of Desert Cathay*, 1912

Baby Sylvia was also a great favourite with Father Hendricks, by now old and ailing, and who made his painful way to see her the day before he died of cancer in June 1906. 'Alone in his ramshackle house,' wrote Stein, 'he had persistently rejected all offers of nursing and help, so there was no-one to witness the end. It was a pathetic close to a life which was strangely obscure even to the Abbé's best friends.' After the funeral Stein set off for Khotan and the southern arm of the Silk Road, which eventually led him to Tunhuang where he was to make the most spectacular discoveries of his career.

German archaeologists from the Ethnological Museum in Berlin also made a number of fruitful expeditions to Chinese Turkestan between 1902 and 1914. The first, led by Professor Grünwedel, had stayed with Petrovsky when they passed through Kashgar, but this had not been a success. The professor's assistant was Jewish, and the Russian Consul had proved to be abusively anti-Semitic. The second expedition, a couple of years later, was led by the Anglophile Albert von Le Coq, and when he and his colleague arrived in Kashgar after months of excavating along the northern arm of the Silk Road, it was to Chinibagh that they turned for hospitality. They were not disappointed, and like Stein found it 'most refreshing to stay in a European home':

> It is true we had at first to reaccustom ourselves to many habits of civilization. When Lady Macartney had installed me on an English bed in a well-furnished room, I thought I was in Heaven. But after a short time in bed I felt as if I should suffocate; I got up, took my rug, spread it out on the verandah, used my saddle as a pillow and, wrapped in a light fur, slept out in the open air. It was some time, too, before I could get accustomed again to the narrow confines of a bedroom.
>
> Von Le Coq, *Buried Treasures of Chinese Turkestan*, 1928

All the same, it must have been a relief not to sleep among the scorpions, cockroaches and poisonous spiders with which he had had to contend at Karakhoja, or to have his camp surrounded by howling wolves, as at Bezeklik (see TURFAN).

In 1908 the Chinese finally agreed to recognise the British Representative at Kashgar as a Consul, ironically while the Macartneys were on leave in England. Shortly afterwards their old foe Petrovsky died in retirement, a disappointed man. Not only were the Chinese still in charge in eastern Turkestan, but Russia had signed a friendly agreement with the detested British in 1907, putting an end to their rivalry in Central Asia. Macartney's prestige in Kashgar improved steadily as that of Russia declined. The Chinese turned to him increasingly for advice, but their internal problems were becoming insoluble. The fading Manchu dynasty attempted to introduce a few half-hearted and belated reforms in China, but it was the usual story of too little, too late. Finally, at the end of 1911, the Manchu government fell and China was declared a republic.

In remote Turkestan nothing happened immediately, for the Provincial Governor in Urumchi refused to pass on the humiliating news of the Prince Regent's abdication. It was impossible, though, to keep such a thing secret for long, and Chinese soldiers and officials in Kashgar were soon in a state of complete disarray, if not panic. Under Manchu rule all Chinese men had been obliged to wear their hair in a pigtail, and the republicans had cut these off as a ceremonial rejection of the 'badge of servitude'. Some Chinese officials in Kashgar began to follow suit, perhaps hoping to ingratiate themselves with the new administration and hang on to their lucrative posts. Others, particularly the soldiers, were proud of their pigtails and were apt to set upon any 'traitor' who had cut his off. But the Chinese soldiers were sloppy and undisciplined, and the Taotai and his staff knew they could expect little protection in the event of serious trouble. Macartney asked his chiefs in India for an armed guard, for as British Consul he was responsible for all the Indian traders in Kashgar and Yarkand, as well as the Swedish missionaries and his own family and staff. Unfortunately his request had to be turned down for logistical reasons, and this gave the new Russian Consul-General an excuse to reinforce his own guard of Cossacks.

Luckily there was also some happier news for the Macartneys in this momentous year of 1911, for it saw the birth of their third child, Robin, and the elevation of Chini-bagh to the status of Consulate-General. The old house, fond though they were of it, was really too small now for a family of five, plus nanny and governess, when it had also to be used as an office and guest-house, and for official entertaining. The practical Mr Högberg drew up plans for a more suitable building to be erected on the same site, using local materials and workmen, and these were soon agreed by the British authorities. In the middle of all the building work, in May 1912, a revolution broke out in Kashgar. Catherine Macartney gives a vivid description in her memoirs of how they were woken at four o'clock in the morning by the Russian Consul, who begged them to take refuge with him as fighting had broken out in the old town and no one knew what would happen:

> My husband jumped up at once, dressed himself and tried to stuff his revolver in his pocket without my seeing it. He told me to dress myself and the children and rouse the household. My brother-in-law, Donald, was staying with us, also Mr Hunter of the China Inland Mission. It is strange what silly ideas one has at really critical moments. My one thought was that the children and I must be in clean clothes if

we were to be murdered, and to the surprise of the Russians, we all appeared at 4.30 a.m. as though we were going to a garden party, in spotless white! We heard a few shots fired, but otherwise everything was deadly quiet, and it seemed impossible that on that peaceful summer morning anything horrible could be happening.

While they were having breakfast, a message from the revolutionaries was received from the old town, reassuring them that foreigners would not be harmed. The old Taotai, however, his wife and many of his officials had been slaughtered. Back at their own Consulate, the Macartneys ran up 'all the British flags we could find', and advised all British subjects to do the same. (As a result some very eccentric Union Jacks were soon flying over Kashgar, hastily run up by the Indian community.) Catherine's account continues:

About midday one of the city gates was opened, and a number of Chinese refugee officials got out and came to us, hidden in carts driven by natives who had befriended them. We took them in, giving them some rooms in the garden, putting up tents when the rooms were full, till we had as many as we had accommodation for. They were all in a state of terror, for the roads were infested with the revolutionaries, who were going about flourishing horrible three-edged swords, on which were gruesomely suggestive stains. The widow and little son of the murdered Hsien-Kuan [the Taotai's assistant] were among the first to be brought to us. She, poor thing, was in a pitiable plight, for she had seen her husband literally hacked to death, but when they took the boy to kill him, she threw herself on his assailants, imploring them to spare him, and they, having bigger game to pursue, let him go.

Next day the insurrection, which seemed to have more to do with general disaffection than with republicanism, spread to the new town, and the situation began to look ugly. A mob of mutineers and drunken ex-soldiers marched on the old town, bent on looting, rape and the settling of old scores. Macartney received a telegram from a well-wisher warning that Europeans would not be spared. 'So we knew that we had to prepare for the worst,' wrote Catherine.

The British subjects were told to bring their valuables and stow them away in the room that could be best defended, and where we were all to go, if necessary. My husband and his brother even arranged between them how we women and children were to be dispatched if the mob was too strong for us, though this I did not know till long afterwards. Rolls of bandages were prepared, and I packed up the children's clothes and the baby's food into bags in case we found it necessary to run and hide in a place we had already decided upon.

Our servants armed themselves with any kind of weapon they could find – knives, sticks, old swords etc – and even our governess, Miss Cresswell, took the big carving knife and steel to bed with her. Having made all preparations possible, we lay down fully dressed, while Donald and Mr Hunter took it in turns to do sentry duty round the house and garden.

There was no chance of sleep, but it was something to be able to lie down after the day we had been through. All was strangely quiet, and we were getting drowsy, when at midnight three cannons boomed out, making the house vibrate. Up we jumped, and everyone came running, thinking that the attack had begun. We waited and waited, and nothing more happened till at last the cocks began to crow, the birds twittered, and then the old sun shone once more. The relief of hearing natural sounds after a night of such nervous strain is past description.

For some reason – Catherine put it down to the power of prayer – the mob had set out but had then turned back peacefully to the new town. It later transpired that they had all been accepted into the 'New Regiment' just formed by the murderers of the Taotai – whom they had nonetheless buried with due pomp, including the three-gun salute which had so alarmed the inmates of Chini-bagh. The New Regiment, composed of desperadoes and ne'er-do-wells and headed by a pork-butcher called Pien, soon became known in Kashgar as 'the Gamblers'. George knew it was important to show no fear to the revolutionaries, so the next day he and Donald rode into the old town and reminded the new government that they must respect the rights of foreigners. There was no hostility, and after a few days he took his 9-year-old son Eric with him, as well as his brother, much to the delight of the Chinese who showered the lad with sweets and cakes. Donald noticed, however, that one man proffering sweets was holding a severed head in his other hand, still dripping with blood.

For two months the country was governed by the pork-butcher and his pawnbroker assistant. The refugees remained at Chinibagh, camping beneath the protective Union Jacks, and a Russian regiment arrived to 'keep order'. Diplomatically this was a setback for George, who was always at pains to remind the Chinese that Russia would occupy Sinkiang without hesitation if a suitable pretext arose. But Catherine confessed that she felt safer with European soldiers around, even if they were Russians. Gradually things quietened down, and those wily officials of the old regime who had managed to survive the massacres soon bribed their way to new positions of power. The pork-butcher and the pawnbroker were quietly beheaded, and their followers quickly settled for discretion rather than valour. Thanks to Macartney's tact, courage and firmness, no harm came to any of the foreign residents of Kashgar, including the wealthy Indian merchants and money-lenders of the old town. In 1913 the local authorities wrote to the Governor in Urumchi recommending the British Consul for a Chinese honour, saying that his 'conciliatoriness and justice in the treatment of affairs are eulogized alike by officials, merchants and ordinary people'. Macartney also received at last the recognition of his own government for twenty-three years of patient, unflappable diplomacy in the face of every sort of obstacle: he was made a Knight Commander of the Indian Empire.

Catherine's cup was running over, for the new Consulate-General was also completed in 1913.

[It was a] fine building, still of the bungalow type, with the exception of the towers, which overlooked the garden and in which there were two upstairs rooms and a loggia commanding a splendid view over the whole country. The roof was flat and a veritable sun trap, greatly appreciated in winter, when we could mostly get a glorious panorama of the magnificent Pamir Mountains from it. Inside, the large reception rooms opened out of a central hall and could be shut off from our private part of the house. The whole house was centrally heated by hot air circulating in all the rooms from a furnace in a hot air chamber running under the house …

Office buildings worthy of a Consulate comprised several offices; a large court room, in which hung a good picture of our King; and in the centre – with the rooms built round it to protect it from thieves getting in from outside – was the strong room.

Over the main gateway stood a splendid Coat-of-Arms sent out to us by the British Foreign Office, and of which we were immensely proud. The whole property, enclosed by a high wall, was artistically laid out with avenues of acacia trees.

Although Chini-bagh has declined sadly in recent years, the imprint left by the British coat-of-arms can still be made out over the peeling entrance.

The First World War put an abrupt end to Russian intrigues in Kashgar. The Chinese, faced by the novel spectacle of the British and Russian Consuls as best friends and allies, became fiercely hostile and obstructive to both. A tennis court was laid out between the two Consulates, and the English and Russian ladies took turns at providing cream teas for the players. Lady Macartney was sometimes known to wield a tennis racquet herself – to the amazement of the natives – though Princess Mestchersky, wife of the Russian Consul, declined to follow suit. (The Mestcherskys went home on leave in 1917, little knowing the cataclysm that would engulf them. Many years later the Macartneys heard from the Prince that they had managed to escape from revolutionary Russia, but had lost all their possessions. They were living in fairly desperate circumstances in Paris, he working as a waiter and she as a chambermaid. George and Catherine, by then retired, were shocked at the plight of their old friends and gave them discreet financial help.)

The Russian Revolution was slow to reach Sinkiang. Macartney departed, but the acting Russian Consul stayed on and for a while Kashgar became a place of refuge for White Russians from across the mountains. One of these was Paul Nazaroff, a mining engineer who had plotted an anti-Bolshevik rising in Tashkent but had been betrayed and captured. After escaping from prison he had spent many nerve-racking months on the run (he once had to be literally walled up by his protectors to elude a Bolshevik search party) before crossing the border into Sinkiang, where he arrived destitute in 1920. A keen naturalist and amateur geologist, he had always hoped to visit Kashgar, but had never envisaged his present circumstances. 'There stood I upon the threshold, in the city of Kashgar itself,' he wrote later, 'not as a traveller, not as a scientific explorer or mere tourist, but as a poor devil of a refugee, driven out of the socialist paradise of the Bolsheviks, having lost my fatherland, my family, my home, my property, left without a farthing.'

Luckily for Nazaroff, the flag of Imperial Russia was still flying over the Consulate in Kashgar, and he was to spend four peaceful years in the town before fate decreed that he must flee once more. The information he brought with him was of great interest to Percy Etherton, the new British Consul, who waged an unremitting war on Bolshevik infiltration of the area throughout his period of office.

For Paul Nazaroff, after the fraught life he had led as a fugitive, Kashgar seemed very soothing, and he spent many hours bird-watching. The best place, he discovered, especially in winter, was a warm spring next to the British Consulate. Although Kashgar was west of the main line of bird migration from Siberia, geese, duck and snipe would arrive there from the north, together with a few herons – usually the great white but occasionally the common grey. 'Before sunset there fly down the river flock after flock of ruddy sheldrake, their ringing note resounding through the air, a kind of blend between the note of a bugle and a dog's bark.' Nazaroff came to regard the warm spring as his personal bird-sanctuary:

> Great flocks of starlings weigh down the trees and fill the air with their pleasant chatter and whistles, just as they do in London on the cornices of the British Museum. Immense flocks of sparrows settle in spots warmed by the sun, and in the marsh here you may meet with Baillon's crake, which is extraordinarily tame. Its elder brother the water rail resembles it in showing no fear of man. Wrens slip through the bushes, and four or five snipe spend the winter in the marsh. And towards dusk two or three mallards are sure to fly down.
>
> On the clay walls of the British Consulate one could often get a glimpse of the red flash of the wings of the wall-creeper,

a handsome bird industriously collecting spiders and insects hibernating in the crevices. These mountain-lovers have been driven down to the plains by the sharp frosts and deep snows of their own alps. They look like red poppies stuck to the walls. Another beautiful bird is our kingfisher, like a living emerald fluttering over the water.

Nazaroff, *Moved On! From Kashgar to Kashmir*, 1935

But among the honking, whistling and twittering came another sound, mysterious and hard to identify:

It is a pleasant, melodious, soft sound, something like that of the Aeolian harp, but louder. It comes down from the clear blue sky when the air is still, especially in the mornings. It seems to radiate from above, in the air, and gradually die away, like some celestial panpipes. It was only after I had lived many months in Kashgar that I traced these melodious and mysterious sounds to their sources. The folk of Kashgar are great pigeon-fanciers and go in for breeding these birds on a large scale. They are fond of tying little reed-pipes to the tails of some of the stronger birds. When they fly high and come down rapidly or tumble in the air these curious pipings resound from the sky.

(Curiously enough, Captain James Abbott had been puzzled by a similar 'music from the skies' at Khiva in 1839, but there it had been caused by tightly strung kites – see KHIVA.)

Nazaroff found several species of mammal in the Kashgar region which were hardly known elsewhere, including a wild cat, a special type of marten and at least one new species of bat. But the creatures which most endeared themselves to him were the three varieties of hedgehog, all much alike and very attached to mankind, although they were wild:

They are smaller than the European species, more yellowish in colour, with broader ears. If one of these little creatures is attacked by dogs, which set up a terrific barking, it rolls itself up in self-defence, but directly a man appears it runs to him as though to its natural protector. If you pick one up and put it on your lap it will lie there like a kitten and be quite pleased to have its neck tickled, or if you stroke its little velvety tummy it will lower its spines flat so as to have its back stroked. It is really an extraordinary thing, for it is an entirely wild little animal, that has probably never seen a man before, much less been handled by one, yet when captured it will behave just like a kitten that has been civilized, so to speak, from time immemorial.

Unusual animals were sometimes to be found in Kashgar itself, for some of the inhabitants of the old city kept tame ibex or gazelles in their courtyards. Nazaroff used to be visited by an ibex which had acquired a taste for his tobacco and which came to him 'over the roofs of houses and along the tops of walls, like a cat'. Sadly, gazelles did not usually survive for long in Kashgar, for once they found their way into the streets they were invariably brought down by packs of stray dogs.

Life for the Kashgaris themselves was apt to be equally nasty, brutish and short, and during his four years there Nazaroff frequently saw 'bundles of men's amputated arms or feet' nailed to the massive gates of the old city. For Kashgar was now dominated by a bloodthirsty tyrant, General Ma, who was nominally Titai or military commander, but whose powers were in practice limited only by his own caprice. A Tungan, or Chinese Muslim, he was fond of amputations and had a special machine made for punishing minor offenders which sliced off their fingers joint by joint. He was no kinder to his own family, and pretty local girls went in fear of attracting his attention. When one of his wives annoyed him he had her tongue cut out, and another was strung up on a pole and beaten to death, creating a vacancy which no one was anxious to fill.

Eventually Ma's excesses became too much even for the Chinese – whom Nazaroff considered an innately cruel people – and the Governor in Urumchi ordered him to be taken prisoner. This the old tyrant refused to contemplate, and put up a fierce struggle. Wounded, he was dragged to the city gate and shot, his body displayed for general view like those of his many victims in the past. 'His corpse was left there for a couple of days,' wrote C.P. Skrine, the British Consul of the day, 'tied up to a kind of cross for the people to insult and defile, which large numbers of them did with the utmost gusto.' Even in death his face had not lost its fierce scowl.

Clarmont Skrine had arrived to relieve Etherton in 1922 accompanied by his young wife. This caused quite a stir among the European community, for Chini-bagh had not had a lady of the house since Catherine Macartney had gone on leave one day in 1915 only to find her return blocked by the vicissitudes of the Great War. 'So it was not without a little inner trepidation', wrote Paul Nazaroff, 'that our ladies accepted their first invitation to a tea-party in the Consulate garden. But they were at once put at their ease by the unaffected simplicity and perfect tact of their hostess, with whom they all fell in love at once. Tea was laid out under the shade of the lofty trees between clumps of rose-bushes and the lily-pond ... That was a red-letter day for our poor little Kashgar society.' On another occasion the children of the White Russians were speechless with joy when Mrs Skrine arranged for Father Christmas to appear at one of her parties, complete with 'an enormous sack full of all sorts of lovely things from Europe, toys such as they had never even dreamt of before'.

Doris Skrine was also a keen gardener, and took a pride in sending home-grown vegetables to the table every day of the year. She tried breeding chickens but was broken-hearted when a pack of the semi-wild – and very agile – Kashgar dogs managed to get over the garden wall and slaughter her entire brood. She and her husband were both very fond of animals and kept quite a menagerie of pets – another bond with Paul Nazaroff, who wrote of them with great affection. They loved Chini-bagh as much as the Macartneys had done, and the wonderful views from its terrace, overlooking the Tümen valley and beyond to the foothills of the Tien-shan. Doris never tired of sketching and painting them, while her husband became enthralled by Eastern Turki songs, many of which he transcribed as his understanding of the language progressed. 'The Eastern Turkis are a musical race,' he wrote in his book *Chinese Central Asia*. 'The ballad is still a living verse-form, and the troubadours of Artush are famous for their improvizations on any subject. Two days after the defeat and execution of the Titai a ribald ballad, which I took down later, was being sung about him in the streets.'

But professionally Skrine was not as ruthlessly effective as his predecessor, who had been able to report in 1920 that 'so far we have kept Kashgaria clear of Bolshevism'. Gradually it dawned on the White Russians that the Chinese, without Etherton's iron will behind them, would not withstand the tide of Bolshevism much longer, and they began another sad trek in search of adoptive homes. Nazaroff himself travelled to Kashmir in 1924 and eventually to London.

With the departure of the Skrines and the White Russians in 1924, Kashgar lost any pretence at *joie de vivre*, and a year later the Bolsheviks took over the Russian Consulate there. The dour new officials soon made themselves unpopular with both the native population and the Chinese colonialists, who resented their hectoring attitude. As for the British, it must have seemed like Petrovsky all over again, with smear campaigns and blatant propaganda, not to mention spying. Major George Gillan, the new British Consul, found the Bolsheviks actually trying to suborn his own staff. 'They have definitely tried bribery,' he wrote in a secret dispatch to India in 1927, 'apparently on the assumption that I leave my secret papers lying about freely, and have tried other schemes of a comic opera nature which you will relish personally but which I will not commit to paper ... They have also discussed, but I believe abandoned as impracticable, a scheme to catch our mail on the road.' Major Gillan evidently had an efficient intelligence system of his own.

While the autocratic Governor Yang was in charge in the provincial capital of Urumchi, British Indian interests were safe and the Soviets were unable to make much headway, but Yang was assassinated in 1928 and Sinkiang was soon plunged into a bloody conflict between the Han Chinese and the Tungans, or Chinese Muslims. The peaceful native traders of the region, both Turki and Hindu, suffered greatly, and the Bolsheviks were quick to seize the opportunity to introduce 'advisers' and even troops to hasten the collapse of the province (see URUMCHI).

During this time of upheaval and transition Kashgar was visited by a Swedish student who went on to become a distinguished diplomat and Central Asian scholar. Gunnar Jarring was at that time studying Turkic languages at Lund University under Dr Gustav Raquette, who had been a missionary in Kashgar when the Macartneys were there. 'Coming to Kashgar in 1929 was like coming from the present to the Middle Ages,' wrote Jarring.

> There were no cars, no motorcycles, not even a bicycle. No electric lights illuminated the dark, narrow passages in the bazaar districts. There were no newspapers, no printed books

– scribes sat cross-legged and copied manuscripts in neat Arabic characters. The water carrier walked around with his heavy load of water contained in a sheep or goat skin. Dyers hung their skeins of yarn on rods on top of the flat roofed mud houses. Their section of the bazaars was painted blue, yellow, red and mauve, and those cheerful colours were repeated in the clothes they wore.

At that time you could still find examples of ancient East Turkestan textile products – embroidered fabrics or carpets from Khotan, Yarkand or Kashgar. However, the imported textiles from Tashkent and other Soviet textile centres were already taking over. Those new fabrics had flowery patterns and glaring colours.

No one in those days expected to complete the purchase of a rug during the course of one day. The pleasurable process of bargaining would be extended over a week or two, or preferably a whole month. Nearly fifty years after his first visit Gunnar Jarring saw Kashgar again, changed almost beyond recognition, and wrote a book encompassing both visits, entitled *Return to Kashgar*.

In 1934 Kashgar was briefly captured by the Tungans, a race Clarmont Skrine had described as 'formidable and unpleasant'. The British Consul and his wife watched from the terrace of Chini-bagh as the Kirghiz and Turkis fled from the old city, pursued by the Tungan soldiers. Suddenly one of the pursuers stopped and took aim at the watching group of white people. Mrs Thomson-Glover, the Consul's wife, described by the writer Peter Fleming as 'a peculiarly indomitable sort of person who had not even bothered to take cover', was shot through the shoulder. Soon after, the Tungans were driven out of Kashgar by the forces of another warlord who had Soviet backing, and an uneasy peace returned.

Peter Fleming, who was travelling through China and chaotic Sinkiang for *The Times*, in company with the Swiss traveller Ella Maillart, found 'Kashgar-les-Bains' the acme of civilisation when he arrived there in 1935. 'Few people', he wrote in his book *News from Tartary*, 'can ever have enjoyed a bath more than we did, who had not had one for five and a half months … We stayed a fortnight in Kashgar, leading a country-house life … In the evening we played tennis with the Russians, or football or volley-ball with the Hunza guard, who numbered fifteen. Twice a week there was polo, organized and led – her bullet-wound notwithstanding – by Mrs Thomson-Glover, and the Hunzas, whose national game it is, performed with great dash. Ella Maillart recalls in her book *Forbidden Journey* the strain of sitting on a chair after months of squatting on the ground, but she revelled in the luxurious smell of black coffee, and the gleam of crystal and silver and flowers on a polished table. She was a keen sportswoman, and was amused to hear that her football playing had given rise to a bazaar rumour that she was really a White Russian man disguised as a woman.

The warlord with Soviet backing, General Sheng Shih-tsai, had by now made himself Governor of Sinkiang, which he ruled despotically and erratically until 1944. With aid from his paymasters he built roads and schools, but he also carried out a reign of terror against Muslim leaders, Turki landowners and foreigners. Life for the British Consulate in Kashgar became very difficult in the 1940s. Nobody wanted to be seen speaking to the staff, or be caught selling them supplies. British Indian subjects were expelled, often at a few hours' notice, and protests by the consular officials were simply ignored. Effectively, the Consulate was boycotted by the Chinese. The British were not the only ones to suffer, for the Swedish Mission was forced to close down at this time, while purges and liquidations decimated the ranks of rich Turkis. In 1942 Sheng abruptly changed sides, evidently thinking the Soviet Union and the other Allies would lose the war, and attached himself to the central government of China – who quietly removed him from office in 1944.

The last of the line of energetic Englishwomen to hold sway at Chini-bagh was Diana Shipton, wife of the distinguished mountaineer. Eric Shipton had already had one posting there from 1940 to 1942 and, despite the difficulties, the lure of the Tien-shan and the Pamirs made him eager to accept when he was offered another posting to Kashgar in 1946. His young wife, the daughter of a Forest Officer in India, was used to lonely places and found her new home surprisingly luxurious, especially after the difficult journey through the Karakoram mountains. (Lady Macartney's old route via Russia was, of course, no longer possible.) Exploring the rooms, she was struck by the traces of the varying personalities of her predecessors. In the drawing-room was a magnificent library of books on Central Asia, while in the upstairs room of one of the towers was a collection, almost as impressive, of crime fiction in lurid dust-wrappers. Someone had brought a gramophone up from India and a motley assortment of records, ranging from Mozart and Brahms to out-of-date dance music. There was also a ping-pong table, a gamebook and someone's (Nazaroff's?) observations of local bird migrations.

Two fatal accidents on the Chini-bagh polo field in the early 1940s had put an end to the sport and, to Mrs Shipton's secret relief, the pitch had been planted with melons by the time she arrived. She loathed riding and had no desire to emulate Mrs Thomson-Glover's equestrian feats. She shared her husband's love of the mountains, however, and enjoyed long walks in the cool of early morning, as well as expeditions to the foothills. She was a high-spirited young woman who loved parties, but entertaining in Kashgar was always a headache, with all the problems of differing languages and cultures, not to mention the unpredictability of the climate. Her book *The Antique Land* chronicles some near-disasters quite up to Lady Macartney's experiences fifty years earlier.

The Sovereign's birthday calls for a specially grand party at British embassies and consulates all over the world, and Kashgar was no exception. Diana planned a charming *al fresco* banquet on the terrace of Chini-bagh, and decorated the garden and flat roof with a host of little oil lamps which would shine 'like so many glow-worms' as darkness fell. Alas, the honoured guests had scarcely begun their meal when the wind blew up and a sudden and violent dust-storm engulfed Chini-bagh, shattering unfastened windows and sending the flower of Kashgar society scurrying for cover. 'In one's own language it is possible to turn a calamity into a joke,' wrote Diana ruefully. 'Through interpreters it is not so easy.'

Indian independence in 1947 removed the *raison d'être* of Chini-bagh, listening-post for British India, and Eric Shipton left in 1948. The following year Mao Tse-tung and his Communists seized power in China and an attempt was made to drag Sinkiang into the twentieth century. Most of Kashgar's ancient walls were torn down, two roads were bulldozed at right angles through the old city, charmless totalitarian architecture sprang up incongruously among the old mud-and-wattle houses and shops, and a sixty-foot statue of Chairman Mao was heaved into position. The Russian Consulate remains as the 'old wing' of the Seman Hotel, and Chini-bagh – after an inglorious period as an overnight hostel for truck-drivers – is being refurbished as a hotel. But its beautiful gardens have gone for ever, and the shades of Catherine Macartney and Doris Skrine must be wringing their hands among the concrete and rubble.

However the call to prayer still wafts down from the minarets of the Id-ga mosque, albeit from a loudspeaker, and if you visit the remaining bazaars of the old town, or the Sunday Market across the river, you may catch a glimpse of the old Kashgar of the merchants and caravan men. Or if you are a romantic, stand on the east-facing terrace of Chini-bagh in the early morning and look towards the Tien-shan mountains, remembering the words of Sir Clarmont Skrine:

> What a joy that terrace was! How pleasant, as one sipped one's early tea, to watch the sunlight flood the valley and listen to the various noises of the morning as they floated up from field and homestead, the harsher ones softened by distance: birds twittering, cocks crowing, women calling to one another, donkeys braying, boys singing, dogs barking, cart-wheels creaking; best of all, that peculiar sound which for us seemed to hold the very essence of Kashgar's charm – the note of the millers' horns as they called to their customers to bring their grain for grinding. To us the gentle sounds which floated up in the morning from the little mills by the river were as 'the horns of Elf-land faintly blowing'.

KHIVA
The Freeing of the Slaves

At Khiva the river Oxus is hard frozen during four months,
although the latitude corresponds with that of Rome, and
snow lies for several months ... Yet in summer, the heat at
Khiva is almost insufferable. Linen clothes can scarcely be
borne, and it is impossible to sleep beneath the roof. People
exposed to the sun die in consequence.

Major James Abbott, *Narrative of a Journey
from Heraut to Khiva*, 1843

Lines of green and gold, and gold and green, beyond which
the walls and minarets of Khiva appeared in sight. Can that be
really Khiva? The scene filled one with a thrill of satisfaction.
All past difficulties and discomforts were forgotten, and
future ones unthought of – the goal was reached.

Ella Christie, *Through Khiva to Golden Samarkand*, 1925

FOR ELLA CHRISTIE, her arrival in Khiva in 1912 was the
realisation of a dream, but prior to the Russian annexation in
1873 to arrive there was often the beginning of a living nightmare.
For Khiva had long been a city of evil repute, and one of the two
great slave markets of Central Asia, Bokhara being the other.
Turcoman raiders from the Kara Kum desert could be sure of a
fat profit from their human cargo, snatched from the shores of the
Caspian, 500 miles away, or from a lonely caravan trail. Russian
men were always in demand as workers, although Persian women
were highly prized for the harem. 'The Tekke tribes, the most
savage of all the Turcomans,' remarked the Hungarian traveller

Vambery, 'would not hesitate to sell into slavery the Prophet himself, did he fall into their hands.'

Present-day Khiva, since 1968 a silent museum-town, almost deserted apart from the tourists who are taken there on excursions, has little in common with its bustling earlier self. Its narrow streets used to be so crowded with men and camels that visitors – from Ibn Battuta in the fourteenth century to Ella Christie in the early twentieth – all complained that it was well-nigh impossible to move at all. Now its mosques and *medressehs*, or colleges, have been rebuilt to a lifeless perfection, and even its ancient walls have been replastered with new mud, giving it the air of an abandoned stage-set. But in Khiva, unlike Samarkand, there are at least few modern intrusions, and if imagination can supply the noisy, colourful crowds of merchants, the groaning camels and the heaps of fruit, the spices, tea and bales of cloth, then one can experience something of the timelessness of a Central Asian caravan town.

Khiva, in the oasis of Khorezm, first came into prominence after Genghis Khan had reduced the capital, Gurganj, 150 miles to the north, to a heap of smoking ashes in 1219. But it had existed as a staging-post on the Silk Road – Kheivak Well – since at least the sixth century. East-bound caravans would halt there before travelling on to Bokhara and Samarkand. Others would be heading south to Merv and then westwards through Persia to the eastern Mediterranean. Some would travel north to the Aral Sea and then across the desert to the Caspian city of Astrakhan. Khorezm, or Chorasmia as it was known to the Greeks, was a fertile country on the lower reaches of the Oxus, bounded by the deserts of Kyzyl Kum and Kara Kum and by the Sea of Aral, and it had passed through the hands of many conquerors – including the ubiquitous Alexander the Great. In AD 711, it fell to the Arabs who were astonished by the luxuriance of its vegetation in summer and the severity of its winters. As a result they were able to send choice melons and grapes to the Caliph in Baghdad, packed in ice which was stored underground in blocks in summer.

Khorezm was part of the huge Seljuk empire in the eleventh century and was still part of a large Turkic confederation at the beginning of the thirteenth, including Persia, most of Afghanistan and all of Central Asia to the west of the Syr-darya, or Jaxartes river. In 1219 it is said that the ruler of Khorezm mortally offended Genghis

Khan by shaving the heads of his envoys, but perhaps the Mongols simply wanted an excuse to invade. At all events, the revenge was terrible, and nothing was left in Gurganj but a heap of skulls. While some of the Mongols swept on to conquer the rest of Central Asia, the Middle East and eastern Europe, others were left to administer the new territories, and by the fourteenth century Khorezm was ruled by the Blue Horde. Racially they were no longer pure Mongols, for they had interbred with the Turkish tribes who still inhabited the region, and the Arab traveller Ibn Battuta, who went there in the 1330s, described them all as 'Turks'. He was entertained by the Governor of Gurganj – evidently now rebuilt – to a feast which included several tables devoted entirely to fruit: 'Pomegranates prepared for the table, some of them served in vessels of gold and silver with golden spoons, others in vessels of glass with wooden spoons, and wonderful melons.' In winter, however, many plants – and especially vines – had to be buried in the earth in order to survive.

At the end of the fourteenth century Khiva and Khorezm were captured by Tamerlane, and after his empire broke up they became the property of the Uzbek Khans, a warlike grouping of former nomads. Their main occupation, according to the Elizabethan merchant Anthony Jenkinson, who passed through their territories in 1558, was fighting among themselves. Gurganj, he reported, had been constantly fought over and had changed hands four times in the previous seven years. Everyone was very poor as a result, and Master Jenkinson found few customers for his bales of cloth. When not fighting, the inhabitants liked hawking, or simply sitting around plotting. Jenkinson formed a very low opinion of them. Khiva became the principal city of the Khanate at the end of the sixteenth century, when the Oxus suddenly changed its course, possibly as a result of a minor earthquake, leaving Gurganj stranded in the desert. (Central Asian rivers are nothing if not capricious: the Oxus, or Amu-darya, seems originally to have flowed into the Caspian rather than the Aral Sea.) The ruins of Gurganj, today known as Kunya Urgench, can still be seen, although they are now the other side of the border, in Turkmenistan.

Khiva quickly acquired an unsavoury reputation, partly because of its slave trafficking but also on account of the cruelty and duplicity of its rulers. Strangers ventured there at their peril in the eighteenth and early nineteenth centuries, and anyone who had the misfortune to arrive there in winter had the extra burden of the cold to endure. Captain James Abbott, who was detained as the guest of the Khan of Khiva for several uncomfortable weeks in the winter of 1840, suffered miserably from being confined to one room:

> The air was searchingly cold. In England, nothing is known approaching to the chill of the Khiva winter. My towel, hung up to dry in the small room warmed with a large fire of charcoal, instantly became a mass of ice. If the door was left open, the passage of the wind was detected, as it blew over any liquid, by its sudden conversion to a solid form, and there was no thaw excepting in spots where the sun-beams accumulated.

These sunbeams also produced a rather magical effect on the moisture in the atmosphere:

> The sun now shone cheerily through the cutting air, lighting in its passage myriads of minute particles of mist (small as the motes of the sun-beam, and invisible like them excepting in the brightest light): which the intense chill of the air was continually freezing, and which, falling in an unceasing shower of light, gave sparkle to the atmosphere that savoured of enchantment. This effect I have observed only at Khiva.

Abbott had been sent from Herat, in Afghanistan, to Khiva on a delicate mission. The British government was becoming increasingly worried about Russia's intentions in Central Asia, then a sort of no man's land ruled by a lot of petty chieftains and situated uncomfortably near to Britain's commercial gold-mine, India. Russia's southern border was somewhat vague at this period, and Russian citizens in the outlying regions were constantly at the mercy of the 'man-stealing Turcomans', as one writer described them. This alone gave the Tsar an excuse to send exploratory expeditions to the Central Asian khanates, and even to Afghanistan, traditionally regarded as the gateway to India. However, the first Russian expedition to Khiva, in 1717, had been a disaster. On arrival the Russians had been welcomed and persuaded to split up into smaller groups, on the pretext that there was nowhere big enough to accommodate them all together. The treacherous Khivans had then fallen upon the Russians and slaughtered them.

A century later, in 1819, Captain Muraviev had spent an anxious seven weeks locked in a fort there, but had finally been well received by the Khan, who evidently feared reprisals from his powerful neighbour if Muraviev came to any harm. The young Russian officer was shocked to receive secret messages from Russian slaves in Khiva, revealing that there were 3,000 of them held in bondage, often in conditions of the utmost degradation and hardship. His own position being extremely precarious, he could do nothing to help them, but he returned to St Petersburg burning with indignation on their behalf. His discreet enquiries and observations had convinced him that Khiva could easily be taken by a full-scale expedition, but it was another twenty years before the Tsar felt able to undertake one.

In the autumn of 1839 General Perovsky set out from Orenburg with 5,000 troops and 10,000 camels on the long trek through steppe and desert to the sinister mud-walled town on the Oxus. It was at this point that Captain Abbott was hurriedly dispatched from Herat to forestall the Russian plot. If Abbott could persuade the Khan to release all his Russian slaves, it was reasoned, then Perovsky would have no excuse for annexing Khiva. Many of the slaves, of course, were not Russian. On his way across the wilderness from Merv, Abbott overtook a melancholy procession of men, women and children from Herat, being led to Khiva by their Turcoman captors:

> The men are chained together by the throats at night, so that rest is scarcely possible, whilst the contact of the frozen iron with their skin must be a torture. My heart is full of heaviness, when I think of all the heart-rending misery of which this system is the cause. Alas! he who once enters Khiva abandons all hope, as surely as he who enters hell. His prison-house is girdled with trackless deserts, whose sole inhabitants are the sellers of human flesh.

Sending ahead an emissary to the Khan, assuring him that the English wished for friendly relations with Khiva, Abbott approached the city with many misgivings. 'My present position', he reflected, 'was one of interest and deep anxiety. I had been sent to execute what might well appear an impossibility, and my fame, as well as life, was staked upon the venture.' Abbott spoke a little Persian, but had no information on the manners and etiquette of the Khivan court, had few gifts to bestow and was provided with a small and distinctly unimpressive retinue. 'I confess,' he wrote later in his book, 'the case appeared to me as desperate as possible.' On entering the city he was surprised to hear a pleasant melodic sound, resembling 'the distant music of a hundred Aeolian harps'. Much later he discovered the source of this extraterrestrial music:

> Seeing some children on the road with their paper kites, I approached to examine the contrivance by which these toys emit a musical sound whilst floating in the air. The kite is square, formed upon two diagonals of light wood, whose extremities are connected by a tight string, forming the sides of the square. Over the whole paper is pasted. A loose string upon the upright diagonal receives the string by which the kite is to be held, and a tail is fastened to its lower extremity. The transverse diagonal, or cross-stick is then bent back like a strung bow, and fastened by a thread or cat-gut. Of course, every breeze that passes the kite vibrates this tight chord, and the vibrations are communicated to the highly sonorous frame of the kite. And, as numbers of these kites are left floating in the air all night, the effect is that of aerial music; monotonous, but full of melancholy interest.

Abbott was received politely by the Khan who, however, had only the haziest idea of what or where England was. In fact it was only with difficulty that Abbott convinced him that the English were not a minor tribe belonging to the Tsar of Russia, and that he himself was not a Russian spy. The Khan's astonishment knew no bounds when he learned that the King of England was actually a young woman, and there was much sniggering among the courtiers when Abbott tried to explain that her future husband would be a consort, not a king. 'Do you always choose women as your kings?' enquired the Khan incredulously. And what about ministers and officers, did they have to be women too?

Abbott had many audiences with the Khan, who wanted to know about his beliefs in magic, religion and astrology, as well as about England's military strength. In the course of one of these conversations the Khan remarked pleasantly that he had been obliged to execute his last two European visitors. They too had claimed to be English, but he had been convinced that they were Russian spies. Mastering his indignation with difficulty, Abbott suggested that imprisonment would have been sufficient, for 'God alone can restore life'.

> 'It is certainly a pity,' said the Khan, with a good-humoured smile, and in the tone in which mere mortals speak of the death of rats, 'but they were Russians and spies.'

On hearing that an expeditionary force had been sent by the Tsar the Khan agreed, in theory, to relinquish his Russian slaves, but before long news reached the Khanate that Perovsky's force had met with disaster. Severe snowfalls had unexpectedly engulfed the expedition, and both men and animals had died of exposure in their hundreds. Halfway to Khiva General Perovsky had been forced to turn back, losing more and more of his force with every day that passed. Apart from the horrors of frostbite, snow-blindness and scurvy, the weary column was now accompanied by a sinister rearguard of wolves, waiting to pounce on any stragglers. One-fifth of the men perished and only about a thousand of the baggage animals survived. Emboldened by this news, the Khan of Khiva sent Abbott packing, saying only that if the Tsar promised not to send any more expeditions against him, then he would agree to release the slaves.

Meanwhile the British in Herat had heard nothing of Abbott's progress – the Khan having intercepted all his mail – and feared the worst. At this same time the ill-fated Colonel Stoddart was being held in a filthy dungeon by the Khan of Khiva's neighbour, the Emir of Bokhara, and Central Asia was clearly a most perilous place for an Englishman. Nevertheless, in June 1840 another resourceful officer was sent to Khiva, this time with more success. Lieutenant Richmond Shakespear saw the city under far more favourable conditions than the hapless Abbott, for it was now early summer. He kept a diary which was later published in *Blackwood's Magazine*, under the title 'A Personal Narrative of a Journey from Herat to Orenburg', in which he recorded his observations of Khiva:

> There is a fort of some size here, but of no strength. All the houses are made of mud, the outer walls being solid and the inner partitions supported by wooden framework;

they are of a considerable size, and the rooms are lofty, but unornamented, and without windows. If sufficient light cannot be procured from the doorway, a hole is knocked in the roof. Water is so near the surface that it is necessary to lay a foundation of wood or stone for all the walls. The gardens in the neighbourhood of the town are very numerous, and appear to be kept with much care. The bazaar was crowded, the streets narrow and dirty; the climate is delicious.

Perhaps Shakespear reaped the benefit of Abbott's dignified behaviour, for he was allowed much more freedom than his predecessor, and was also granted an immediate audience with the Khan, 'a good-natured, unaffected person of about forty-five years of age'. The most impressive buildings in the town were the Muslim *medressehs* – 'showy buildings, ornamented with coloured tiles, which have a gay effect' – but the lack of firm foundations gave all Khiva's edifices a rickety appearance. 'The minarets all slope from the perpendicular, and the walls are in general separated at the corners of the buildings.' This instability, together with the ravages of fire, explains why most of the buildings to be seen in Khiva today date only from the nineteenth century. 'The chief beauty of Khiva', wrote Shakespear in his journal, 'consists in the luxuriant growth of the trees, and in the number and extent of the gardens.'

There is a gap in Shakespear's journal between 30 June and 3 August. 'I have been too busy with office matters to resume this rambling journal,' he explains, and indeed he had, for by this time he had somehow persuaded the Khan to part with all his Russian slaves. There were a number of last-minute hitches when various nobles, including the Khan himself, tried to hang on to a special favourite, but Shakespear was uncompromising: it was all or nothing. Finally, in the middle of August, he set out with 416 grateful Russians and marched them across the desert to Fort Alexandrovsk on the Caspian, where he handed them over to the astonished Commandant. 'All the sufferings fell to my lot, all the laurels to his,' commented Abbott later, with a hint of asperity. He, incidentally, had had an extremely unpleasant time after leaving Khiva, having been attacked, wounded and robbed of everything by brigands in the desert. Shakespear, predictably, went home to a hero's welcome and a knighthood.

For a while the Russians left Khiva alone. Their immediate pretext for an annexation had been removed with the freeing of the slaves, and in any case it was too remote, too difficult to reach in safety from either Orenburg or Fort Alexandrovsk. But its hour would come once the Tsar had a bridgehead in Turkestan, for the massacre of the 1717 expedition and Perovsky's catastrophe in 1840 had not been forgotten. In the meantime a certain amount of trade developed between Russia and the khanates of Central Asia, and the more daring of the Khivan merchants travelled to the northern Caspian port of Astrakhan and thence up the Volga to the famous annual fair at Nizhny-Novgorod. Indeed, as silk and cotton cloth were among the merchandise travelling north, it could be said that the Volga was a modern arm of the Silk Road.

In 1858 a Russian mission went to Khiva and Bokhara, led by a young officer named Nikolai Ignatiev. A passionate advocate of a forward policy for Russia in Central Asia, he did not always see eye to eye with his Foreign Ministry, but his journey was supported enthusiastically by the War Ministry. Although ostensibly his visit was a simple return of courtesies – both rulers had been guests at Alexander II's coronation in 1855 – Tsarist documents of the day make it clear that one of the real aims was 'the destruction of the harmful interference of the English who are trying to penetrate Central Asia and lure it into their sphere of influence'. In support of this Great Game manoeuvre no expense was to be spared in the giving of gifts. An organ was considered a suitable offering for the Khan of Khiva, and was carried 750 miles by camel from Orenburg to the desert kingdom.

Ignatiev spent six weeks in Khiva, trying in vain to persuade the suspicious and vacillating Khan – a much younger half-brother of the Khan seen by Abbott and Shakespear – to sign a treaty of friendship. Memories of the treachery his predecessor had met with in 1717 kept the Russian awake at night, and at times the mission seemed doomed to much more than mere failure, as the Khan waxed hot and cold – but mostly cold:

> Our situation in Khiva from the very beginning of our visit was extremely uncomfortable. Under pain of execution it was forbidden for the local inhabitants to visit or even to speak

to us. Armed Khivans guarded our living quarters and were located on the flat roofs of the clay buildings where we had our meals. They were with us day and night, inspecting us through the windows or openings in the ceilings.

Ignatiev, *Mission to Khiva and Bokhara in 1858*

On the infrequent occasions when they were allowed out of their quarters, the local people cursed them and made threatening gestures. Another nasty habit was the loud banging of drums outside their doors, sometimes in the middle of the night. Ignatiev saw very little of the city, and wrote despairingly to his father: 'My negotiations go extremely slowly and I really do not know when I shall get out of this terrible country.' Eventually he did, and the Khan's unpleasant behaviour no doubt hardened Russian hearts, for the next decade saw the start of a prolonged campaign of Russian conquest throughout Central Asia.

Khiva's evil reputation, meanwhile, grew if anything more horrible, for the current Khan was weak, sadistic and fanatical. (There was a high turnover of Khans of Khiva, the previous two having died in mysterious circumstances after reigning for only a few months each.) It may seem surprising in the circumstances that any foreigner should choose to go there, but the summer of 1863 saw the arrival of the Hungarian orientalist Arminius Vambery, heavily disguised as a Muslim dervish. He had set out from Persia with a party of pilgrims returning from Mecca, and so effective was his disguise that they regarded him as even more devout than themselves. He had spent a number of years studying in Constantinople, and was posing as a Turk, but he had plenty of heart-stopping moments when his identity was challenged by strangers who were more familiar with European features than his simple companions. His cool nerves, allied to a thorough knowledge of the Koran, enabled him to survive these encounters, and even the Khan of Khiva asked for his blessing. This rascally individual, with his cruel and degenerate appearance and effeminate voice, made Vambery shudder inwardly. His repugnance was not lessened when he came upon eight of the Khan's prisoners having their eyes gouged out, the executioner wiping his knife blade each time on the beard of his victim.

Vambery himself, having been graciously received by the Khan, was treated everywhere with kindness and hospitality, but it was a nerve-racking time and he was not sorry to leave after a month. At least his caravan was now in better shape, for the Khan had ordered all the pilgrims to be given riding asses, and their foodbags had been filled with bread and flour. Two years after Vambery's clandestine visit to Central Asia, the Russians captured Tashkent and settled down in earnest to colonise the region. General Kaufmann, Governor-General of the new Russian province of Turkestan, took Samarkand and Bokhara in 1868, and in 1873 he was ready to tackle remote Khiva.

Just to be on the safe side, the Russians decided to attack the Khanate from five different directions at once. The five columns, comprising a total of 10,000 men, would converge from the Caucasus, from Orenburg, from the Caspian, from Fort Kazala on the Syr-darya, and finally from Tashkent. General Kaufmann was in overall command, and would himself lead the Tashkent force. The Russians were not keen for the rest of the world to see what they were up to, having denied any intention of annexing the Khanate, so journalists were strictly barred from accompanying the expedition. This proved to be more of a challenge than a deterrent, of course, and at least two resourceful reporters set off at once. David Ker of the *Daily Telegraph* was finally thwarted by the Russians, after months of traipsing around the desert on false trails, and ended up fuming in Tashkent. His American rival had better luck and rode into Khiva with the triumphant invaders.

James MacGahan worked for the *New York Herald* under its great, if eccentric, editor Gordon Bennett. Although only 29, he had already won his journalistic spurs during the Franco-Prussian War, and he spoke French and German fluently. He also spoke some Russian, having a Russian wife. Perhaps as a result, he always got on well with the Russian officers with whom he now played hide-and-seek in the Kyzyl Kum desert. Naturally, they were obliged to oppose his efforts to catch up with the elusive General Kaufmann, but they were generous with food, drink and fodder, and without their covert assistance he would probably have perished. As it was he had some very close shaves.

MacGahan had set out from St Petersburg in March 1873 and on 29 May he finally caught up with his quarry on the banks of the

Oxus. Kaufmann was so astonished that this ragged and dishevelled young man had managed to cross the Kyzyl Kum single-handed that he relented completely and allowed him to accompany the final stages of the Russian campaign. After their weeks in the desert the Khorezm oasis seemed like paradise both to MacGahan and to the Russians, with its tree-lined streams and its apricots, mulberries, apples and cherries. And after a few inconclusive skirmishes in the desert, the Russians were looking forward to a good battle for the city of Khiva. But they were deprived of this pleasure. The Khan, seeing he was surrounded on all sides, offered his unconditional surrender on 9 June, though the Turcomans among his troops were as eager for a scrap as the Russians, and fierce scuffles continued in the north of the town until the two sides were prised apart by their respective leaders.

The way was now clear for General Kaufmann to enter Khiva in a dignified manner, and receive the formal submission of the Khan and his predominantly Uzbek subjects. MacGahan, like a good reporter, followed close behind:

> It was now about noon, and in ten minutes we were in sight of the renowned city. We did not see it until we were within less than half a mile, owing to the masses of trees everywhere that completely hid it from our view. At last it broke upon us, amid the clouds of dust which we had raised. Great, heavy mud walls, high and battlemented with heavy round buttresses, and a ditch, partly dry, partly filled with water, over which we could see the tops of trees, a few tall minarets, domes of mosques, and one immense round tower that reflected the rays of the sun like porcelain ... As we passed through the long arched gateway we left the dust behind us, and emerging from this, found the city before us.
>
> MacGahan, *Campaigning on the Oxus and the Fall of Khiva*, 1874

Gradually, as they passed along the narrow, winding streets, they became aware that nervous eyes were watching them:

> We began to see small groups of men in the lateral streets, in dirty ragged tunics and long beards, with hats off, bowing timidly to us as we passed. These were the inhabitants, and they

were not yet sure whether they would all be massacred or not. With what strange awe and dread they must have gazed upon us as we passed, dust-covered and grimy after our march of 600 miles over the desert, which they had considered impassable. Grim, stern, silent and invincible, we must have appeared to them like some strange, powerful beings of an unknown world.

Then we came upon a crowd of Persian slaves, who received us with shouts, cries, and tears of joy. They were wild with excitement. They had heard that wherever the Russians went slavery disappeared, and they did not doubt that it would be the case here.

Finally they reached the main square in front of the Khan's palace:

One side of this square was taken up by the palace, a huge rambling structure, with mud-battlemented walls about twenty feet high; opposite was a new *medresseh* not yet finished; the other two sides were filled up by sheds and private houses, while at the south-eastern angle of the palace rose, beautiful and majestic, the famous sacred tower of Khiva. It was about thirty feet in diameter at the bottom, and tapered gradually to the top, a height of about 125 feet, where it appeared to have a diameter of fifteen feet. It had neither pedestal nor capital, nor ornament of any kind, but its surface was covered with burnt tiles, brightly coloured in blue, green, purple and brown on a pure white ground, arranged in a variety of broad stripes and figures, the whole producing a most brilliant and beautiful effect.

But there was no sign of the Khan who, it appeared, had fled ignominiously. Kaufmann and his party entered the audience chamber and were served with refreshments by an elderly official.

Imagine a kind of porch entirely open to the court, thirty feet high, twenty wide, ten deep, and flanked on either side by towers ornamented with blue and green tiles, in the same way as the large tower on the square; a floor raised six feet above the pavement of the court, the roof supported by two carved, slender, wooden pillars, the whole resembling much the stage of a theatre, and you will have a very good idea of the grand hall of state, wherein the Khan of Khiva sits and dispenses justice.

That night MacGahan explored the palace and, climbing a steep and narrow stairway, emerged on the battlements and gazed down on the city:

> It was now near midnight, and the silent, sleeping city lay bathed in a flood of glorious moonlight. The palace was transformed. The flat mud roofs had turned to marble; the tall slender minarets rose dim and indistinct, like spectre sentinels watching over the city. Here and there little courts and gardens lay buried in deepest shadow, from which arose the dark masses of mighty elms and the still and ghostly forms of the slender poplars. Far away, the exterior walls of the city, with battlements and towers, which in the misty moonlight looked as high as the sky and as distant as the horizon. It was no longer a real city, but a leaf torn from the enchanted pages of the *Arabian Nights*.

Walking round the palace battlements, MacGahan found himself looking down on the women's quarters. The Khan, in his haste, had left his entire harem behind. The ladies ranged from 'sweet young girls of fifteen' to 'old toothless hags, apparently a hundred and fifty', and MacGahan was very taken with a girl of about eighteen with large dark eyes and a 'noble appearance'. Descending cautiously in the pitch dark – he dared not strike matches for there were piles of gunpowder in the labyrinthine passages – the young American eventually joined the bolder girls for an illicit midnight feast of tea and sweetmeats. The dark-eyed beauty knelt at his feet and seemed to be imploring his help. They gazed into one another's eyes, but in the absence of a common language he could elicit little beyond her name: Zuleika. 'I never in my life before so much regretted my ignorance of an unknown tongue,' he wrote frankly in his book. Mrs MacGahan must have been relieved to learn that her husband's *inamorata* led the women out of the palace later that night and placed them under the protection of the Khan's aged uncle.

After an interval the craven Khan was induced to return to his capital and take nominal charge of affairs, but there was little doubt in anyone's mind that Khiva had now effectively become part of the Tsar's empire. Indeed, it was not long before St Petersburg decreed that no foreigners were to travel in 'Russian Central Asia'. This was too much for one young officer of the Household Cavalry. Captain Frederick Burnaby began immediately to plan a trip to Khiva and beyond on his next long leave.

Just before setting out at the end of November 1875, Burnaby met MacGahan for some last-minute advice. 'It is to be done,' reckoned the American, 'though the odds are rather against you.' Everything would be possible as far as Fort Number One – Kazala, at the mouth of the Syr-darya – but then the Englishman would have to make a dash for it. And so it proved. The railway took him as far as Syzran, on the Volga, where a travelling companion offered to share a sleigh with him as far as Samara (modern Kubyshev). 'You had better put on plenty of clothes,' advised the Russian, for there was a stiff wind and twenty degrees of frost. There were also wolves about, but when Burnaby tried to put on his revolver belt over the extra layers, he found it would not fit round his by now Herculean proportions. He was a big man to start with – six foot four in his socks and weighing fifteen stone – and he felt that both he and his stout companion looked less like men than like the Colossus of Rhodes, as they set off through the snow.

Burnaby was a good linguist and had picked up Russian during a long leave in 1870 spent in Moscow, Kiev and Odessa. He and his jovial friend had a capital time together, and no lack of minor adventures, until just short of Samara where Burnaby had to branch off for Orenburg. 'I was sorry to shake hands with him and to say good-bye,' admitted the gregarious Burnaby. 'He was a very cheery companion, and a drive over the steppes alone and without a soul to speak to for several hundred miles was not an inviting prospect.' But he was soon busy buying a sledge, hiring a driver and laying in provisions for the next step of the journey. From now on Burnaby encountered nothing but trouble: official obstruction, incompetent drivers, delays and accidents, and above all, the most vicious and unrelenting weather. It was a constant battle for any human being to stay alive in these conditions, and in the end disaster struck. Burnaby fell asleep in his sleigh and awoke in agony:

> A feeling of intense pain had seized my extremities; it seemed as if they had been plunged into some corrosive acid which was gradually eating the flesh from my bones. I looked at my

finger-nails; they were blue, the fingers and back part of my hands were of the same colour, whilst my wrists and the lower part of the arm were of a waxen hue. There was no doubt about it, I was frostbitten, and in no slight degree.

Burnaby, *A Ride to Khiva*, 1876

The driver took one look and drove hell-for-leather for the next post-station. It was seven miles away, and the sweat poured off Burnaby, in spite of the intense cold, as the pain crept up to the glands under his arms, and he experienced an agony unimagined in all his years of soldiering. At last they arrived, and the swift action of some Cossack soldiers saved him from a double amputation, although the cure was almost as painful. They massaged his hands and arms repeatedly with naphtha – the only spirit available – until they were raw, but at least the sensation had come back. He then had to plunge them into a tub of ice and water. 'The more it hurts the better chance you have of saving your hands,' the Cossacks assured him. They refused to accept anything from Burnaby beyond his heartfelt thanks, insisting: 'Are we not all brothers when in misfortune?' It was several weeks before Burnaby's arms were fully healed, and by then he was in Khiva.

As MacGahan had predicted, Burnaby reached Kazala safely, and even spent the Russian Christmas as the guest of the District Governor. But the Russian authorities now did everything in their power to dissuade him from going on to Khiva. The Oxus was frozen, they pointed out, which enabled the Turcoman bandits to raid on both sides of the river, while the Khivans themselves were very dangerous people and the Khan might well gouge out Burnaby's eyes. All things considered, Burnaby had better go to Petro-Alexandrovsk with a Cossack escort, and the Colonel at the fort there could decide whether it was safe for the Englishman to continue. Burnaby thanked the Governor heartily for his advice, and set about purchasing or hiring the animals and equipment necessary for a journey to Petro-Alexandrovsk, although he had no intention of going there. Dispensing with the Cossack escort at the last minute, on the grounds that they would freeze to death in their thin uniforms, he set out on 12 January 1876, with a Kirghiz guide, three baggage camels in the charge of a Turcoman driver, various riding horses and a quantity of frozen cabbage soup.

Once his little caravan was well clear of Kazala, Burnaby induced the guide to take the road to Khiva by a judicious combination of threats, promises and bribery. He knew that time was limited, for the Russians would soon realise what he was up to when he failed to arrive at Petro-Alexandrovsk, and he was determined not to be thwarted so close to his goal. Sending ahead a suitably effusive message to the Khan, the convoy approached the fabled city, and Burnaby was overjoyed to meet his messenger returning with two Khivan ministers bearing an official welcome. In the distance he could see 'richly-painted minarets and high domes of coloured tiles' towering over a belt of trees. MacGahan had first seen the city in a haze of heat and dust, but now, on a bright January day, everything was crystal clear:

> We now entered the city, which is of an oblong form, and surrounded by two walls; the outer one is about fifty feet high; its basement is constructed of baked bricks, the upper part being built of dried clay. This forms the first line of defence, and completely encircles the town, which is about a quarter of a mile within the wall. Four high wooden gates, clamped with iron, barred the approach from the north, south, east and west, whilst the walls themselves were in many places out of repair.
>
> The town itself is surrounded by a second wall, not quite so high as the one just described, and with a dry ditch, which is now half filled with ruined debris. The slope which leads from the wall to the trench had been used as a cemetery, and hundreds of sepulchres and tombs were scattered along some undulating ground just without the city. The space between the first and second walls is used as a market-place, where cattle, horses, sheep, and camels are sold, and where a number of carts were standing, filled with corn and grass.
>
> Here an ominous-looking cross-beam had been erected, towering high above the heads of the people with its bare, gaunt poles. This was the gallows on which all people convicted of theft are executed; murderers being put to death in a different manner, having their throats cut from ear to ear in the same way that sheep are killed.

Burnaby noticed that the streets were clean and the richer houses adorned with polished bricks and coloured tiles. He estimated the population at around 35,000. There were nine religious schools, or *medressehs*, and these were all decorated with 'frescoes and arabesque work' and surmounted by high, coloured domes. After riding through the tortuous streets of the bazaar, he was conducted to a nobleman's dwelling, where he was later called on by the Khan's Treasurer. The Khan was anxious to know his business, and was most surprised that he had not been stopped by the Russians. Next day he was allowed to call on the Khan, with all due pomp and ceremony. Six men on horseback accompanied him, and four others on foot:

> After riding through several narrow streets where, in some instances, the housetops were thronged with people desirous of looking at our procession, we emerged on a small flat piece of ground which was not built over, and which formed a sort of open square. Here a deep hole was pointed out to me as the spot where criminals who have been found guilty of murder have their throats cut.
>
> The Khan's palace is a large building, ornamented with pillars and domes which, covered with bright-coloured tiles, flash in the sun, and attract the attention of the stranger approaching Khiva. A guard of thirty or forty men armed with scimitars stood at the palace gates. We next passed into a small courtyard. The Khan's guards were all attired in long flowing silk robes of various patterns, bright-coloured sashes being girt around their waists, and tall fur hats surmounting their bronzed countenances. Good-looking boys of an effeminate appearance, with long hair streaming down their shoulders, and dressed a little like the women, lounged about, and seemed to have nothing in particular to do.

In fact their official duty was dancing before the Khan who, like all Central Asian princelings, had a weakness for *bachas*, or dancing-boys.

After an interval, Burnaby was ushered into an ornate marquee standing in a courtyard, and found himself face to face with the latest Khan, a youngish man with a twinkle in his eye, who had been on the throne for ten years. 'I must say I was greatly surprised', admitted the Englishman, 'after all that has been written in Russian newspapers about the cruelties and other iniquities perpetrated by this Khivan potentate, to find the original such a cheery sort of fellow.' The Khivan knowledge of geography, however, had not progressed much since Abbott's visit thirty-six years earlier. Was England the same place as Germany? asked the Khan. When shown a map of the world he asked where India was. Burnaby showed him Khiva, and India below it. 'No,' said the Khan, who happened to be facing south, that couldn't be right. 'I am in Khiva and India is over there.' He pointed ahead of him. Burnaby tried to explain the mysteries of orientation with the help of a pocket compass, much to the consternation of the court officials who clearly thought this was some small, but infernal weapon.

Burnaby's gracious reception by the ruler ensured him the deference and co-operation of the populace, and he was able to go wherever he liked. He visited the prison, which had only two inmates, and one of the *medressehs*, where rows of boys were memorising pages of the Koran, and admired the Khan's summer palace and garden. After a couple of days, however, the Russians caught up with him and he was escorted unwillingly to Petro-Alexandrovsk. The Khan was sad to lose his unusual guest so soon, and expressed the warm wish that he and other Englishmen would visit him in the future. Burnaby had his usual jolly time with the Russian garrison, who seemed to bear him no ill-will in spite of his tricking them, then reluctantly turned for home. He was disappointed not to have seen more of Central Asia – he had hoped to get as far as Merv – but at least he had seen forbidden Khiva, and he had plenty of material for a book.

Whether the Khan was as pleased to see his next English visitor is not recorded, but it seems unlikely, for it was an evangelical clergyman who turned up in October 1882, armed with Bibles and a long list of questions. The Revd Henry Lansdell had already distributed 50,000 religious tracts and Bibles in Siberia in 1879, and was firmly under the protection of the Russians, so the Khan had perforce to make the best of it. He graciously accepted a copy of the Bible in Persian and a New Testament in Arabic, but as he only spoke Uzbek – a form of Turkish – it is doubtful whether he ever looked at either. A senior official was assigned to answer the missionary's questions, but Lansdell's underlying disapproval of the local way of life was a barrier to cordial relations. The rapport the easy-going Burnaby had felt for the Khan, despite his faults, was impossible for a man of deep religious convictions. Still, a fat two-volume work resulted from Lansdell's peregrinations round Central Asia, and the missionary societies which sponsored him were well pleased.

Another eccentric surprised the Khivans just before the turn of the century, for Robert Jefferson arrived on a bicycle after pedalling 6,000 miles from Catford in south London. He was partly inspired by Burnaby (who had by then been killed fighting in the Sudan), but 'the real reason why I rode a bicycle to Khiva', he revealed later, 'was because so many people said it was impossible.' It says a lot for his machine – a British-made Rover – that it survived the journey intact despite the most punishing treatment. For west European roads were mostly cobbled at that time, while further east they degenerated rapidly into stretches of mud, ruts and pot-holes, and from Nizhny-Novgorod, in central Russia, 'all idea of a made road ends'. However, the cycling papers had spread word of his trip, and in many places he was met by cheering members of local bicycle clubs.

In his entertaining book, *A New Ride to Khiva*, published in 1899, Jefferson describes his send-off from the small Volga town of Simbirsk whose most famous son, Vladimir Ilyich Ulyanov, better known as Lenin, led to its being renamed Ulyanovsk in 1924.

> The whole of Simbirsk turned out to see me off. The half-dozen cyclists of the town accompanied me across the Volga, trailed with me through deep sand for ten versts, and left me to my own devices. Samara, I learned, would take me at least four days, but for the sake of God, said everyone, 'do not miss the road; there is nothing right or left of that trail, not a house – nothing!'

Jefferson had already cycled in Siberia, where 'at least one had telegraph poles and verst-posts to guide one', but here there was nothing. The melancholy road to Samara was just a 'bare, gaunt, desolate land-track'. Soon the heat produced mirages and he began to fear for his sanity when one day

> I was startled by seeing in the sky a Russian church upside down. It was so distinct that it seemed real. There were the cupolas and the domes, the windows, the tiny graveyard and its cluster of crosses. I could see where the green and pink wash had peeled off the walls. For a minute it trembled in the atmosphere and

155

then, like the passing of a rainbow, it went. A mirage, of course, and when I reached the next village I had a look at its church, but it was not the replica of the one I had seen in the sky.

Next day, after riding out of a little village, he saw something ahead which stopped him in his tracks:

Off to the left and low down on the ground I perceived what at first looked like a big, black wave of water rolling along towards me with great rapidity. Bigger and bigger it grew, mounting higher and higher as it advanced, and as it neared I saw its billows inflected with colours of all descriptions. It spread out north and south as far as the eye could see, and now, when near in, it was sky high.

For a while he watched fascinated, thinking some much-needed rain was on the way, but then he heard a low moaning sound coming from afar, and he was suddenly filled with terror:

A presentiment that something was going to happen possessed me, and seizing my bicycle I mounted with all rapidity and sped back in the direction of the village. Nearer and nearer came the cloud, now so high and sinister, while louder and louder had the moaning become. The top of the cloud bent over and circled under. The next moment it was upon me. With a roar, a boom, the great wave enveloped myself and my bicycle. It was not rain, it was sand.

Fortunately, both Jefferson and his cycle survived this frightening experience, but he was now nearing the furthest extremities of Christian Russia and once he reached Orenburg, where 'the civilization of the West holds out its hand to the barbarism of the East', the authorities insisted he must travel with an escort. The Orenburg cycling club gave him a marvellous reception, and a band played God Save the Queen as he arrived in the town. Orenburg in 1898 was the end of the railway and the end of the post-track. To Jefferson it also seemed like the end of the world. From now on he would have to cycle laboriously through the burning sand of the Kazakh steppe and the Kyzyl Kum desert.

Their first sight of a bicycle had an electrifying effect on the nomads:

My bicycle was looked upon with alarm and dismay and, when I approached an encampment the Kirghiz, mounting their horses, made for me with a rush, rending the air with their screams and shouts, and cracking their long whips in fury.

This was not the only time Jefferson was grateful for his escort. On another occasion he was bitten by a poisonous spider and began to lose consciousness, but was saved by the presence of mind of his guide who cut the poison out swiftly with his knife.

When his little party reached the Oxus, Jefferson was met by an emissary of the Khan of Khiva and conducted to the city. It took a tedious five hours to be towed across the river, which was two miles wide at this point and full of islands. (Khiva itself was now some miles from the wandering river.) When he entered the legendary city the inhabitants at first fell about at the sight of his bicycle, but were soundly whipped by the Khan's officers for their impudence. After his gruelling journey, Jefferson should have felt elated at reaching his goal, but his overwhelming feeling was disappointment, for Khiva was in a sorry state. The walls had been allowed to crumble and debris was lying everywhere. Miserable dogs and beggars, both covered in horrible sores, were to be seen at every corner:

> Gratified as I was at having completed my cycle ride to Khiva, I yet felt a strange, unaccountable desire to get out of it as speedily as possible. The gloom, the wretchedness, the utter decay on every hand filled me with anything but inspiring feelings. I had read Burnaby and several other writers who have visited the city in previous years, but my first glimpse convinced me of one thing, that I saw Khiva in a far different state to that in which it presented itself to them. The suggestion of a doctor in Petro-Alexandrovsk that the Russians were simply waiting for Khiva to die out had here ample corroboration and, during the three days I remained in the city, it became patent to me that Khiva is absolutely doomed to obliteration within a few short years.

Jefferson met the Khan's chief minister, a very old man with a long white beard, who remembered Dr Lansdell but could not recall either Burnaby or MacGahan. He it was who had been given the task of answering Lansdell's questionnaire, so perhaps it is not surprising that the missionary was imprinted on his memory. Over the twenty-five years since the Russian conquest, he and the Khan had watched helplessly as the once-rich city had steadily declined. The Russians had imposed a crippling 'war indemnity', which the Khivans now had great difficulty in paying, for the old caravan trade had fallen away with the coming of the Transcaspian railway. The line from Krasnovodsk, Ashkhabad and Merv went on to Bokhara, Samarkand and Tashkent, but ignored Khiva. As the Khanate was still nominally administered by the Khan, the Russians simply shrugged their shoulders at the poverty and squalor, and concentrated on building a Russian town around the fort at Urgench. This lay on the Oxus, some twenty miles north-east of Khiva, and became its port once the river had shifted eastwards.

Happily, by the time Ella Christie visited Khiva in 1912 the town had been patched up and cleaned up, and the atmosphere was altogether more cheerful. A Russian official – a Colonel Kornilov – had been appointed as the Khan's adviser some years previously, partly to collect the war indemnity which was still being paid off, but also to help the Khivans to put their house in order. He and his wife were kind and energetic people, on good terms with the Khan and the local population, and they insisted that Mrs Christie stay with them. They spoke no English, and the Scottish anthropologist had only the most basic Russian, but with goodwill and a bit of French they got on famously, despite a few cultural differences. Mrs Christie never got used to the idea of a communal bath-house, and there was the problem of what to call each other. 'Mrs Christie' was too formal for the Russians, while 'Ella' was far too familiar. What was her father's name? they enquired. 'John' was converted to the Russian 'Ivan', and the patronymic 'Ivanovna' formed: Ella Ivanovna was her new name. Mrs Kornilov, whose father's name was Anatoly, was to be called Natalya Anatolyevna. In fact Mrs Christie found this too much of a mouthful, and decided to call her new friend Natalya An.

The Kornilovs' house was just outside the city, clean and spacious and usually filled with the delicious smell of baking. To Ella Christie's delight, it was surrounded by a garden full of nightingales. Natalya An had many friends, one of whom was midwife to the royal harem and lived in a tiny house right in the bazaar. Another lived in a small

German colony at Ak Mechet, nine miles outside Khiva, and Mrs Christie spent a day there. They were all Mennonites, dressed soberly in black and white, and their settlement was run on the lines of a co-operative. Jefferson had also visited the Germans in 1898, for the colony had been in existence since the 1880s, when they had left their former homes on the Volga and followed in the wake of General Kaufmann's conquest of Central Asia. They were very industrious, and supplied the Khan with all manner of wooden objects, including doors, water troughs and pipes. Ella Christie's book, *Through Khiva to Golden Samarkand*, was not published until 1925, after the cataclysms of the First World War and the Russian Revolution. 'In the upheaval of the world's catastrophe,' she wrote then, 'one often wonders how it fared with the colony. Was it still a haven of peace or a harbour of war?' Happily, they did somehow survive, and the Swiss traveller Ella Maillart came across some of them in Khiva in 1932.

Having spent a busy week in Khiva, Mrs Christie took her leave of the Kornilovs:

> After a week of great kindness I had at length to say farewell to my hospitable friends, and their orchard with its singing birds. Natalya An looked quite sad as we left and, as parting gifts for the journey, she gave me a bag of loaves, a fruit cake, a box of dried pickled cabbage and a bag of camel wool. Kind Natalya An, who could then have dreamt of such a fate awaiting you?

For Natalya Anatolyevna and her husband were brutally murdered by the Bolsheviks when Khiva fell to this last in a long line of conquerors. For a while the territory of the Khanate survived as the small Republic of Khorezm, with Khiva as its capital, but in 1924 even this vestige of its identity vanished. The western lands became part of Turkmenistan, while those to the east, including Khiva itself, were taken into the fringes of Uzbekistan. In 1968 the wicked old town underwent its final transformation and became a conservation area.

MERV AND BAIRAM ALI
Stepping Stone to India?

If you meet a viper and a Mervi, kill the Mervi first.

> Central Asian saying

Merv, at this time, is only a refuge for marauders ... but if it pass into the hands of Russia it will regain its former splendour. But the question will not rest there, that Russia will take Merv merely, and hold it quietly, but she will take the Murghab river also, and march up to it, and thus possess all the country.

> Prince Iskander Ahmed of Afghanistan, writing in the 1870s

MERV, THE QUEEN of the ancient world, is now little more than a memory. Even the name has disappeared locally. The modern Russian town on the Murghab river was renamed Mary under Stalin, and the ruins of the magnificent Silk Road city lie ten miles away at a place called Bairam Ali. Old Merv, or Merou, is in fact a series of ruined cities, strewn over several miles on what is today a desolate plain. But it was not always an arid waste. Pliny wrote in the first century AD that this district was the most fertile part of Asia, and Herodotus talks about a great lake to the north-west of Merv. Geographers believe that the Oxus, or Amu-darya, used to flow west into the Caspian Sea and that what is now the Kara Kum desert used to be a rich alluvial plain. Only after the Oxus changed its course, perhaps as a result of an earthquake, and flowed north into the Aral Sea, did what is now Turkmenistan become a desert.

Legend has it that Merv was founded by Zoroaster, the father of fire-worship, who lived around the sixth century BC. Under Darius it was known as Margush, under Alexander the Great as Antiocheia

Margiana. For many years a province of Parthia, it nonetheless became a centre of Nestorian Christianity with its own bishop, before being conquered by the Arabs in the eighth century, and then becoming the renowned capital of the Seljuk Turkish empire in the eleventh. Two of the most prestigious Seljuk emperors, Alp Arslan and Sultan Sanjar, are buried there.

Alp Arslan, the 'valiant lion', conquered the Roman empire in Asia in 1072. A famous soldier, he was also a good man who was fatally stabbed by a captive he had just pardoned. He ordered the following inscription to be placed over his tomb at Merv: 'O ye who have seen the glory of Alp Arslan exalted to the heavens, repair to Merou and you will behold it buried in the dust.' The historian Edward Gibbon commented: 'The annihilation of the inscription, and the tomb itself, more forcibly proclaims the instability of human greatness.' Sultan Sanjar, grandson of Alp Arslan and also a just ruler, had the misfortune in about 1150 to be captured by his traditional foes, the nomads of Khiva, and held captive for four years. In his absence they despoiled his city, torturing the inhabitants for good measure, just in case they were concealing any of their wealth. Many were killed, and others were carried off into slavery. When Sanjar eventually escaped and made his painful way across the desert, he thought he had mistaken his route. For where was his beautiful capital and his flourishing oasis? Faced by an abomination of desolation, Sultan Sanjar collapsed and died of a broken heart.

The basis of Merv's prosperity was water, and in the ruins of the old town the ancient irrigation channels can still be made out. For the Seljuks had built a mighty dam on the Murghab river, thirty miles south of Merv, and guarded it with a fortress. Canals had carried the precious water in all directions, thus enabling the oasis to expand and flourish and allowing the rulers to surround the royal palace with groves and gardens. After the attack by the Khivans, Merv had scarcely been restored to prosperity when the arrival of the Mongols led to yet another sacking. Tuluy Khan, youngest and most brutal son of Genghis, razed the city to the ground in 1221, returning a few days after his first onslaught to finish off the handful of survivors who had crept back to their wrecked homes. Anything worth taking was looted by the horde. Only the blue and turquoise glint of smashed tiles lying in the dust, and the shards of iridescent glass, bore silent witness to Merv's past splendours.

After the Mongol devastation Merv came under the dominion at various times of the Uzbek Turks and different dynasties of Persians, and was frequently fought over by the rival rulers of Khiva and Bokhara. When no one else was in control, it was camped in by nomads. Finally, in the eighteenth century, a strong man emerged who repaired the dam and built himself a citadel and a new town out of the ruins of ancient Merv: his name was Bairam Ali Khan. This remarkable man was a Persian, although his mother had been a princess of the Salor Turcomans, and under his stern but wise rule Merv once more saw peace and prosperity. Even the unruly Turcomans, for whom the greatest honour was to be included in an *alaman*, or raiding party, kept at a respectful distance from their kinsman.

But it could not last. Merv's strategic position at the gateway to Khorassan, Persia's rich northern province, was bound to make it a target for warlike invaders from the north. The next to cast greedy eyes on the oasis was an Uzbek of the Mangit tribe, the Amir Masum, later to be known as Shah Murad of Bokhara. The Uzbeks had come from Mongolia in the thirteenth century with Genghis Khan's hordes, with whom they interbred. The Mangits settled around Bokhara and soon became leaders of the ferocious Uzbek clans who took over much of western Central Asia in the ensuing centuries. In theory subject to the Golden Horde, the rump of the Mongol empire based in southern Russia, the Uzbeks grew bolder as the Mongols declined. In 1783, Masum declared himself King of Bokhara and set about carving out his own empire.

First, he decided, Merv must be taken, and then all Khorassan would be at his mercy. In 1785 he set out at the head of 6,000 mounted warriors, and by a skilful ruse lured Bairam Ali and his men into an ambush, where the ruler of Merv was slain. But his son Mohammed Khan took over, and the city defied Masum, confident that it could sit out an indefinite siege. However, by treachery Masum gained control of the fortress guarding the great dam, and he then destroyed the barrage itself. First flooded and then totally deprived of water, the inhabitants of Merv had no choice but to surrender. Most were carried off as slaves to Bokhara, and the wide, flourishing oasis shrank to a small settlement on the banks of the Murghab. Once again old Merv became a dusty heap of ruins surrounded by the endless sands of the desert.

In 1840 an Englishman, Major James Abbott, was one of the first Europeans to set eyes on the fabled Merv, and he was not impressed. He found the oasis 'more dreary than the desert itself' although he was quick to note its strategic importance:

> The present Merv is an assemblage, upon the Murghab, of about one hundred mud huts, where a considerable Bazaar is held … The trade passing through is very considerable, Merv connecting Bokhara and Persia, Khiva and Afghanistan. Indeed the position of Merv is so important, that it never will be long abandoned and might, with judicious care, rapidly rise from its dust into wealth and consequence.
>
> Abbott, *Narrative of a Journey from Heraut to Khiva*, 1843

Abbott only glimpsed the ruins of ancient Merv on the eastern horizon, and made out the remains of a mosque and several forts, for he was detained on the banks of the Murghab by the Sarik Turcomans who were currently masters of the oasis. Alternately goaded by insults or assailed by 'sympathisers' who tried to lure him into indiscretions or criticisms of Islam, the blunt soldier had difficulty in keeping his temper. Only the thought of the unfortunate Colonel Stoddart – the British officer languishing in a verminous dungeon in Bokhara at that time – enabled him to maintain an appearance of dignified imperturbability (see BOKHARA). The Turcomans, of course, had very little idea who the English were, and as Abbott had few gifts to bestow on them, they were not inclined to treat him with much respect. Luckily they were too cautious to do him any real harm and, after presenting him with a horse as a token of their esteem, they finally let him go on his way to Khiva. 'I bade farewell to Merv', Abbott admitted in his book, 'with no wish ever again to behold it.' After a mile his gift-horse went lame.

The Sariks – like their kinsmen but enemies, the Tekke Turcomans – were notorious brigands and slave-raiders, and their chief prey were the Persians. Periodically the Persians would lose patience and make a determined effort to subdue their Turcoman tormentors, and thus stem the pitiful flow of Persian men, women and children to the slave markets of Khiva and Bokhara. The trouble was, the nomads seemed quite happy to abandon any of their own people who were taken as hostages, and if they were driven out of one place they simply reappeared from somewhere else. The Persians managed to clear the

Tekke out of Sarakhs, but they were no better off for the Tekke simply ousted the Sariks from Merv and made that their new base. In 1860 the Shah declared in a rage that he would wipe the Tekke from the face of the earth, and sent an army to Merv. The Tekke were not especially renowned as warriors – their tactic was rather to make lightning raids in semi-darkness – but when fighting for their survival they were like the fiends of hell. (Russia too was to discover this twenty years later at the Akhal oasis – see GEOK-TEPE.) It was the Persians who were routed:

> Those who had means of escape fled the scene of slaughter, but the infantry and artillery were killed or captured to a man. The victors collected so many prisoners that they did not know what to do with them. A ready market for slaves existed in Khiva and Bokhara, but the prisoners poured in in such abundance that the price of a Persian slave fell to a pound.

This account was given by Colonel Petrusevich, a Russian anthropologist and military surveyor, who made a detailed study of the various Turcoman tribes and who was killed in the last battle of the Tekke at Geok-Tepe.

The Tekke did not attempt to rebuild Merv, but they did construct a mud rampart within which they set up their tents. They also made a new dam on the Murghab and extended the cultivable area of the oasis, though on nothing like the scale of Sultan Sanjar's old irrigation scheme. The Shah of Persia retired to lick his wounds, and Merv was never destined to fall into Persian hands again. But Abbott's prophetic remark about the strategic significance of the oasis was not lost on the two Great Powers of the nineteenth century. For Russia and Britain Merv was the key, not to the riches of Khorassan, but to Herat and ultimately to India.

The British were often regarded by those nations not directly involved as being amusingly paranoid over their Indian possessions, forever panicking about a mythical Russian bogeyman with designs on their precious empire. But in fairness it must be said that Russia's behaviour at this time was equivocal to say the least, and the diplomatic policy professed by St Petersburg was frequently at odds with what actually happened on the frontier. In the course of 'consolidating' her southern border, Russia had quietly annexed Kazakhstan in the first half of the nineteenth century, and had been extending her Central

Asian territories ever since. The whole of Turkestan became a Russian province in the 1860s and '70s, bringing the Tsar's empire 1,000 miles closer to India. Where would it end?

Regarding Merv, and Transcaspia generally, the following statements were all made during the course of the 1870s:

His Imperial Majesty has no intention of extending the frontiers of Russia such as they exist at present in Central Asia, either on the side of Bokhara, or on the side of Krasnovodsk.

Prince Gorchakov, Foreign Minister

Merv, with its water communication nearly complete to Herat, lies only 240 miles from that place, to which it is the key. Strategically, the Russian occupation of Merv would place Herat completely at her mercy.

Colonel Valentine Baker

I rode along the road from Merv to Herat. To conduct an expeditionary force of any strength along that route would be an impossibility.

Colonel Grodekov

There is so little impression of difficulty in my mind, that I would undertake to drive a mail coach from Merv to Herat by this road.

Colonel C.M. McGregor

We should have no difficulty whatever in taking Merv. People talk of the difficulty of getting there: why, our Cossacks could be at Merv in a week if the Government would only allow us.

Russian frontier officer at Petro-Alexandrovsk

Britain tried hard not to upset the Russians, and forbade its officers – including Colonels Baker and McGregor – to visit Merv, but when word reached London that the armies of the Tsar had begun a campaign against the Tekke Turcomans (see GEOK-TEPE), it became clear to even the most charitable observer that Transcaspia was destined to be the next Russian acquisition. In view of Prince Gorchakov's earlier assurance, the British government felt entitled to an explanation. As usual, this was soothing. In July 1879 the British ambassador to St Petersburg was able to report home that the head of the Asiatic Department of the Russian Foreign Ministry had assured him 'in the most positive manner, that there was no intention on the part of the Russian Government to go to Merv, that their object was simply to put an end to the depredations of the Turcoman tribes in the neighbourhood of the Caspian'.

However, within a few short weeks the Russians were already putting a different gloss on the affair, and on 26 August the ambassador had to add a rider to his earlier report:

> M. de Giers intimated that ... although he had told me that an advance upon Merv was not contemplated by the Russian Government, and formed no part of their existing programme, he did not mean to imply that in different circumstances, and in view of unforeseen contingencies, the occupation of Merv might not become necessary; that in fact, the Russian Government had never intended by a solemn pledge, given for all time, to preclude themselves from ever going to Merv.

It is hard to avoid the impression that the Russians were simply running rings round the British. The different circumstances – totally unforeseen, of course – having duly presented themselves, Merv was annexed by the Tsar in February 1884. But three years before that, and quite unknown to the Tsar or Queen Victoria, the Mervis had tried hard to fly a Union Jack from their ramparts and had insisted on appointing an Irishman as their ruler.

Edmond O'Donovan, former Irish agitator, French foreign legionnaire and now special correspondent of the London *Daily News*, had gone to Central Asia to report on the Turcoman campaign. Blocked by the Russians, who wanted no witnesses, he arrived clandestinely at the Akhal oasis just in time to see the fall of Geok-Tepe. Hurrying on to Merv, which he was convinced would be next on the Tsar's shopping list, he found himself regarded with the deepest suspicion and was lucky to escape with his life. For the Turcomans were quite unable to understand the concept of a newspaper correspondent, and assumed he was spying – most likely for the Russians. After all, one European looked much like another as far as they were concerned.

O'Donovan was hustled into a hot and airless tent made of sky-blue canvas, into which the entire population of the oasis – not to mention those visiting the bazaar – seemed to follow him. They stared at him and his gear with fascination, and discussed vociferously whether his throat should be cut immediately or later, for news of their kinsmen's defeat at Geok-Tepe had already reached them and Russophobia was at its height. Although he did not know it then, O'Donovan was to spend three weary weeks there under house, or rather tent, arrest, and it would be six months before he was allowed to leave the oasis altogether. Next morning he woke up to find the tent already crammed with Turcomans, who had been squatting there patiently, gazing at their uninvited guest and waiting for him to awaken. Presently, so many people crawled under the edges of the overflowing tent that all the pegs were pulled out and the whole thing collapsed, nearly smothering the Irishman.

O'Donovan wanted to write to the British authorities in Meshed, across the border in Persia, but the mere sight of his writing things caused an uproar. He was sternly forbidden to put pen to paper, on pain of having his throat cut, but he managed to write secretly to Meshed, and to keep a diary, by waiting until dead of night and then writing under a blanket. As a reporter, he was most eager to see what the mysterious Merv was like, but in these early days he was kept firmly inside the stifling tent, 'in case the dogs should bite you'. The total lack of privacy and the feeling of 'living in the interior of a much-patronized peep-show' was very trying, but when he protested to the old man appointed as his minder, the latter was mystified. Why should he mind being looked at? It wouldn't do him any harm.

After a week he was summoned to attend a council of the elders, held in a large open space seemingly surrounded by the entire population. There was an unnerving hush when he arrived, and poor O'Donovan feared his last moment had come. However, after an hour's interrogation he was taken back to his tent-prison, from where he could hear the clamour of heated discussions which would presumably decide his fate. After a nail-biting interval he was escorted back to hear the decision of the elders. He was not to have his throat cut, he was very relieved to learn, but he would remain their prisoner until the British authorities in Persia sent confirmation that he was not a Russian spy. There was nothing O'Donovan could do in the meantime but sit it out, gathering as much information as he could on Tekke manners and customs, and consoling himself with the thought of the bestseller he would write once he was free.

O'Donovan had arrived in February, and with every week the temperature grew more furnace-like. Surrounded as it is by desert, Merv has an extreme climate variously described by European travellers as 'intolerable', 'insufferable' or plain 'abominable'. O'Donovan soon adopted the loose native dress, and once the Turcomans were reassured as to his nationality he was allowed to move to a traditional dome-shaped tent made of willow wands and felt, which was slightly cooler than being under canvas. His hosts were in no hurry to let him go, but he was now allowed more freedom and began to make a covert plan of his surroundings, taking discreet bearings when possible with a prismatic compass. The Tekke were clearly very alarmed at the Russian conquest of the Akhal oasis – the other main Tekke stronghold – and were doing their best to fortify Merv. A huge rampart was being constructed on the banks of the Murghab, every male inhabitant being obliged to play his part in the toil.

O'Donovan was proudly shown a number of cannon captured from the Persians in their battles of 1860. The Turcomans had great faith in these weapons, but their wooden supports were all rotting away and the guns looked to O'Donovan as if they had been spiked. By keeping his head, and by the judicious handing out of presents, money and medicine, O'Donovan came to be regarded by the Tekke as their trusty friend. One of his rewards was to be taken on a two-day visit to the ruins of old Merv, something he had long wished to do.

We came in view of an immense wilderness of ruined buildings, forming a semi-circle in front of us to the north and south. Between us and the domes stretched in an apparently unbroken line for four or five miles a belt of ruined wall and shattered houses, apparently the remains of former suburban villas and gardens. Even still nourished by the scanty rains and still scantier moisture of the earth itself, the withered gardens displayed remnants of former greenness, choked with masses of ruin. Snakes swarmed on every side and, save these, black eagles, sparrow-hawks and vultures were the only living creatures to be seen.

O'Donovan, *The Merv Oasis*, 1882

Colonel Petrusevich had also remarked on the absence of life in the steppes of Central Asia:

> Without water existence is impossible, and thus in the wastes to the north of Akhal and Merv neither birds nor beasts are to be found. Only where there are wells may be observed a few small members of the feathered race, fluttering about the well-tops in quest of water. The wells are sometimes very deep, nevertheless the birds fly right down them for water.

Exploring the ruins methodically, and taking covert compass bearings which enabled him later to draw a plan of the whole site, O'Donovan was able to distinguish the remains of three separate cities. Giaour Kala was reputed to be the oldest:

> The whole of the area within the ramparts is littered with the debris of broken tiles and earthenware vessels, many of the fragments exhibiting the most beautiful tints, and in some cases prismatic colours. I did not come upon an entire utensil of any kind.

In Sultan Sanjar's city, the next in age, there was hardly one brick left standing on another, apart from the imposing mausoleum of the Sultan himself. O'Donovan was also puzzled to see vast numbers of large holes dug everywhere. He knew that this was the city sacked by the Mongols, but this did not explain the wholesale dismantling of the site. His Turcoman companions were able to provide the explanation: the damage was caused by souvenir-hunters and treasure-seekers. For Sultan Sanjar was revered as a saint and his tomb had long been a place of pilgrimage. It was also on a regular trade-route and 'a caravan scarcely ever passed by the place without many of its members trying their fortune by digging holes, in the hopes that they might perchance stumble upon a pot of gold or jewels'. Bairam Ali, the most recent of the ruined cities, had been laid waste barely a century before, and the remains of its high battlemented walls still surrounded the ruins of mosques, palaces, houses and baths.

Although he continued to find the lack of privacy excruciating, O'Donovan gradually became accustomed to Tekke conventions and no longer had to worry constantly about inadvertently committing some frightful *faux pas*. Religion remained the principal minefield, however. If he joined the Turcomans in their prayers it might be considered blasphemous, yet if he simply ignored them and went about his business this might be construed as an insult. In the end he decided that the safest course was to dismount, if he was on horseback, and stand still in a respectful manner. But he could not win, and even this was criticised. Nothing if not quick-witted, however, when O'Donovan was reproached for never praying by one of Merv's leaders, he replied loftily that Christians – unlike Muslims – prayed all the time. 'You snatch a few minutes from your occupations to pray to your Creator,' he said. 'Our life is one continual prayer.'

As time went by, the Turcomans became more and more friendly towards O'Donovan, each faction trying to outdo the others, until he was created a Khan or leader, and finally – in spite of his protests – actually appointed Ruler of Merv. The truth was that the fear of being annexed by Russia was so strong that the Tekke were only too willing to declare their allegiance to Queen Victoria provided she would defend them. Some scraps of red, white and blue cloth were produced, and O'Donovan was asked to draw the design for the British flag. The bizarre thought of a Union Jack flying over the Merv oasis, and the awful diplomatic repercussions – not least to himself – were too much for even O'Donovan's sense of adventure. He explained as tactfully as he could the need to ask permission first, and the advisability of doing nothing to antagonise the Russians, who were so much nearer than Queen Victoria. By now he felt a pressing need to get away from the place before he got into any more scrapes, but this was easier said than done.

Finally, after innumerable delays and excuses, and by dint of engineering an urgent summons from Tehran to attend 'consultations', Merv's one and only Irish ruler rode out of the oasis on 29 July 1881 and crossed thankfully into Persia. His own book is now very hard to find, but Fitzroy Maclean gives a most entertaining account of his adventures in *A Person from England*. Sadly, O'Donovan's next assignment was his last, for he was killed in the Sudan in 1883 in the campaign against the Mahdi.

One of the last things O'Donovan had heard as he rode out of Merv was the fear expressed by many of the bystanders that 'it was the utmost folly to allow me to go away, because immediately I had left the oasis the Russians would come in'. Perhaps the Mervis overestimated O'Donovan's power to keep the Russian army at bay, but there was no doubt that their days of independence were running out. Tsar Alexander II had been assassinated in March, and his son – the new Tsar Alexander III – had invited a number of the Akhal Tekke chieftains to his coronation in St Petersburg. They returned to Transcaspia just after O'Donovan's departure, and their descriptions of the wealth and magnificence of the Russian capital, and the huge numbers of soldiers and artillery in evidence, gave their Mervi kinsmen pause for thought. The Mervis were also unsettled by the apparent prosperity of those Tekke who had become Russian subjects, and some of them began to venture west to Ashkhabad, where the bazaar was now full of alluring European goods. The Russians realised that if they played their cards right, they would be able to take Merv by stealth.

The deed was achieved by a Russian officer who was himself a Muslim, a native of the Caucasus. For his first visit, in February 1882, Lieutenant Alikhanov posed as a merchant who could supply Merv with undreamt-of luxuries if they would agree to trade with Russia. The poor Khans, on the one hand dazzled by the Russian consumer goods and on the other fearing greatly for their independence, were in a quandary. Alikhanov profited by their indecision in making a quick survey of Merv's defences during his early morning walks and, once this was completed, he left. A year later Merv was obliged, under threat of invasion, to accept the suzerainty of her old enemy Khiva, which was now a Russian protectorate. Then, early in 1884, Alikhanov turned up again at the oasis, this time in full uniform and accompanied by a detachment of armed men. Rather than have their city destroyed, he suggested to the Khans, would it not be better to accept the beneficent rule of the Tsar? The Mervis had, perforce, to bow to the inevitable. Within two years Merv and Bairam Ali were stations on the new Transcaspian railway, which would in due course connect up all Russia's vast possessions in Central Asia.

At least the Pax Russica, and the advent of the railway, meant that Europeans could now travel to Central Asia without taking their lives in their hands, provided they were granted permission from St Petersburg. This was not always given, but as long as you had time and the right connections, you were likely to be successful. One of the first was a French civil engineer called Edgar Boulangier. He admits cheerfully in his book *Voyage à Merv* that his trip was quite unpremeditated. At the beginning of August 1886, finding Paris intolerable, he bought a ticket for Constantinople and boarded the Orient Express. In Bucharest, however, he discovered that Turkey had just imposed quarantine restrictions because of a cholera scare, so he decided to visit the Caucasus instead. In Tiflis he found that his acquaintances had left town for the summer, and it was here that he conceived the idea of going to see the great unknown of Transcaspia and of travelling on the new military railway, which had just been completed as far as Merv. A fortunate introduction to a Russian prince enabled him to obtain the necessary permits, and on 3 September Boulangier found himself in Krasnovodsk.

The railway had not yet been officially declared 'open', and conditions were apt to be a trifle primitive. There was as yet no droshky service from Merv station, and the Frenchman had to set out on foot to find a hotel in the new Russian township which had been hastily constructed. Choking on the fine dust which enveloped him in a cloud, and into which his feet sank up to the ankles, he made his way to the principal hotel. It was full. A young Polish railway worker who spoke French and a little Turki offered to help, and they tramped laboriously round all five of the town's hotels, but to no avail. They were all full of soldiers and administrators who were busy organising Merv along Russian lines. In the end Boulangier was given a room in a barely finished new hotel, still full of workmen but already colonised by the local bugs and creepy-crawlies. A particularly repulsive specimen scuttled away into a crack in the floor when he lifted the blanket to inspect his bed.

A week earlier, Boulangier was told, when temperatures were still in the 40s centigrade, there had been a plague of scorpions and other poisonous insects, but now that it was autumn they had crept back into their holes. He was advised to boil all water before using it, as the first European settlers had developed painful sores and abscesses. 'You have been warned,' comments Boulangier drily in his book, 'if your holiday plans take you to this little paradise which was nearly fought over by two great nations.' Shrugging off the discomforts of his situation, he sent his card to the Governor of Merv, who was none other than Alikhanov, now promoted to Colonel. One feels there was a certain poetic justice in his appointment to this dusty and bug-ridden 'paradise', in view of his duplicity to the Khans. Boulangier found him sheltering from the heat in a huge tent, adorned with Persian hangings and Turcoman rugs.

Boulangier also called on General Annenkov, whose railway battalions were busy extending the Transcaspian line towards the Amu-darya or Oxus, and whose headquarters was currently at Merv. Although the General had quite a large and handsome house at his disposal, he used this mainly as an office, preferring to live on the special train used by the railway engineers. That way he was always in the right place at the right time to direct work personally on his beloved railway. Delighted to have a visitor who was technically literate, Annenkov invited Boulangier to travel east with him to see how the line was progressing, and in the course of this they stopped off at Bairam Ali to inspect the ruins of old Merv. As an engineer, Boulangier was amazed that such ambitious architecture could be undertaken in the complete absence of stone for building. The thought of the slow, laborious process of making all those millions of sun-baked bricks filled him with awe.

Two years later the Honourable George Curzon, future Viceroy of India, travelled the length of the newly opened railway, which now terminated at Samarkand. Merv, he found, had actually dwindled in size and importance since the Frenchman's visit:

> The present Merv consists only of the rickety town which the Russians have built, and which is inhabited mainly by Persians, Jews and Armenians. A visitor in 1886 describes its population as 3,000; but it cannot now be more than one-third of that total. The reason of the diminution is this. From the time of the annexation in February 1884, and while the railway was being pushed forward to Amu-darya, Merv was the headquarters of General Annenkov and his staff. There was a sudden inflation of business, shops were run up, merchants came, and the brand-new Merv fancied that it had inherited some aroma of the ancient renown. A club-house provided a centre of social reunion, and was the scene of weekly dancing and festivity. For the less select, a music-hall re-echoed on the banks of the Murghab the airs of Offenbach and the melodies of Strauss. The Turcomans, attracted by the foreign influx, flocked in large numbers from their settlements on the

oasis, and drove an ephemeral but thriving trade. But with the forward movement of the railway battalion, and still more with the occupation by the line of Bokhara and Samarkand, this fictitious importance died away ... Whether or not the glory of Merv may revive will depend upon the success or failure of the schemes for the regeneration of the surrounding oasis, which are now being undertaken.

Curzon, Russia in Central Asia, 1889

Nine years after Curzon's rather disapproving visit, Merv was descended upon by a positive bevy of English tourists. A mixed party of twenty turned up in Transcaspia in November 1897 and were conducted on a Cook's tour of the province in a special train. The charming Russian officers appointed as their guides and companions made sure that their impressions of Russian hospitality were highly favourable, and at every halt they were greeted with receptions, balls and spectacles. The English entered into the fun with great enthusiasm, toasting their hosts in halting Russian (rapturously received) or only slightly less halting French, and cheerfully submitting to tours of Russian improvements. No doubt the Russians, who for their sins or merits had been posted to Central Asia, were delighted to see some congenial new faces, but there was probably a hidden political agenda too. For in this Great Game era it behoved Russia to present the face of a benevolent provider of schools and sanitation rather than that of an aggressive conqueror of territory.

At least one of the Englishmen wrote a book about his unusual holiday. Mr J.T. Woolrych Perowne describes a typical day of sight-seeing and entertainment at Merv:

When we got up in the morning we found that, as at Ashkhabad so here, a programme had been arranged for us, so we took our places in the droshkies which were ready waiting and started out to visit a Merv village. It lay some twenty minutes away on the other side of the Murghab, which we crossed by a rather crazy wooden bridge, which apparently does duty for trains, carriages and pedestrians alike. It was a glorious day, but the dust was as thick as a sand storm and nearly choked us all as we drove. Just on the other side of the river lies the modern Russian town, if indeed we could call such a small settlement a town, and high over the houses loom the mighty unfinished mud walls of the fort which was built under forced labour by the Tekkes after the fall of Geok-Tepe.

After seeing the village, which reminded some of them of Egypt, and hearing some native flute music, which they thought 'weird in the extreme', they were hurried off to watch one of the spectacular mock-battles between Cossacks and Turcoman cavalry so beloved of the Russians in Central Asia (see ASHKHABAD). There followed an al fresco luncheon with much drinking of toasts and a number of cordial speeches. A glittering ball at the Club rounded off the day.

Next morning their train took them to Bairam Ali, whence they embarked on a droshky drive around the ruins of old Merv. 'The traveller who expects to see ruins such as those of Greece or Rome', warns Perowne, 'will be bitterly disappointed as he drives across the waste that once must have seen the flourishing cities of so many dead centuries.' The Glory that was Greece and the Splendour that was Rome could not, he felt, be matched by the Desolation that was Merv. In fact, as their Russian hosts seemed to be quite ignorant of Merv's past, the visit meant little to the English group:

> Our drive lasted about four hours, during which we drove through a desolating wilderness of ancient crumbling walls and gateways, with here and there a meaningless ruin standing up gaunt and bare against the sky. No ivy or creepers are here to make decay picturesque, or ruins romantic. A desolation of miles of shapeless mounds and enormous brick city walls do not raise much emotion in a Westerner's heart ...

If beauty is in the eye of the beholder, so it would appear are size and importance, for in only a year the oasis of Merv seems to have changed out of all recognition. John W. Bookwalter, an American businessman, was not interested in ruins, but he saw new Merv – which Perowne could hardly bring himself to call a town – in a quite different light:

> Like all the new Russian towns, the city is laid out with great regularity, the streets running at right-angles and fringed on both sides with rows of beautiful trees. The private residences are elegant, with all the modern improvements, and almost

always located in the middle of a great square, forming a splendid park. A handsome boulevard of several miles in length, and ornamented by a double row of trees on either side, extends through the city. Owing to the richness of the soil, bright sunshine, and an abundance of water for irrigation, the creation of a beautiful park or delightful boulevard in this genial climate is the work of only a few years. From the extent and solidity of the improvements seen everywhere, the Russian has evidently entered this country with great confidence, and to stay.

Bookwalter, *Siberia and Central Asia*, 1899

It is hard to believe that he is talking about the same place as Curzon or Perowne. Admittedly, the purpose of his book was to persuade Americans to trade with Russia, which he saw as an up-and-coming nation with a huge untapped market for American goods. 'In my travels throughout this great empire', he claimed, 'it was impossible for me not to observe everywhere the many evidences of Russian fondness, and even partiality for, American goods.' Perhaps as a result he tended to see even arid Transcaspia through rose-tinted glasses. Nobody else has ever called Merv's climate 'genial'. Perowne had described the land between Merv and Bairam Ali as being covered with cane-brakes and juniper bushes, but to the imaginative Bookwalter it was an impenetrable jungle inhabited by tigers. At least they were agreed on the desolation of old Merv. 'Not a single human inhabitant now dwells in this silent city,' Bookwalter informed his readers. 'The ghoulish hyena and noisy jackal find their lair in what was once the glory and home of nearly two million people.'

Perhaps the American writer Michael Myers Shoemaker, who travelled in this area in 1902–3 and published an engaging book entitled *The Heart of the Orient*, should have the last word:

The glaring hot day draws to its close as our train approaches the ancient city. Already the atmosphere has taken on that wonderful golden glow which in the still air of the desert heralds the approach of night and marks the passing of the sun. As I gaze from the carriage window at Bairam Ali, as far as the eye can reach spread the ruins of the wonderful city – mile after mile of crumbling arches, tottering towers, and ruined mosques. In the clearness of this air distances are annihilated and ruins miles away are as distinctly visible as those nearer at hand. One stands awe-struck as one's eye roves over the vast desolation. The silence is so intense that even the puffing engine of our train seems impressed by it and grumbles in a monotone.

No sign of life in all the desolate prospect save some lonely floating vultures, and even they, turning from the desolation of Merv, soon vanish in the distance, and as they go the day departs, while from the vast ocean of black sand stretching away to the eastward far beyond the city the moon rises slowly ...

Two millions of people lived here once, and now you cannot even find their graves, while these ruins of the palaces and houses they once inhabited are sadder than any grave. All is vanity. Truly as I gaze outward into the deepening shadows tonight I fully appreciate that all is and has ever been – vanity.

SAMARKAND
City of the Scourge of God

Samarkand – the home of Tamerlane, the home of all the romance and poetry in the East …

Michael Shoemaker

I climbed by a narrow twisting stairway to the top of the Shir Dar and from there I looked down on the sun-baked Registan and beyond it on the fabled city of Samarkand, on the blue domes and the minarets, the flat-roofed mud houses, and the green tree-tops. It was a moment to which I had long looked forward.

Fitzroy Maclean

OVER THE ENTRANCE to the Gur Emir mausoleum in Samarkand is this inscription: 'Here lies the Illustrious and Merciful Monarch, the most Great Sultan, the most Mighty Warrior, the Lord Timur, Conqueror of the World'. As it has been estimated that Timur, or Tamerlane as he is more widely known, was responsible for the deaths of seventeen million men, women and children, many of whom were massacred with indescribable brutality, not everyone would have agreed with the word 'merciful'. But illustrious he certainly was, and a mighty warrior, and in his lifetime he created a city which was renowned as the 'Mirror of the World', the 'Garden of the Blessed' or simply 'The Fourth Paradise'. Even now, the name Samarkand is for many people synonymous with Tamerlane's power and splendour.

But although it is this medieval town which we still glimpse today, the oasis on the Zarafshan river – the name means 'strewer of gold' – has been inhabited for at least 40,000 years. And no wonder:

Bokhara is a city of the plains, low lying, desert encircled; but Samarkand stands high, tucked away under the foothills of the mountains, embedded in a veritable Garden of Eden, in a land literally flowing with milk and honey, where all the fruits of the earth seem to grow in profusion and to perfection, where man finds life easy and the climate is perfect.

Douglas Carruthers, *Beyond the Caspian*, 1949

A short distance to the north-east of Tamerlane's city lie the ruins of its classical predecessor, fabled Afrasiab – Maracanda to the Greeks – the capital of the Sogdian empire. That empire came to an end when, after a fierce fight, Alexander the Great captured Maracanda in 329 BC, one of a succession of invaders. But the Sogdians were survivors, and they continued to criss-cross Central Asia with their caravans, their language becoming the lingua franca of the whole region. From time to time their activities would be interrupted by a wave of horse-borne nomads from the north, who would pour down on the tempting oasis from the Hungry Steppe. Various tribes of Huns and Turks plundered Samarkand over the years, but each time the Sogdians would return to their despoiled city, patch up the walls, rebuild the warehouses and carry on trading. As an important staging-post on the Silk Road, Samarkand became famous as a centre of trade and manufacture, renowned for its glass and fine paper, its caravanserais crowded with jostling merchants and camel trains, its warehouses packed with rugs, spices and bales of silk.

During the seventh century AD, when Samarkand was part of a Turkish khanate (and Europe was in the Dark Ages), the Chinese Buddhist pilgrim Hsuan-tsang visited the town on his way to India. Sa-mo-kien, he reported, was a flourishing city, whose inhabitants 'set a good example to their neighbours in their observation of the laws of morality and decency'. Another Chinese traveller remarked on the early education of Sogdian boys, from the age of 5, in reading, writing and the arts of commerce. 'The majority of the inhabitants', he explained, 'consider the receipt of profits to be an excellent pursuit.' About half the population, according to Hsuan-tsang, were engaged in trade and the rest in agriculture, although the frescoes uncovered by Soviet archaeologists at Penjakent, near Samarkand, depict scenes of battle and feasting – perhaps a portrayal of Sogdiana's glorious past.

At the beginning of the eighth century Samarkand fell to the armies of the Arab Caliphate, and the Sogdians and Turks were driven out or forcibly converted to Islam. For a century it became an Arab city, with mathematicians and astronomers rubbing shoulders with merchants, and women were now obliged to veil themselves from head to foot in public. The rule of the Caliphate soon declined, but henceforth the grip of Islam tightened on Central Asia, not to be challenged until the twentieth century. The earlier religions of Buddhism, Zoroastrianism, Manichaeism and Nestorian Christianity which had put down roots as they passed along the Silk Road were now ruthlessly suppressed by the mullahs, who demanded a fanatical adherence to the new creed.

After the departure of the Arabs, Samarkand was ruled by the Samanids, a Persian dynasty, and later by the Seljuks, the new tribe of Turks who carved out a mighty empire for themselves in the eleventh century. Finally, like so much of Central Asia, the city was devastated in 1220 by the pitiless hordes of Genghis Khan, and this was the end of the ancient site of Afrasiab and Maracanda. When the town was next rebuilt, from the rubble of its predecessors, it had shifted south-west to the site still occupied by the old town today.

But it was not until the fourteenth century that Samarkand took on the appearance we now associate with it – the soaring minarets and the domes of glistening turquoise and cobalt blue. Tamerlane's long reign, from 1370 to 1405, was almost entirely taken up by military campaigns, but in the course of conquering most of the known world he never forgot his beloved capital, and always sent back the best artists and craftsmen of the countries he had defeated, together with vast armies of slaves for the manual work. Architects, brick-glaziers, ceramic tile-makers and mosaic-workers flowed in from Baghdad, Damascus, Shiraz, Isfahan and Delhi, while one of Tamerlane's many wives brought cultural influences and skilled craftsmen from her native China. Whenever the Emperor returned from a military expedition he would immediately go and inspect the progress of his latest monument, and if anything displeased him the architects would be publicly hanged in the market place. Tamerlane was not a patient man: he wanted results. Sometimes he bribed his slave battalions with chunks of meat. When no amount of bribery or flogging could achieve the miracles he sought, he imported ninety elephants from India to help the work along. Thus was the Timurid style of architecture born.

One of the first monuments Tamerlane undertook in Samarkand was the Shah Zindeh complex, a mosque and series of mausoleums on the outskirts of old Afrasiab. According to legend, a Muslim saint named Kasim-ibn-Abbas was martyred here at the end of the seventh century by the infidel inhabitants of Afrasiab, and would arise at the appropriate moment as the defender of Islam. ('His failure to appear when the Russians took Samarkand has somewhat shaken his reputation,' remarked Ella Christie, who travelled there just before the First World War.) But in fact Islam seems to have hijacked an earlier Zoroastrian or Manichaean legend about a 'living king' who was merely sleeping in his tomb. In any case it gave Tamerlane the excuse to embark on what many visitors have described as his greatest achievement. 'In these sepulchres', wrote the explorer Douglas Carruthers, 'the enamelled tile-work, for which Samarkand is chiefly famous, reaches the highest pitch of perfection.' To Rosita Forbes, writing in the 1930s, the court of Shah Zindeh 'might have been steeped in sea-water. All the blues from turquoise to the deepest sapphire were reflected in the incomparable mosaics of this deep, quiet pool of colour contrasted or blended with the rich browns and golds of the earthen walls. Sea and sand with sunshine caught between them.'

Further west, the vast and imposing Bibi Khanum mosque and accompanying *medresseh* or college seem to have been erected between 1399 and 1404, possibly in memory of the Emperor's Chinese wife, though some say more prosaically that it was to commemorate his triumphant Indian campaign. Built on a gigantic scale, the main doorway was 135 feet high, but the design was far too ambitious for an earthquake zone and the mosque began to collapse soon after it was completed. It has been claimed that it was also damaged by Russian shell-fire during their campaign of Central Asian conquest in 1868, but the dome – though cracked – was still more or less intact when Carruthers first saw it during his long visit in 1907–8. Sadly, while he was there another earth tremor dislodged 'the greater part of it', and he reflected that 'it will never be seen again as I saw it'.

The immense marble lectern which used to stand under the Bibi Khanum's dome, supported on nine feet, has now been placed in the courtyard outside. Legend has it that the Chinese queen, a zealous convert to the faith of her lord and master, used to stand before it and read from an enormous Koran. A Russian traveller records seeing a huge book there in 1770 when he visited Samarkand, although he did not realise what it was. The Koran had disappeared by 1841 when the orientalist N. V. Khanikoff was there, but he noted that 'the chief merit of the marble pulpit at present consists, according to the superstitious belief of the inhabitants, in curing for life pains in the backbones, provided the patient manages to crawl under it'. Early twentieth-century visitors heard a variant of this superstition: crawling under the lectern was a cure for infertility in women.

In 1404 Tamerlane began his last architectural extravaganza, the Gur Emir, which he was never to see completed. It was originally intended to serve as a mausoleum for his favourite grandson, the Crown Prince Mohammed Sultan, who was killed in battle in Persia in 1403, but it eventually became the tomb of Tamerlane himself. However when work began, he was still a revered, and feared, emperor to whom other nations sent ambassadors laden with placatory gifts. Don Ruy Gonzales de Clavijo, envoy of the court of Castile, has left this description of Tamerlane's Samarkand:

> The city is surrounded on all sides by many gardens and vine-yards, which extend in some directions a league and a half, in others two leagues, the city being in the midst. Among these gardens there are great and noble houses, and here the lord Timur has several palaces. The nobles of the city have their houses amongst these gardens, and they are so extensive, that when a man approaches the city he sees nothing but a mass of very high trees. Many streams of water flow through the city and through these gardens, and among these gardens there are many cotton plantations and melon grounds, and the melons are good and plentiful; and at Christmas-time there is a wonderful quantity of melons and grapes.

De Clavijo was dazzled by the opulence of Tamerlane's court. Jewel-encrusted gold and silver lined his walls, he banqueted from golden tables, drank from a golden cup and dressed in silks and sables. His nine wives, also adorned in silks and precious stones, embellished their faces with a paste of white lead so that their skin looked like paper. But Tamerlane was visibly an old man now, and the Castilian noticed at one feast that 'he was so old his eyelids had fallen down'. So much food was served at a banquet that 'it would have lasted for a year', and etiquette demanded that a cup of wine be drained at one draught, the cups being constantly replenished by an attendant. The title of *bahadur*, meaning 'valiant drinker', was conferred on whoever managed to imbibe the greatest quantity of wine without becoming unconscious. Perhaps it was just as well that wine was only permitted on special occasions. De Clavijo wisely preferred to stick to sweetened mare's milk. Tamerlane was said to 'have visions', but whether these resulted from physical or mental infirmity or from too much feasting, we shall probably never know.

What made this son of the steppe, of mixed Mongol and Turkish blood, embark on this orgy of building? As the writer Margaret Craig-McKerrow has said: 'Genghis Khan came and conquered and destroyed, but Timur conquered, remained and left behind him enduring monuments to fame.' She hazards her own guess as to his reasons: 'It was, perhaps, as compensation for his own ugliness that he created so much beauty around him.' For Tamerlane was one-eyed, crippled in his right leg and arm, and reputedly the ugliest man in Asia. It is said that he once flew into a towering rage after seeing his reflection in a mirror. He was, of course, a Muslim and many of his buildings had a religious significance, but perhaps his compulsive need to build vast and grandiose edifices was as much a defiant rejection of his humble nomadic origins as a desire to glorify God. For over his palace at Kesh, his birth-place, was the inscription: 'Let he who doubts our power and munificence look upon our buildings'.

In any case, in a part of the world where conquerors came and went with monotonous regularity, most of them soon to be forgotten, and where entire civilisations could rise and fall and be obliterated, Tamerlane should have died a happy man. Neither he nor his works would ever be forgotten. But his restless spirit could not be happy while there were countries still unsubjugated, and the great land of China lay outside his enormous empire. 'And shall I die and this unconquered?' are the words plausibly put in his mouth by Christopher Marlowe in his great melodrama. So the 69-year-old tyrant gathered up his armies and prepared to mount a new campaign. Greatly to the relief of the Chinese, Tamerlane was struck down by a fever on his way east, and soon he 'coughed like a strangled camel and foamed like a camel dragged backwards with the rein', in the words of his followers. His doctors had to admit to the Emperor: 'We know of no cure for death.' So the Scourge of God lost his final battle, not on the field of conquest, but lying in a tent with a winter storm raging outside.

The Emperor's body was carried back to Samarkand and laid in state in the Gur Emir mausoleum, where slaves from China, Persia and India were still at work. Hans Schiltberger of Munich, who happened to be held captive in Samarkand at this time, recounts the following story:

> After Tamerlane was buried, the priests that belonged to the temple heard him move every night during a whole year. His friends gave large alms, that he should cease his howlings. But this was of no use. They asked advice of their priests, and went to his son and begged that he would set free the prisoners taken by his father in other countries, and especially those that were in Samarkand, who were all craftsmen he had brought to the capital, where they had to work. He let them go, and as soon as they were free, Tamerlane did not howl any more.

There was a legend that if Tamerlane's body were ever to be disturbed, a catastrophe would befall the world, eclipsing even the horrors he had himself unleashed. On 22 June 1941, while Professor Mikhail Gerasimov was examining the skeleton, Germany invaded the Soviet Union, and what Russians call the Great Patriotic War began.

Tamerlane would certainly have been gratified if he could have heard the paeans of praise – not to mention purple prose – uttered by Western visitors to his capital, even though they saw his monuments in a much reduced state. Some, like the Hungarian scholar Vambery, got to Samarkand in the 1860s in disguise and at great risk to their lives. Others went in the 1870s in the wake of the Russian conquest. And once the Transcaspian railway reached the city in 1888 there was a steady stream of eager visitors, starting with the Hon. George Curzon. Everybody was bowled over by Samarkand. Eugene Schuyler, the American Consul at St Petersburg, wrote: 'I look back to Samarkand with feelings of special pleasure, and consider it one of the places in the world to which I would gladly return at any time or under any pretext.' It seemed to him 'a living remnant of a far-off world'. Douglas Carruthers, who went on to be a distinguished explorer and naturalist, was in his twenties when he went there, and although his book *Beyond the Caspian* was not published until forty years later, it brims with the enthusiasm of a young man. Here are his descriptions of first Bibi Khanum and then Shah Zindeh:

> To see it to the best advantage one should go beyond the city's precincts, out to the waste place where old Maracanda stood. One should go at even, when the sun sinks low, and watch the pageant as it passes out over the Kyzyl Kum desert. One should wait till the great turquoise dome, reflecting the dying rays, turns pure amethyst, and remain until the whole vast pile stands silhouetted against the after-glow. Then – when the roar from the distant bazaars dies down and the air is heavy with a golden haze, when twilight falls and ghosts of all Time come up out of Afrasiab to walk with you – then you will have seen and felt the work of Timur's hand and stood in awe.
>
> But choose high-noon on a hot summer's day to wander through the courts and alleys of Shah Zindeh, which is Samarkand's chief treasure. There you will be struck dumb, if you have any feeling at all for design and colour. No adequate description has yet been given of the glories of those tombs of Timur's faithful followers, perhaps because it is impossible to do justice to the unrivalled wealth of coloured tile and porcelain with which they are adorned.

Ella Christie, an intrepid Scotswoman who made two journeys alone to Central Asia just before the First World War, found the Gur Emir most memorable:

> Crossing a slight ravine from the Citadel we come in sight of the Gur Emir, or tomb of Tamerlane, built by himself and dedicated to his friend and tutor, Mir Sayyid Baraka, who is buried near the pupil who did him such credit and honour. Surrounded as it is by trees, chiefly poplar, I can never forget the sight of that fluted blue dome rising far above the delicate spring green. On the stone path leading up to the chief portal I found a little group of natives in gay-coloured *khalats* seated playing chess – a peaceful, undisturbed spot in which to meditate on their moves – and so absorbed were they in their game that my presence passed unnoticed ...

As one enters the great portal, or *piktash*, as these arches are called, there is a passage, obscurely lighted, off which open two chambers, in one of which are buried female members of the family of Tamerlane, and in the other his son Shah Rukh and his family. Then comes the vaulted octagonal hall, 115 feet in height. Beneath its dome is a white marble railing enclosing seven tombs, the centre one of which is that of Tamerlane, and is of dark green jade, made darker by the contrast of the six others, which are of white marble. This block of jade measures six feet in length, seventeen inches wide and fourteen inches thick. It is the largest known specimen of that stone in existence, and was said to have been the gift of a Mongol princess.

Ella Christie, *Through Khiva to Golden Samarkand*, 1925

Medieval visitors to Tamerlane's tomb were convinced that the dark green slab was an enormous emerald. Fitzroy Maclean, who saw it in the course of an illicit visit in 1937, described it as nephrite. The young Maclean, who had temporarily shaken off his secret police shadows, hastened to see the sights before they caught up with him and sent him back to Moscow where he was working as a diplomat. Wandering about the outskirts of the town, he suddenly came upon 'the splendid ruins of the Bibi Khanum mosque', with its 'one immense crumbling arch ... poised perilously above the surrounding buildings'. Nearby he found the Shah Zindeh complex, but here he was not welcome:

Near the Bibi Khanum two or three incongruous modern buildings in the Soviet style have already made their appearance and will no doubt be followed by others. Passing by these and along the main street out into the country I came to a dusty hillside, littered with graves and gravestones all crumbling into decay. Down it ran a walled stairway with, on either side, a row of small mosques of the most exquisite beauty. In these lie buried the friends and contemporaries of Tamerlane. From some, the blue tiles have disappeared completely, leaving a rough crumbling surface of pale sun-baked clay sprouting here and there with tufts of grass. At the top of the stairway stands a larger mosque, the tomb of Kasim-ibn-Abbas ... After him the mosque, for centuries a

place of pilgrimage, is called Shah Zindeh – the Living King.
Climbing over the wall, I wandered in and out of the mosques
until I was eventually turned away by an angry Uzbek woman
ably seconded by an idiot boy. Sight-seeing, it seemed, was
not encouraged in Samarkand.

Maclean, *Eastern Approaches*, 1949

In Tamerlane's day, what is now the *registan*, or public square, was the
commercial centre of Samarkand, a bustling bazaar with caravanserais
for the many merchants who passed through the city. It was Tamerlane's
grandson and successor, Ulugh Beg, who built the first mosque and
medresseh there, in the fifteenth century. He was a scholarly man, with
a passion for astronomy, and the building dearest to his heart was the
Observatory he designed and had built on a hill in the 1420s. It was a
three-storey tower, topped with a dome, and contemporary travellers
did not hesitate to compare it with the awesome dome of Saint Sophia
in Constantinople. Inside was a marble sextant of gigantic proportions,
which enabled Ulugh Beg and his astronomers to draw up a catalogue of
the stars that still astonishes scholars with its accuracy. But the Emperor's
encouragement of science, and interest in the work of Western scholars,
made him many enemies among the Islamic clergy. The dangerous
notion that truth could be discovered through knowledge instead of
through religious instruction did not suit the *mullahs* at all, for it clearly
undermined their influence and power. Ulugh Beg himself hardly
helped matters by such pronouncements as: 'Religions disperse like
mist; kingdoms decay; but science remains for all time.' Like Galileo's
theories and his persecution by the Inquisition two centuries later, Ulugh
Beg's ideas could not be tolerated by the religious authorities. He was
assassinated by his own son in 1449, dervishes wrecked his Observatory,
and his fellow scientists fled for their lives.

Fortunately one of them escaped to Constantinople with a
bundle of manuscripts and was able to publish there Ulugh Beg's *New
Astronomical Tables*. This work caused such a sensation that it was
quickly republished in Cairo and Damascus and, in the seventeenth
century, in Oxford, Paris and other European centres of learning. The
site of the Observatory was forgotten after a generation or two, for
the dervishes were careful to leave no trace of this heretical edifice,
and was only rediscovered in 1908 after painstaking research by the

Russian antiquarian Vladimir Vyatkin. To his excitement, the lower half of the great sextant, sweeping down into the earth and flanked by a staircase, had survived with all its calibrations. The upper half, of course, like everything above ground, had been smashed to smithereens and all traces had long since disappeared. A museum now marks the site where Ulugh Beg once gazed at the stars.

The gracious city of Tamerlane and Ulugh Beg was not destined to be left intact for long. A new wave of nomadic invaders, the Uzbek Turks, swept down from the Hungry Steppe at the beginning of the sixteenth century, bringing death and destruction in their wake. By 1505 Shaybani Khan was in control of the whole of Transoxiana, the land between the Oxus and the Syr-darya, and the Ferghana valley to the east. In the course of this shake-up, Prince Babur, a descendant of Tamerlane's third son and erstwhile ruler of the eastern part of his empire, was obliged to renounce his claims to Turkestan. Instead, he turned his attention to the conquest of Hindustan, and so the upheavals of Central Asia led to the founding of the Mogul dynasty in India. Samarkand gradually declined, and after Shaybani's line went the way of all conquering dynasties the whole region collapsed into anarchy.

As if invasion and internecine strife were not enough, Samarkand was also assailed by serious earthquakes in the seventeenth century. But at least these led to the creation of the *registan* in the form we know it today, for the old caravanserais had to be completely demolished, making room for the *medressehs* of Shir Dar and Tilla Kari. Curzon called the *registan* 'the noblest public square in the world', and he was not given to hyperbole. Michael Shoemaker, an American travel-writer, shared his enthusiasm:

> In the old city there is what I have never seen in Oriental towns before – until reaching Teheran, where it is not nearly so imposing – a great square, and I know of no more picturesque spot in the East. Three stately buildings called medressehs, or universities, rise around it, a picturesque jumble of domes, alcoves, and fretted gateways, all covered with porcelain tiling of turquoise blue and dark blue on a ground of yellow, while minarets out of the perpendicular complete the fantastic effect.
>
> Shoemaker, *The Heart of the Orient*, 1904

The earthquakes which skewed the minarets terrified the inhabitants so much that most of them ran away, and for much of the eighteenth century Samarkand was a ghost town, frequented, it was said, by a solitary religious recluse. Towards the end of the century it was forcibly repopulated at the command of the Emir of Bokhara, and a polyglot population of Uzbeks, Tajiks, Persians, Arabs, Indians and Jews resulted. Happily, the buildings were patched up and the walls repaired, the canals cleared and the gardens replanted, otherwise medieval Samarkand might have crumbled away entirely. During the nineteenth century the whole of western Central Asia came under the covetous gaze of a rapidly expanding Russia, and Tsarist missions began to penetrate this mysterious region. In 1841 when Nikolai Khanikoff was there, Samarkand still had the typical appearance of a Central Asian town, with a citadel, high mud-brick walls, lookout posts and six gates, which were locked at sunset, but inside the walls Khanikoff found the city in a sorry state, for 'the present generation not only do not erect anything new worthy of description, but are ever busy in destroying the monuments of former grandeur'.

In 1868 both Samarkand and Bokhara surrendered to the forces of General Kaufmann, and were taken under the Tsar's 'protection'. Samarkand's walls were demolished, as was most of the old citadel built by Tamerlane and containing the *koktash*, the grey marble coronation stone of the Timurids. A new fortress was put up by the Russians in roughly the same place, and this came to mark the border between the old town and the new Russian one which began to grow up next to it. The prospect of fabled Samarkand being open to Western visitors caused a *frisson* of excitement around the world. Schuyler spoke for many when he wrote:

> There is no place in Central Asia, the name of which has so impressed the imagination of Europe as Samarkand. Surrounded by a halo of romance, visited at rare intervals, and preserving the traditions of its magnificence in a mysterious impenetrability, it long piqued the curiosity of the world ... The news of its capture by the Russians in 1868 excited a glow of interest, like the awakening of some half-forgotten memory ... At last, we thought, the curtain is to be drawn aside.
>
> Schuyler, *Turkistan*, 1876

The Russians now began to attempt the daunting task of preserving what was left of the old monuments. Their efforts were not helped by the persistent earth-tremors, of varying severity, which plagued the region. There had been a particularly bad one shortly before J.T. Woolrych Perowne visited Samarkand in the winter of 1897:

> The recent earthquake has left its mark everywhere, and in a few years – it cannot well be longer – there will hardly be left anything of antiquarian interest in Samarkand. It is all very well for irresponsible writers to decry the Russian authorities, and say they have no care for the historic buildings of which they are now the guardians, but it only needs the most casual glance to assure oneself that these buildings are practically past restoration or repair. Whatever may have been the case a hundred years ago, patching now would be quite useless in my opinion – everything is too far gone. Then again, the recurrence of earthquakes, the last only in September 1897, would at once destroy again what had been restored, and the money spent would have been only wasted.
>
> Perowne, *Russian Hosts and English Guests*
> *in Central Asia*, 1898

Perowne was not alone in thinking the ruins were beyond repair. An American businessman, John Bookwalter, who was there shortly afterwards referred to the old town's 'mouldering ruins, most of them in the last stages of decay'. The historians Francis Skrine and Denison Ross, writing in 1899, had no hesitation in blaming the Russians, however:

> The Russians must be held responsible for the forlorn state of the Bibi Khanum. When they entered upon their glorious inheritance the power of disintegration might have been arrested. But they were content to see the stately mosque degraded to the base uses of a cotton-market and a stable.
>
> Skrine and Ross, *The Heart of Asia*, 1899

Ella Christie was inclined to agree, although some crude repair work had been carried out by the time she went there in about 1912:

> The Russians have done a certain amount of preservation, but a great deal more might have been achieved, and much has

gone that might have remained intact. The mere prohibition of removal of tiles is not sufficient when the material in which they are set is fast crumbling to dust. Where the various melon-shaped domes are concerned, cement moulded to the original form has been the medium employed, and this preserves any coloured portions left.

Lack of money was certainly one problem, but the total indifference of the inhabitants to their artistic heritage was an even greater obstacle to preservation. And there was no improvement in the years following the Russian Revolution, when everything to do with the past tended to be rejected as bad. Still, the impact of Samarkand was stunning even in the most inauspicious conditions. Margaret Craig-McKerrow went there in 1931 on an Intourist tour, and her great dread was that the city would have become entirely Sovietised. The drive from the station did nothing to reassure her, for every road seemed to be called Karl Marx Street or Lenin Boulevard:

> However, we soon passed through the great gate of the fortress into the old town and got down at the Registan, the public square. There one was at once in the heart of Asia, in the days of Tamerlane. One thinks of all the fine squares and plazas of the world, but perhaps there is none to equal the sad beauty of this great space, surrounded by the remains of three magnificent buildings, still well enough preserved to give an idea of their pristine loveliness of life and colour.
>
> Craig-McKerrow, *The Iron Road to Samarkand*, 1932

The Soviet authorities soon had second thoughts about exposing their Central Asian colonies to the gaze of Westerners, and the Intourist tours came to an abrupt halt. Samarkand became a closed city to all but fellow-travellers, who could be relied upon to see things in the correct light. Without a special permit – and your 'papers' were inspected by every petty official who crossed your path – you had to rely on bluff and cunning if you wanted to follow the Golden Road. A few fearless souls managed to do so, among them Ella Maillart, Ethel Mannin and Fitzroy Maclean. Maillart, the Swiss sportswoman turned traveller, camped in a cell in the

Tilla Kari mosque in 1932 and found herself witnessing the show-trial in the *registan* of a group of *basmachi* – the anti-Bolshevik, pan-Islamic guerrilla group – nineteen of whom were sentenced to death. After the verdict had been pronounced, there was 'a cry, a prolonged howl ... The women rush forward, passing underneath the cord ... the confusion is heart-rending. Their swords drawn, the militiamen force a passage through the *khalats* and turbans, and the women, forcibly torn away, are removed to a distance from their men' (see DUSHANBE for more on the *basmachi*).

Mlle Maillart made friends with some students who were most surprised at her interest in the old buildings, and gave her extremely misleading information about them which she was too tactful to correct. While she was wandering about the ruins of the Bibi Khanum she noticed a daring Uzbek clambering around in the very heights, busily removing all the wood he could carry, quite oblivious to the incidental damage he was causing:

> He is collecting wood for himself, which he drags away from the beams supporting the brickwork of the vault. The wood is smooth, hard, and raspberry-coloured. The man goes off with his booty, leaving the ground strewn with glazed tiles.
>
> Maillart, *Turkestan Solo*, 1934

At least by now the donkeys and horses, and the cotton-market, had been cleared away, although this was probably for reasons of safety rather than in the interests of preservation.

Ethel Mannin arrived in Samarkand in the middle of a bitterly cold night in 1935 and was rewarded by seeing the *registan* for the first time by moonlight. After a nightmarish train journey, and in spite of the paranoia induced by her lack of 'papers' – which meant she had no chance of a bed for the night – she was overwhelmed by the magical quality of the old town. 'There is a splendour of pale blue towers and arches reaching up to the blazing stars,' she wrote. 'Samarkand by moonlight! How is it possible to care very much where we lay our heads for the rest of this fantastic night? We blunder along over the cobbles, and now we do not feel our weariness, or the steely coldness, for we walk in an enchanted land.' Next day, after snatching a little rest on a hard bench at the railway station, she hurried back to see the *registan* by daylight:

Façades, minarets, cupolas, archways – all are blue, delicate blue-green and deep pure cobalt. Moonlight mists it all to a pastel softness, but in sunlight it is glitteringly brilliant, sea-green, sky-blue, dazzling. Before the tiles began to fall away, leaving ugly patches of yellow-brown clay, it must have been a flawless dream of beauty, but even in ruins it is the perfect introduction to the wonders of Samarkand.

Mannin, *South to Samarkand*, 1936

But some of the minarets had been chained into position to stop them crashing down, and she felt that Tamerlane had been far too impatient in achieving his instant masterpieces:

When Tamerlane himself commanded that there should be beauty and splendour, human imagination and human energy were strained to the utmost. At his command blood flowed and beauty flowered. But a mortal and perishable beauty, doomed to perish out of its due time and become again a part of the dust of Asia.

How amazed all these earlier visitors would be if they could see the city now, with many of its monuments so rebuilt and restored that they are almost reproductions, and standing amid the incongruous paraphernalia of a modern metropolis. One wonders too what Professor Vyatkin would have thought – he who tracked down the site of Ulugh Beg's Observatory in 1908 and who stayed on, even after the Soviet coup, as Director of Antiquities until his death in 1934. He must often have wrung his hands over the lack of funds which prevented him from preserving his beloved monuments or from carrying out scientific investigations. For in his day the only archaeologists in Samarkand were at best amateurs, and at worst indiscriminate treasure-seekers. Ella Christie came upon one of the former, a Russian sign-painter, who spent all his spare time digging up old pots. 'He was a real enthusiast', she wrote, 'and worked for the love and interest in such discoveries.' Intrigued, she went to the site of ancient Afrasiab to see for herself:

On the hill itself, amid the mounds of rubbish and debris, are to be found specimens of whole and broken fragments of pottery and glass. There is no organized plan of excavation, and the natives dig as they like, without any scientific knowledge, so that for the one perfect specimen that may be unearthed many others are smashed in so doing. On one spot I gathered up the fragments of what had once been five glass bowls of classic shapes and treasured them as much for the exquisite iridescent colouring of the pieces as for their historic interest.

Her Russian friend had amassed a collection of about a thousand perfect and imperfect specimens and was anxious to find a good home for them. Mrs Christie acquired five 'for the South Kensington Museum', and she later heard that the remainder had gone to the National Museum in Kiev. What befell them during the chaos of the revolution, civil war, and the destruction of the Second World War is not known. In 1937 when Fitzroy Maclean was there, Afrasiab was still 'a desolate, undulating plain, sprinkled with crumbling ruins', but since then the site has been excavated by Soviet archaeologists, and Sogdian wall-paintings, amongst other things, have been uncovered.

Inevitably the Soviet period brought many changes to Samarkand. The Russian new town, which hardly existed at the time of Schuyler's visit, and was described by Bookwalter as 'presenting the appearance of having been literally carved out of a dense forest of poplars and acacias', was modernised and industrialised. The unmade or cobbled streets, bordered by 'running streams of pure, clear water, drawn from the mountains', and with tall trees interlacing overhead, made way for modern highways. The camel had to give place to the truck and the tractor. Samarkand, for centuries a jewel of the Silk Road, one-time capital of the Conqueror of the World, more recently subject to the Emir of Bokhara, became for five years the capital of the Uzbek Soviet Socialist Republic. However, in 1930 this modern prize was snatched from her by ambitious Tashkent.

But nowhere else – not Tashkent, nor even Bokhara or Khiva – can ever supplant the city of Tamerlane as the place to which we would all, in Schuyler's words, be glad to return at any time or under any pretext. For the footprints of a giant are still visible there. No ugliness, said Ethel Mannin, can invade this triumphant beauty: it lifts the gaze from the squalor of the pavements to the everlasting blue to which its minarets aspire. Even in its decline, thought Douglas Carruthers, Samarkand was like some fair lady looking out from the seclusion of her garden on to the wilderness around her. Like Carruthers we can climb the mound of old Afrasiab and watch the sun sink behind the shattered frame of the Bibi Khanum, and then see in our imagination the dark cloud on the horizon and hear the thunder of hooves which heralded another raid by the nomads of the north.

And thanks to James Elroy Flecker, who died of consumption before he could see the fabled city for himself, we can also hear the quiet footfalls of the unnumbered legions of merchants and pilgrims who made their way along the Silk Road to Samarkand:

> Sweet to ride forth at evening from the wells
> When shadows pass gigantic on the sand,
> And softly through the silence beat the bells
> Along the golden road to Samarkand.

> We travel not for trafficking alone
> By hotter winds our fiery hearts are fanned
> For lust of knowing what should not be known
> We make the golden journey to Samarkand.

THE SILK ROAD

One enters into a great sandy desert, where neither water nor grass is to be found. It is necessary to look at some high mountain in the distance, and seek for abandoned bones, to know how to guide oneself and recognize the path to be followed.

Hsuan-tsang, AD 629

Khotan is a province lying between north-east and east, and is eight days' journey in length. The people are subject to the Great Khan, and are all worshippers of Mahommet. There are numerous towns and villages in the country, but Khotan, the capital, is the most noble of all, and gives its name to the kingdom. Everything is to be had there in plenty, including abundance of cotton, with flax, hemp, wheat, wine and the like. The people have vineyards and gardens and estates. They live by commerce and manufactures, and are no soldiers.

Marco Polo, c. 1254–1324

B Y THE SECOND century BC, following the destruction of Carthage in the Punic Wars, Rome was the undisputed master of the Mediterranean. As they fought their way into the Near East the Romans began to hear of a mysterious country far to the east – the Land of Silk – whose rulers were clad in a shimmering cloth unknown anywhere else in the world. What they did not realise was that China, under the Han dynasty, was a highly developed nation with a central government at its capital, Chang-an (Sian), and a population even greater than that of the Roman empire. As for the Chinese, they had never heard of Rome, for the only people they were aware of to their west were the nomadic Hsiung-nu or Huns, who roamed between Mongolia and the Pamirs and who were a constant threat to their frontiers.

But in 138 BC the Chinese Emperor Wu-ti decided that he could no longer tolerate the impudence of these barbarians, whose brilliant horsemanship usually enabled them to escape from their raids unscathed, and he looked for allies. In the far west, he had heard, was a people – the Yueh-chih – who also hated the Huns, and he sent off an expedition to make contact with them. The young man chosen to lead this dangerous mission would no doubt have been astonished to learn that his name would be recorded in the world's history books, and that his epic journey would be China's first tentative step along what came to be known as the Silk Road. Chang-Chien's initial problem, of course, was how to get from Chang-an to the land of the Yueh-chih on the other side of both the Gobi and the Taklamakan deserts without being intercepted by the Huns.

He set out with a hundred men and a caravan laden with gifts, but scarcely had he crossed into Kansu than he was captured by the enemy. Detained for ten years, the luckless Chang was given a wife to keep him happy, and raised a brood of half-Hun children. Eventually he managed to escape with a handful of his original companions, and they doggedly resumed their interrupted journey. We do not know their route, but after marching for 'many periods of ten days' they were delighted to reach Khokhand, in the Ferghana valley. Here at last, after a decade of living a primitive life in tents, were proper towns with houses and farms, merchants and craftsmen. The little state had several thousand inhabitants, ruled over by a prince who had heard of the rich land of China and was eager to welcome its emissary.

His people were now mainly settled, but their nomadic past was still apparent in their passion for horses. Chang-Chien, who had developed an experienced eye, regarded them as almost the equals of the Huns at horsemanship and archery, and he was astonished at the size and speed of their horses. But he was anxious to continue his journey, for he had a mission to accomplish and the Yueh-chih were still a long way off. Reluctantly, the Prince of Khokhand allowed the Chinese travellers to depart, and provided guides to the adjoining country of Kang-chu, or Khorasmia, north-west of the Ferghana valley. Its people were peace-loving nomads who roamed the steppe between the Aral Sea and the lower reaches of the Oxus and the Syr-darya rivers, paying tribute when necessary to their more powerful neighbours.

Finally the determined Chang reached his objective. The Yueh-chih, he found, were a partly nomadic people living in a vast and prosperous land comprising, roughly, what came to be Russian Central Asia and the western end of Chinese Turkestan. Their capital was more or less where Khiva stands today. But their ruler was hesitant about joining China in an alliance against the Huns. His people had settled down in their rich new territory and had no desire to bring themselves to the attention of their old enemy. While the Prince thought matters over, Chang busied himself making enquiries. Until this time China had assumed that the rest of the world was composed entirely of barbarians. Now it appeared that there were other civilisations – albeit inferior ones – far to the west, beyond the domains of the Huns. Apart from the Yueh-chih and the people of Khokhand, Chang learned that there was a country called Bactria to the south, a powerful land called Parthia to the west, and a numerous people who lived in a hot country near to a 'Western Sea'.

Somewhere far away, he was told, to the north of Parthia, lay another great country which Chang called Li-chien in his reports. None of the Yueh-chih had been there, for the Parthians would not allow anyone through their territory. Modern scholars believe this was an early reference to Rome. At length Chang realised he would never persuade the Yueh-chih to join a military alliance with China, so he decided to move on and visit the people of Bactria. Here, too, he drew a blank militarily, for the Bactrians were poor warriors. They were, however, experienced merchants and were eager to trade with China. In fact Chang was surprised to see 'cloths and bamboo' which reminded him of home: the Bactrians explained that they had acquired them in the southern land of India, and that they had been brought across the sea from a land to the east. Chang realised that this must be one of the independent states of south China. Clearly, there were interesting possibilities for trade here.

The problem was, would a caravan from Chang-an ever get to Bactria? It seemed highly unlikely. Not only would it have to run the gauntlet of the ubiquitous Huns, but as it approached Bactria it would have to pass close to the hostile land of Tibet, which was swarming with murderous bandits. Chang spent over a year gathering information in Bactria and then set out for home. Miraculously, he managed to avoid the attentions of the Tibetan bandits, but once he emerged from their territory he had the supreme ill-luck to be captured again by the Huns. This time, happily, his detention lasted less than a year, for he was able to escape while they were engaged in a struggle for the clan leadership. When he at last reached Chang-an he had been away for thirteen years and was greeted like one returning from the dead. Only one of his original companions was still with him.

The Emperor Wu-ti was a man of vision. He dreamed of expanding his empire westwards, of spreading Chinese influence throughout the world. Now he knew that only the barbarians stood in his way. If other nations were too craven to help him, he would beat the Huns on his own, even if it took him years. The first step was to acquire some of the 'heavenly horses' Chang-Chien had come across in Khokhand, and then to induce his farmers by threats or bribes to become horse-breeders. At the same time he would make approaches to the rulers of southern China and see if they would allow him to join in the trade with India. Soon envoys and caravans laden with Chinese goods were setting out from Chang-an for the west and south. Many fell into the hands of the Huns and the Tibetans, but Wu-ti spared no expense in sending out replacements and backing them up with armies. With such determination he was bound to succeed, and in the end he did.

China's prosperity at this time – the height of the Han dynasty – was inextricably linked with silk, for this was the heyday of sericulture there. Apart from being woven into fine cloth, silk was employed for bowstrings and fishing lines and for stringing musical instruments. Garments were padded with silk floss, lengths of silk were used as currency for the payment of taxes, and a special method of weaving had even produced a waterproof material for the transportation of liquids. No other nation had discovered the secret of silk production – even in the first century AD Pliny and the Romans still believed that silk grew on trees – and the Chinese were determined to keep things that way. Small wonder, then, that once word of this wonderful new fabric spread to the West, there was an immediate and ever-growing demand for it.

What China wanted in return was mainly horses. Although Wu-ti established many stud-farms near his capital and ordered his farmers to grow lucerne for fodder (the seeds of this plant had been brought back by the thorough Chang-Chien from the Ferghana valley), it was a long time before supply could begin to meet demand. It has been estimated that Wu-ti lost over 100,000 horses in his campaigns against the Huns between 121 and 119 BC alone. But the art of Han China makes it clear that the 'heavenly horses' quite supplanted the small local ponies from this time. Once the Huns were subdued, trade with the western parts of Central Asia began to flourish, and the route through south China was abandoned as too hazardous. Instead the Chinese extended the Great Wall westwards to Tunhuang and policed the Silk Road with garrisons, for the barbarians were never far away.

The term 'Silk Road' is a modern one, coined in the nineteenth century by the German geographer Ferdinand von Richthofen. It was not, of course, a single road but a vast network of trade routes stretching from Chang-an to the eastern Mediterranean. Once a caravan had passed through the Great Wall at Jiayukuan, the traditional border of China proper, there was a choice of routes depending on the ultimate destination of the merchandise and the fluctuating fortunes of the settled peoples and the barbarians. The most northerly trail led from Anhsi to the oasis of Hami and then followed the northern foothills of the Tien-shan or Celestial mountains to Khorasmia – the oasis south of the Aral Sea which was later to contain the great city of Khiva. From there the track divided: southwards lay Samarkand and Bokhara, and beyond them Merv and Parthia, while the northerly trail passed across the mouth of the Volga, as it flowed into the Caspian, and thence to the Greek settlements on the Black Sea. The advantage of this route was the relative abundance of water and grass, the disadvantage the fact that it lay in the path of all the nomad migrations.

Other routes from Anhsi skirted the Taklamakan desert, either to the north via Turfan, Kucha, Aksu and Kashgar, or to the south via Tunhuang, Cherchen and Khotan. If you went north there was the risk of being raided by the Huns, while to the south you might fall prey to the Tibetans. One route actually struck out from Tunhuang right across the fearsome Lop desert to Lou-lan and then Turfan, but there nature was the enemy, and many a caravan disappeared without trace in the howling sandstorms known as *karaburans*. When the Great Wall was extended to Tunhuang, two new gates were made at Yang Kuan and Yumen Kuan. Caravans bringing jade to China from Khotan always used the latter, and this was how it acquired its name of Jade Gate.

Once merchandise destined for the West had safely reached the Stone Tower, it was past the half-way mark and the worst stages of the long journey were over. No one can be quite sure today where the tower stood, although it was a well-known landmark in the second century AD when the Alexandrian geographer Ptolemy was compiling his famous map of the world. A number of places in Central Asia have names which can be translated as 'tower of stone' – including Tashkent – but the Silk Road archaeologist Sir Aurel Stein thought the most likely candidate was Tashkurghan, on the eastern slopes of the Pamirs, above Yarkand. From here the caravans could proceed to Merv via either Samarkand and Bokhara or Balkh, and thence to Tyre, Palmyra or Antioch, or else branch south through the mountain passes to Kashmir and India.

Although some of the merchandise travelled the whole route, it changed hands many times on the way, increasing in value in the process, because the merchants only traded on their own particular sectors. As most of the Silk Road passed through either desert, steppe or mountain, its existence depended on there being an established string of caravan towns at regular intervals, where goods could be bartered, animals watered and shelter provided. Many of these staging-posts became prosperous entrepôts, especially those near an intersection of routes, like Kashgar and Yarkand, Bokhara and Samarkand, or Merv. Some, like Khotan and Turfan, became the capitals of city-states. Inevitably such conspicuous wealth was a constant temptation to Central Asia's 'other culture', the nomadic peoples who roamed the steppe with their herds, and for whom raiding and plundering were part of their way of life. On the whole, when China was strong the barbarians behaved themselves, for fear of reprisals. But the garrisons of the Western Territories were a very long way from home, and their ranks were often brought up to strength with deported criminals or political offenders. Although the Huns had formally submitted to China in 52 BC, they were quick to exploit her disarray when a usurper snatched the throne of the Han Emperor in AD 25, and again in AD 220 when the dynasty finally collapsed. Thus trade ebbed and flowed, according to conditions, but there were usually merchants willing to try their luck, for the rewards could be very great once East and West had developed an appetite for each other's exotic products.

Tradition has it that the first Romans to encounter silk were the seven legions of Marcus Licinius Crassus at the battle of Carrhae in 53 BC. They were pursuing the Parthians across the Euphrates when the enemy horsemen suddenly wheeled round and unfurled their dazzling silken banners. Momentarily blinded, the Romans were mown down by a hail of arrows, and 20,000 dead were left on the river bank. Within ten years, however, silk banners and canopies were being used for triumphal processions in Rome, and demand was so great that silk was bartered for its weight in gold. This had such a disastrous effect on the Roman balance of payments that in AD 14 the Senate was forced to issue a decree drastically restricting its use.

One of the chief beneficiaries of the trade in silk was Parthia, which controlled the western outlets. In fact, the rapacity of the middlemen was one of the main incentives to the Romans to find a sea route to the east, and during the first century AD they succeeded in doing so. It was a three- or four-month journey in all, via Alexandria, the Nile and some overland stages across the Egyptian desert to the Red Sea. It could only be undertaken at certain times of year, for it depended on using the monsoon winds to steer the ships from the mouth of the Red Sea to north-west India. The sea route proved to be no safer than the caravan trails, and many a cargo was lost in storms and many a crew sold into slavery. As slaves comprised the labour force of the ancient world, demand was endless. But goods brought by sea were cheaper, and this option certainly had to be used during those times of trouble when the land route was closed.

At the end of the first century AD, however, the land route was regularly in use, for the four great empires of the day – the Roman, Parthian, Kushan and Chinese – had brought stability to the Middle East and Central Asia. A great deal besides silk was now being traded. Eastbound caravans would carry corn, wine, oil, gold, iron, woollen and linen textiles, glass and asbestos, while westbound ones would bring arms and armour, fur, lacquerware and mirrors, and of course bales of silk. In the midst of all this trading there was also a gradual interchange of ideas and influences.

Pliny had written earlier that 'the great number of men who sail the seas do so for love of gain, not love of knowledge', and the Tyrian geographer Marinus now said much the same of the merchants who plied the Silk Road. 'They concern themselves only with their own trade, care little for exploration and are often given to boastful exaggeration of distances,' he complained, adding that those he had interviewed 'brought back not a single piece of worthwhile information'. Perhaps it was just as well that not all the travellers were merchants. For soon men of religion – whether pilgrims, missionaries or refugees – were bringing to Central Asia the creeds of Buddhism, Zoroastrianism, Manichaeism and Nestorian Christianity. And with religion came manuscripts, art and architecture.

Buddhism reached China as early as the first century AD, when the Emperor Ming-ti became a convert after seeing a vision, and thereafter bands of holy men regularly tramped the long road to India in search of sacred texts and greater knowledge. Many of these Chinese pilgrims halted in Gandhara, a Buddhist kingdom of the Kushan empire, situated in what is now north-west Pakistan. The Kushans were Indo-Scythians, probably descended from the Yueh-chih, and their empire encompassed northern India, Bactria and Sogdiana – in modern terms, Pakistan, Afghanistan, Uzbekistan and Tajikistan. Gandharan art was already a blend of Indian Buddhist and Greek, for Alexander the Great had encouraged his generals to settle there and take local wives in the fourth century BC. The addition of Chinese ideas led to the birth of a new school of art, to be rediscovered in the twentieth century by Sir Aurel Stein and given the name Serindian.

The spread of Buddhism through the oasis towns around the rim of the Taklamakan desert led to a spate of building. Monasteries, shrines and temples proliferated, for not only could rich merchants pray or give thanks there for the safe passage of their caravans, but all gifts and endowments, however humble, gained 'merit' for the donors. If a Buddhist believer acquired enough merit during his life, he would be spared a similar, or worse, reincarnation on earth when he died. The kingdom of Khotan, when visited in AD 399 by the Chinese Buddhist traveller Fa-hsien, boasted fourteen large monasteries, some embellished with gold and silver leaf and precious stones, and 'several tens of thousands' of priests. Nestorian Christians, who denied the divinity of Christ and were as a result anathematised at the Council of Ephesus in 432, fled eastwards to Persia, Central Asia and eventually China, building and decorating churches as they progressed. And Manichaeans, who were persecuted by Christians and Zoroastrians alike, took refuge in the region, bringing their own distinctive art-forms with them.

Further west Buddhism spread throughout the empire of the Kushans, from Bactria to Khorasmia and the Sea of Aral, taking with it the Graeco-Buddhist art of Gandhara. In fact Soviet archaeologists have found Kushan coins as far north as the Caspian steppes and along the lower reaches of the Volga. They have also discovered Roman art alongside that of Gandhara at the fortress of Toprak-Kala, on the right bank of the Oxus or Amu-darya, 150 miles from the Aral Sea. Rome had broken the power of the Parthians, and the great land of Persia was now ruled by the Sassanids. The Persians were never converted to Buddhism for they were fanatical Zoroastrians, believing in purification by fire in the constant battle between Good and Evil. They had no love for their neighbours, and would allow no foreign merchants to cross their territory. As Rome declined, Persia took control of the trade routes and monopolised the trade in silk, and Byzantium, the new capital of the Eastern Roman empire, became as good a customer for silk as Rome had been. The Church, discarding the austerity of the early Christians, had acquired a taste for pomp and ceremony, decorating its buildings with mosaics, frescoes and silken hangings, and adorning its priests in silk brocade vestments.

At this time northern China was devastated by the Huns and the Chinese Annals fall silent during the troubled times of the third and fourth centuries. It seems likely that the overland Silk Road became unusable again and that silk had to be brought by sea from southern China via India by Persian merchants. Persia was powerful enough to dictate that only certain cities might be used as centres for the exchange of silk, no international deals being permitted anywhere else. The purchaser – usually a Syrian merchant – had to pay an immediate *ad valorem* tax of 12 per cent, and further taxes were imposed on the raw silk at every frontier, and frequently at every bridge and main road. The final price soared as a result, but the Church and the Byzantine court remained eager customers.

Around the year 440 the overland route through Central Asia seems to have opened up again. By now the Kushan empire had collapsed and there were a multitude of small city-states to the west of China. The Sogdians, always indefatigable merchants, were at the forefront of the revitalised trade, and were soon conducting caravans to the Chinese capital. But the new freedom of travel and the forging of new diplomatic links had an unforeseen side-effect. A Chinese princess was given in marriage to the ruler of Khotan and, unwilling to forgo the pleasure of wearing silk garments, she smuggled some silkworm eggs out of the country in her elaborate coiffure. The secret, jealously guarded by the Chinese for centuries, was out at last and Central Asia added silk-weaving to its existing skills of making hand-knotted woollen rugs and wall hangings.

But although raw silk could now be obtained outside China, it was a long time before anyone could rival Chinese weaving techniques. As well as the most sumptuous brocades, they had devised a costly cloth, known to the Romans as *opus plumarium*, in which tiny birds' feathers were interwoven in the silk. It seems likely that the techniques and styles of weaving of West and East met and blossomed in Central Asia, for Sir Aurel Stein found a silk cover on a manuscript at Tunhuang which incorporated narrow bands of finely woven silk in the Chinese manner and broader bands of heavy silk damask decorated in the Sassanid style.

In the middle of the sixth century silkworm eggs reached the court of Justinian in Byzantium, now renamed Constantinople, reputedly hidden in the hollow staff of a Nestorian monk. In theory this should have led to the collapse of the Persian monopoly and a decline in the trade of the Silk Road, but the Emperor's determination to keep the production of silk cocoons as a royal prerogative meant that the new industry never developed. So the Persians clung on to their lucrative customs duties for a little longer. But their supremacy in western Asia was about to be challenged by a formidable new foe, the latest wave in the stream of nomadic conquerors from the east. In about 550 the Western Turks became the overlords of Central Asia, driving the remnants of the Huns into northern India. The Sogdians, however, as the region's master traders, were tolerated and employed by the Turks, and a joint mission was sent to Persia. The arrogant Persians responded to these overtures by slaying the ambassadors, so the Turks sought their revenge by forming an alliance with Byzantium.

This was a serious setback for the Persians, for the Emperor could now obtain silk from Sogdiana using a route which skirted the Aral Sea, crossed the mouth of the Volga, passed north of the Caucasian massif and arrived at Trebizond on the Black Sea. It was a dangerous route, but it cut out Persia altogether. As it happened, the Sassanids in Persia were in any case reaching the end of their power, while China, at the other end of the Silk Road, was emerging again as a unified nation, having assimilated or pushed out its Hunnish invaders. Now that the Western Turks had brought stability to Central Asia, commerce could again prosper and art flourish. Precious stones such as lapis lazuli and diamonds travelled along the Silk Road at this time from India to China, together with dancing girls from Khotan and musicians from Samarkand, for the Tang dynasty (founded in 618) devoted considerable effort to the enjoyment of life. Religious tolerance prevailed for 200 years under the Tang, and Buddhists, Nestorians, Zoroastrians and Manichaeans were all allowed to build their own temples and churches in China at a time when in the West Franks and Saracens were busy slaughtering each other as infidels. At the same time the native Chinese religions of Taoism and Confucianism continued to flourish. In the ninth century they prevailed over the 'foreign' creeds which were actually banned in the year 845.

But in the meantime a new and terrible religion had arrived on the Silk Road, bringing destruction and death. For centuries the civilised world of Rome, Greece and Byzantium had had good reason to fear the barbarians of the north. Now they were attacked from the south by the tent-dwelling followers of Muhammad. The King of Persia fled to China and the Arabs took control of the silk trade. For the Arabs, like everybody else, were beguiled by the softness and sheen of silk garments, and the market expanded. Strictly speaking, Muslims should not wear silk. The Prophet had a horror of luxury and once tore off a silken gown while praying, overcome with revulsion. But his followers soon lost this inhibition, and the stories of the *Arabian Nights* often describe in detail the beautiful costumes of the heroes and heroines, made of rich brocade and cloth-of-gold. Soon there were Chinese silk weavers working in Baghdad, capital of the Caliphate.

By the ninth century the merchandise of the Silk Road was travelling through a new empire in Central Asia, that of the Khazars. This Turkic people had established a large territory north of the Caspian and Black Seas, bounded to the west by the Dnieper and to the east by the Ural river. Its capital, Itil, on the lower Volga, was home to merchants of many nationalities and religions: Persians, now converted to Islam, Greek Christians, Syrian Jews, and pagan Slavs and Vikings from the north who traded in furs. These shaggy creatures were described by the fastidious Persians as 'the most disgusting savages the world has ever seen', which is somewhat reminiscent of what the Chinese had said of the Huns. The Khazars themselves were semi-nomadic and had no distinct civilisation of their own, but they provided a stable region for the transit of caravans, and made a prosperous living from the tolls they exacted. Originally Shamans or spirit-worshippers, they resisted the blandishments of both Christian and Muslim missionaries, but were finally converted to Judaism by refugee Jews from Khorasmia – by then a Muslim area. This was naturally a great help to the Jewish merchants who now ran an international trade network extending from Central Asia to Moorish Spain. For although frequently persecuted in Christian Europe, Jews were at that time tolerated by Muslims, and indeed used by both sides as go-betweens in the silk trade.

Many luxury goods now travelled along the Silk Road. As well as silk, which was always in demand, there was a regular traffic in gold and silver coins, mainly bought by China, incense, perfumes and spices, and precious stones. Pearls from the Persian Gulf, coral from Algeria and emeralds from Africa were all traded in the bazaars of Central Asia. There was also a thriving trade in human flesh, the Caliphate being described by one scholar as 'a bottomless pit swallowing up slaves of all ages, irrespective of race or sex'. The slave-traders were generally Muslims or Jews, and kidnapping was frequently resorted to when prisoners of war failed to meet the demand. The Muslim custom of the harem meant that young women – especially Circassians, Greeks and Slavs – fetched a particularly high price, and there was also a brisk traffic in small boys. But anyone would do, for slave-labour was the standard means of constructing large edifices, propelling ships and keeping armies up to strength.

Like all its predecessors, the empire of the Khazars had its day and was then swept aside, some of its remnants being later absorbed by Kievan Rus, a Christian kingdom which had succeeded the Vikings in Russia. Information about relations between East and West at this time is scanty, although the Chinese Annals of the Sung dynasty mention visits by embassies from Byzantium in 1081 and 1091. Shortly after this the Crusades brought great political changes to the Near East, and control of the trading centres of the eastern Mediterranean – Acre, Tripoli, Beirut, Tyre and Sidon – passed from the hands of the Syrians,

Greeks and Jews to those of the Italians. The merchants of Venice, Genoa and Pisa had long been trying to break the Muslim monopoly of the cloth and spice trades, and the Christian victories in the Levant gave them the opportunity they had been waiting for.

By the time of the Second Crusade in 1146, the Catholic Franks had come to look upon the Orthodox Byzantines as heretics and near-enemies. In the infamous Fourth Crusade of 1204 Constantinople was actually sacked by its supposed allies. Familiarity with the Muslims, on the other hand, had removed some of the fear and mystery, and direct commercial relations between Christendom and Islam had resulted. In fact, while the Crusades were at their height the Genoese had managed to obtain some useful trade concessions from Muslim rulers. Even the Mongol conquest of Central Asia in the thirteenth century did not deter the Italians for long, and the Polo family were soon tramping the Silk Road. Marco Polo took the southern arm around the Taklamakan desert, noting that the road was very sandy and that 'much of the water you find is bitter and bad'. The people were peace-loving merchants who had learned by experience to make themselves scarce when danger threatened:

> When an army passes through the land, the people escape with their wives, children and cattle a distance of two or three days' journey into the sandy waste; and knowing the spots where water is to be had, they are able to live there, and to keep their cattle alive, whilst it is impossible to discover them; for the wind immediately blows the sand over their track.

But the brutal subjugation of so much of Asia by the Mongols had its benefits for travellers, previously at the mercy of brigands, and it was said that a young girl could walk from one end of the Mongol domains to the other with a pot of gold in her hands without being molested.

Kublai Khan, grandson of Genghis, sat on the throne of China from 1260 to 1294 and for the first time the splendours of the Chinese court were seen by Westerners. Not only merchants made their way there, but also monks, for the Emperor's mother was a Nestorian Christian. In fact the new Yuan dynasty was tolerant towards all religions and was a patron of the arts, but the Chinese – with centuries of culture behind them – could never reconcile themselves to these rulers who only a generation before had been barbarians.

The Chinese aristocracy kept aloof from the Mongol ruling class, and the Yuan relied heavily on support from the Muslim states of eastern Turkestan. Trade with Central Asia flourished as a result, but this was to rebound on the merchants when, after a century, the Chinese managed to drive their overlords back to the steppes in 1368. The new Chinese dynasty of the Ming banished the Uighur traders – for so long associated with the hated Mongols – and concentrated on reuniting and consolidating the Chinese nation.

Further west the Mongols were well ensconced in Russia, where they became known as the Tatars, but in Central Asia they had interbred with the Turks. This in turn led to a new race of conquerors and a new empire on the Silk Road – that of Tamerlane. When he first made Samarkand his capital in about 1370 it was still in ruins from Genghis Khan's conquest, but by the time of his death in 1405 it was arguably the most beautiful city in the world. It was also a hub of commerce, and the bazaars crowding its centre were filled with merchants trading spices from India, leather and furs from Tatar Russia, silk from China, rubies from the Pamirs, turquoises from Persia and pearls from the Gulf, as well as the luscious produce of Samarkand's own market gardens.

During the course of the fourteenth century most of the Mongols and Turko-Mongols were converted to Islam, and the militancy of the new religion began to alarm China. Tamerlane, even in old age, was in Marlowe's words a 'monster that hath drunk a sea of blood, and yet gapes still for more to quench his thirst', and was preparing a campaign against China when he died in 1405. The Uighurs, too, were becoming aggressive, and Turfan began to wage war on any neighbouring oases which were still, like Hami, Buddhist. The Ming dynasty took fright, and towards the end of the fifteenth century slammed the door and banned all caravans from 'Uighuristan' from entering China.

The great days of the Silk Road had come to an end, for its *raison d'être* had disappeared. China was now a closed country, Rome had long gone, and Byzantium had fallen to the Ottoman Turks in 1453. The south China coast was infested with Japanese pirates, but in any case silk was now produced in Europe, which had emerged from the Middle Ages and was entering its Renaissance. Lyons was the new centre of the silk trade. Naturally there was still trade in Central Asia, and even Ming China kept up limited relations with the Uighurs of Turfan, who provided the blue dye for their porcelain. But there was no longer any 'through traffic' and commerce was reduced to the mainly local. Anthony Jenkinson, a merchant from the City of London, had high hopes of selling woollen cloth to China in the sixteenth century, but got no further than Bokhara. Although Ivan the Terrible had defeated the Tatars in Russia and Jenkinson had been warmly welcomed in Muscovy, Central Asia had become a perilous place for outsiders, and the Englishman's experiences east of the Caspian were enough to discourage any European from going there for a very long time.

For about 300 years the region continued to be a sort of no man's land, ruled by an assortment of petty despots whose main occupation was waging war on one another. Few Europeans went there by choice, although numerous Russians had the misfortune to be abducted from the borderlands and end up in the slave markets of Bokhara and Khiva. The seventeenth century saw a number of severe earthquakes, and Samarkand was so badly affected that its inhabitants fled, leaving it deserted for a hundred years. Some of the great monuments of the Silk Road were thus destroyed yet again, while others simply fell into neglect and disrepair. Further east, the oases of the Tarim Basin were reclaimed for China in the eighteenth century by the successors to the Ming dynasty, the conquering Manchus, but there was little to be seen by then of their Silk Road glory.

It was only in the nineteenth century, when suddenly Central Asia acquired a political significance, that Europeans began to travel there again. As Tsarist Russia and British India expanded, they found themselves separated only by this unmapped region inhabited by wild tribesmen. Both sides set about surveying the passes, and sending 'friendly' missions to the native rulers, and in the course of all this the crumbling splendour of the old caravan cities of the Silk Road was gradually revealed. By the 1890s, when Russia had constructed a railway across her newly annexed territories of Transcaspia and Turkestan, Western visitors were able to see in relative comfort the ruins of Merv, the caravanserais of Bokhara and the cracked blue domes of Samarkand.

At about the same time European archaeologists began to venture into Chinese Turkestan, where the Muslim population had been augmented by Han Chinese communities deliberately planted there by the Manchu administration. The southern branch of the old Silk Road, linking the oases of the Tarim Basin with the bazaars of northern India, was still in use, and there were communities of Indian traders to be found in Kashgar, Yarkand and Khotan. Merchants from Andijan – now part of Russia – brought their goods to all the northern oases stretching from Kashgar to Urumchi, and both Russia and Britain posted representatives in Kashgar to look after their countries' commercial and diplomatic interests. They were also helpful to the archaeologists who now began to excavate some of the ancient sites, many long abandoned and half-buried in the Taklamakan desert. Although they knew that an ancient Buddhist civilisation had preceded the Islamic one, their discoveries exceeded their wildest dreams. They soon unearthed Buddhist, Manichaean and Nestorian shrines, and centuries-old manuscripts documenting daily life in the towns and garrisons of the early days of the Silk Road.

They have since been criticised for removing vast quantities of wall-paintings, objects and manuscripts from Central Asia, leaving many sites completely denuded. But as a result, examples of the wonderful early art of the Silk Road can now be seen in all the great museums of the world.

TASHKENT
Tsarist Bridgehead

Tashkent ... refuge of damaged reputations and shattered fortunes.

Lord Curzon

It was nearly midnight when I started out to explore. In the old town the dimly-lighted *chai-khanas* opening on the street were still filled with squatting Uzbeks and from all sides the flat native drums throbbed rhythmically in the warm Eastern-smelling darkness.

Fitzroy Maclean

A T FIRST GLANCE Tashkent, capital of Uzbekistan and once the fourth largest city of the Soviet Union, seems of little interest, but for the visitor who knows something of its colourful history there is much to stir the imagination. It may be hard today to picture it as a caravan town on the Silk Road, but it is in fact one of the oldest cities of Central Asia, although it has been destroyed and rebuilt countless times in its 2,000-year history. The most recent in this long line of calamities was the disastrous earthquake of 1966, which is to blame for the city's 'new-town' appearance. But it had been razed to the ground even more effectively in earlier times by successive waves of conquerors who periodically descended on it. It had the misfortune to lie in the path of all the great east-west population migrations, and its status as a wealthy entrepôt for merchants of silk, cotton, furs, rugs, spices, perfumes and gemstones made it an irresistible target. It was always rebuilt, however, once the marauders were well clear, for its climate and situation were ideal. Tashkent stands in the valley of the Chirchik, whose glacier-fed waters cascade down from the Tien-shan

(Celestial) mountains on their way to join the meandering Syr-darya, and it has always been renowned for its fertility. Plant a fence-post in Tashkent, it has been said, and it will soon sprout leaves.

Tashkent – meaning stone castle – was first referred to by its present name in the eleventh century, when it was an outpost of the Arab Caliphate. The Muslim conquest of Central Asia in the eighth century was good for trade, for although the Prophet had disapproved of rich garments the Arabs – like the Romans and Byzantines – grew greedy for silk. Caravans from China passed through the northern foothills of the Tien-shan to reach Tashkent, and then proceeded to Samarkand, Bokhara and Merv. The era of the Crusades also gave a boost to the luxurious products of the silk trade, and the Frankish kingdoms of the Levant became eager customers. But all this came to an abrupt end in the early thirteenth century when the Arab Caliphate was in its turn trampled under foot by the dread horsemen of Genghis Khan. Tashkent was despoiled and then destroyed. As usual, however, it rose phoenix-like from its ashes, and became the northern stronghold of Tamerlane's mighty empire during the fourteenth century, and on his death in 1405 it was bequeathed to his 10-year-old grandson, Ulugh Beg.

Tamerlane's cities, with their dazzling tiled domes and minarets, were the glory of the Silk Road, and despite all its vicissitudes Tashkent still has buildings in its old quarter which date back to the Timurid period. Perhaps if Tamerlane had lived to achieve his dream of conquering China, the Silk Road would have survived longer, but it was at this time that China shut its doors firmly on the West. The Ming dynasty, having driven its Yuan predecessors back to the northern steppes, concentrated on consolidating and unifying the Chinese nation, which had fallen apart as the Mongol Yuan began to lose their grip. The Central Asian mercenaries who had helped the Yuan to keep control were thrown out, and even Muslim merchants from territories to the west were now regarded as enemies, associated with the long years of subjugation.

Tashkent, and all the other caravan towns, saw a sudden falling-off of trade, and a gradual decline in prosperity, for the bales of precious silk could not now be replaced. In the sixteenth century the city was once more ransacked by an invader from the north – Shaybani Khan, leader of the nomadic Uzbek Turks, who were to give their name to the whole region. Tashkent adapted to this new overlord and built up its wealth again, and so the pattern continued. By the nineteenth century Central Asia in general had become a backwater, untouched by the currents of progress, for the fanatical mullahs practised a debased form of Islam which abhorred enlightenment and welcomed hatred and repression. A blind eye was turned to the depravity and cruelty of the rulers, and to their rapacious campaigns against one another. Tashkent, as a prosperous trading city, was for ever at the mercy of the predatory rulers of Khiva, Bokhara and Khokhand, its merchants being obliged to pay a hefty tribute to whoever was affording them 'protection' at the time.

Some of the bolder spirits amongst them began to look towards Russia for their salvation, for while Central Asia had declined, its northern neighbour had become a great imperial power. It was also beginning to industrialise, and was looking for new markets. A cautious trade developed between Tashkent and Orenburg, the last outpost of European Russia. But the mullahs of Tashkent looked to holy Bokhara for support and were implacably opposed to any dealings with Christians. Pulled one way by the merchants and the other by the mullahs, the city's elders found themselves in a painful dilemma. Russia, in the person of Major-General Mikhail Cherniaev, decided to settle the matter by capturing the city in June 1865.

He was taking quite a risk, for he had not bothered to ask St Petersburg for permission, and he had barely 2,000 men with him. As it happened Tashkent's inhabitants put up a far more determined resistance than he had anticipated, but in the end his superior tactics – and his artillery – won the day. Rather than see their city destroyed totally, the elders decided to submit, conferring on their conqueror the flattering title 'Lion of Tashkent'. Faced with a successful *fait accompli*, the Tsar graciously accepted the city and its environs as an addition to his domains, seeing that it greatly enhanced his prestige in the region and gave Russia a foothold in 'closed barbaric Asia'. A substantial Russian town soon sprang up beside the native one, run by a predominantly military administration. Although Russia's avowed policy at this time was solely to safeguard its southern borders against 'those whose turbulent and unsettled character make them undesirable neighbours', in practice Tashkent was to be the springboard for a relentless drive into the desert khanates. 'Where the ruling class is entirely military,' remarked Lord Curzon, 'and where promotion is slow, it would be strange if war, the sole available avenue to distinction, were not popular.'

The architect of Russia's conquest of Central Asia was General Konstantin Kaufmann, for Cherniaev was regarded as too impetuous and was swiftly recalled, much to his chagrin. Kaufmann lived in considerable style, having a magnificent residence built to his specifications, and he was later criticised in St Petersburg for squandering government funds on needless extravagance. However, Russians of German extraction were always the target of malicious allegations by the Slavophil lobby, so perhaps there was a certain element of envy at work here. For there was no gainsaying Kaufmann's achievements: within ten years he had subjugated Samarkand, Bokhara, Khiva and Khokhand, and had himself become the Governor-General of a vast new Russian province. Turkestan was about half the size of the United States of America, and the now huge Russian empire was 1,000 miles nearer to British India than it had been at the beginning of the century. There was a certain amount of disquiet internationally about Russia's prodigious rate of expansion, and the forgotten region of Central Asia was suddenly under the spotlight.

A diplomat who managed to visit Tashkent in 1873 was the American Eugene Schuyler. General Kaufmann was away conquering Khiva at the time, but Schuyler reported with relish some of the gossip about him:

> The Governor-General or Yarim Padshah (the half-king), as he is called, imitates in the state he keeps the Eastern monarchs by whom he is surrounded. He never rides out, so I am told, without a select guard of Cossacks, and even his wife and children had their escorts ... When the Governor-General returns to Tashkent triumphal arches are erected, all the officials go several miles out of the city to meet him, and he is received with salutes of cannon. The triumphal arches and the receptions are supposed to be the outspoken expressions of popular feeling, but these demonstrations are hardly spontaneous.
>
> Schuyler, *Turkistan*, 1876

Schuyler found New Tashkent a pleasant enough place, with its broad, tree-lined streets and small white villas. In fact it reminded him somewhat of Denver, Colorado. But he noted that 'no-one lives here who is not obliged to do so on account of his official duties. No-one comes to Tashkent to remain …' There was the usual Russian Club, where 'a bad dinner can be had every day', and where balls and concerts were held. To his surprise he found an excellent library attached to the clubrooms, containing 'an exceedingly good collection of books and articles relating to Central Asia' as well as the standard works of European literature. Not that Tashkent was a literary sort of place – far from it. It was at this time a small provincial capital riddled with the usual snobbery and cliqueishness of such places. 'The officers have little resource but gambling and drinking,' wrote Schuyler, 'and in many instances young men have utterly ruined themselves, some even having to be sent out of the country – and a man *must* be bad to be exiled from Tashkent – and others having died or committed suicide.' He was impressed, however, by the standard of law and order in both the old and new towns. 'Crimes are very rare,' he noted, 'and it is possible to walk or ride through any part of Tashkent at any hour of the night without incurring the slightest danger.'

This was certainly a change from the bad old days when the Central Asian cities were a byword for sudden death. But Stephen Graham, writing much later, lamented the inevitable decline of the old town. In his book *Through Russian Central Asia*, published in 1916, he says:

> With the coming of the Russians, the angel of death has breathed on all that was once the grandeur of the Orient at Tashkent. Once there were no Russians in the land, and then what is now old Tashkent was the only Tashkent – it was a great Moslem city. But as the fine Russian streets were laid down, and the large shops opened, and the cathedrals were built, and the gardens laid out, the old uphill-and-down-dale labyrinth of the Eastern city changed to a curiosity and an anachronism. It faded before the eyes … Poor old Tashkent, there is much pathos in its destiny.

At the time of Schuyler's visit in 1873 the old Muslim town was still a thriving place, and the American estimated its population at about 120,000. Most were Uzbeks, but there were also Tajiks,

Kirghiz, Tatars – or Mongols – and even Hindus. The residents were collectively known as Sarts, but this was not a nationality, simply signifying that they were settled as opposed to nomadic. Schuyler thought that Tashkent showed more variety than any other Central Asian town, partly because of its hilly terrain and rushing streams, and partly because of its verdure. 'Everywhere trees are leaning over the walls, for everywhere there are gardens,' he wrote. The fertility and luxuriance of Tashkent's gardens resulted from the proximity of the Chirchik river. Sixteen miles above the city at the village of Niazbek, now the site of a hydro-electric power station, a canal had been dug in antiquity to bring an abundance of water to the settlement, and had been patiently repaired each time it was destroyed by invaders. For water was Tashkent's lifeblood.

Not all European visitors saw old Tashkent with Stephen Graham's romantic eyes. The Sart houses, arranged around internal courtyards, had no windows at all on the outside, which gave them a strange, secretive air to Western eyes. 'Great masses of baked mud, which we dimly perceive to be meant for houses, tower up as if to crush us in their fall', was how special correspondent David Ker described them. 'Viewed from above,' wrote Lord Curzon, 'we see nothing but an inclined plane of dusty roofs, the dearth of colour making it as ugly as are most Oriental towns from the panoramic point of view. The real interest and individuality are confined to the streets and, could we but penetrate their interiors, to the houses.' Schuyler, who had introductions to a number of important native families, was able to do this. He and his companion went to call on a merchant named Doda Mohammed:

> Eventually we arrive at a small door which is half open. On calling out, three handsome lads in long loose shirts, girt with handkerchiefs round the waist, and close-fitting skull-caps, appear with smiling faces, greet us and take our horses. We enter, and find a large courtyard nearly surrounded with sheds filled with horses – the only kind of stable which is used here. We are taken through another door onto still another courtyard, on two sides of which are the balconies of the house. This is the *tish-kari* or man's court, and beyond, through a door and a narrow passage, is the *itch-kari* or

woman's court. Doda Mohammed, being rich, has as many as three courtyards, but no-one who pretends to have a house at all has less than two. For the women must have some place where they can be at their ease, and where men do not enter.

As an American, and a diplomat accredited to St Petersburg, Schuyler encountered few problems in Tashkent once he had convinced the authorities that he was not an English spy. For the Russians were very keen to keep any British observers well away from Turkestan while they quietly incorporated the Khanate of Khiva into their empire. David Ker, correspondent of the *Daily Telegraph*, fell foul of these military regulations (in spite of arming himself with a false American passport), and ended up in Tashkent a frustrated and disappointed man. During months of traipsing around desert and steppe, suffering privation, illness and persecution, he had always found himself prevented from catching up with General Kaufmann's forces. At least in Tashkent, he hoped, he would not be ejected or imprisoned, and he might even get a bath.

At length, through all the surroundings of the genuine East – massive walls standing up white and bare in the blistering sunshine, turbaned greybeards squatting in the shadow of low-browed archways, and tapering trees outlined against the blue summer sky – we reach a great rampart of baked earth, pass through the gate, and are in Tashkent. It is Friday, 15th August 1873, and I am four thousand miles east of England, having travelled, one way and another, seven thousand four hundred and forty miles since I left London on 8th March.

Ker, *On the Road to Khiva*, 1874

The 'dismal' hotel, however, reminded him of a deserted stable, having no food, no drink, no furniture and no bath. The mail awaiting him at the Post Office brought him no comfort: his editor was not interested in excuses, why was he not at Khiva? 'My reward', fumed Ker, 'for six months of anxiety, illness, imprisonment, and subterfuge worse than all – is the credit, in my own country and among my own people, of being a liar and a villain.' After posting off an indignant dispatch, he hired a droshky and Cossack driver and ventured into the old town 'through dust, and heat, and dogs and offal, and all the loathsome minutiae of a genuine Eastern town'. Forced to abandon his cab once he reached the maelstrom of the Great Bazaar, he plunged

> into the welter of strange figures – gaunt dervishes, with the brand of the desert still upon them; veiled women, imprisoned in close-fitting umbrella-cases of blue cotton; greasy pastry-cooks, over whom the flies swarm with a comfortable assurance of congenial pasture; shaggy porters waddling under huge baskets; brown paunchy children, in the minimum of clothing and the maximum of dirt; and bare-limbed water-carriers, poising their bulging skins on their brawny shoulders, like caricatures of Atlas.

Ker soon departed for England, eager to rescue his reputation and to write his book. Kaufmann, the author of his misfortunes, returned victorious from his campaign, and life in Tashkent returned to normal. The foundations for a splendid new cathedral were laid, not far from the old wooden Orthodox church, but Kaufmann did not live to see it completed. He died in 1882 and was buried with due pomp in a garden nearby. The central square of the Russian town was named after him, and a large statue erected in his memory. The traveller Stephen Graham described it in 1914:

> The Kaufmann Square is, I suppose, the noblest position in the new city, all the avenues and prospects being used to frame the monument which stands there. This is the statue of General Kaufmann, who took possession of the land for the Russians. On one side of the monument is a fierce, dark, enormous, two-headed eagle in stone. But between its claws this year a dove had its nest. From behind the eagle General von Kaufmann stands and looks over his new-conquered country. On the other side of the monument there is the following inscription: 'I pray you bury me here that everyone may know that here is true Russian earth in which no Russian need be ashamed to lie.' Rather interesting that this should be said by a Russian with a German name.

A later visitor, Colonel F.M. Bailey, watched the Bolsheviks demolish this monument in 1919. The square was then renamed Revolution Square.

General Cherniaev, having triumphantly outlived his detested rival, was at last given the post he had long coveted, that of Governor-General of Turkestan. He hastened to Tashkent and set about dismantling as many of Kaufmann's achievements as possible, ostensibly to save money for the Tsar. The library could go, for a start, he decided. Many of the books were by dangerously radical writers, and there were even humorous journals and popular newspapers lying around. A few books were deemed worthy of preservation and removed to the museum, but thousands of volumes were dispersed, some ending up in the bazaar. Kaufmann's sophisticated chemical laboratory was the next victim of his economy drive, followed by the silkworm-breeding and experimental cotton farms.

After a couple of years of intemperate behaviour and public outcry, Cherniaev was hurriedly recalled to St Petersburg and pensioned off. 'You quarrelled with everyone,' sighed Tsar Alexander. 'You could not remain there.' His successor, General Rosenbach, was reputed to know 'as little about Turkestan as about Zululand', but he smoothed ruffled feathers by reinstating the library and the farms, and set about recovering the laboratory equipment which was by now scattered all over the old town, much of it broken. His economies seem to have been more effective than those of Cherniaev, moreover, for he reduced Turkestan's budget deficit by 28 per cent.

In 1888 the Honourable George Curzon stayed with General Rosenbach after an extensive tour of Central Asia via the new Transcaspian railway. He was entertained very simply – an improvement, Curzon felt, on the 'reckless extravagance which used formerly to prevail' – in the residence built for Kaufmann. He was impressed by the garden:

> Behind the Government House at Tashkent extends a beautiful garden, in which a military band plays, and to which the public are admitted three times a week. It contains shaded walks and sylvan retreats, a respectable cascade formed by an artificial dam, and a pit for bears, which was kept filled by Cherniaev, who had a craze for animals, until one of his pets nearly bit off the leg of a Kirghiz.
>
> Curzon, *Russia in Central Asia*, 1889

As yet, Tashkent was not connected to the Transcaspian line, and Curzon had to travel across the Hungry Steppe from Samarkand – a distance of 380 miles – in the standard Russian conveyance, a tarantass. This 'sorrowful and springless vehicle' reminded Curzon of a ramshackle wooden boat on wheels, and he confessed to hankering after his second-class railway compartment 'as eagerly as did the Israelites in similar surroundings after the flesh-pots of Egypt'. But it was only a matter of time, he predicted, before the railway line was extended, for strategic reasons if nothing else. For this was the era of the Great Game, and Curzon was typical of his generation in suspecting Russia of casting covetous eyes in the direction of India.

By the time that Miss Annette Meakin visited Tashkent in the winter of 1901, Curzon's prophecy had come true: she and her elderly mother arrived at Tashkent's new station, and not in one of Curzon's ordinary second-class compartments, either. The station-master at Ashkhabad had charmingly insisted on providing a 'special' carriage for their exclusive use, an honour indeed. In a few years' time, he told them, they would be able to travel to Tashkent in a far more expeditious manner, for a new railway line was being built from Orenburg which would bring the former caravan town to within three days' journey of Moscow.

Miss Meakin, musician, classicist and Fellow of the Anthropological Institute, had already made a study of the Tatars of Kazan and the Crimea (the remnants of the Mongol Golden Horde), the tribes of northern Siberia, and the Muslims of Morocco, Egypt, Turkey and Palestine. She had been the first Englishwoman to cross Siberia by the new Trans-Siberian railway in 1900, and went on to become a prolific author. Arriving in the depths of winter, the Meakins found Old Tashkent an impossible place to explore on foot:

> The streets are paved by nature with the same clay as that with which the houses are built, so that they are inches deep in powdery dust in summer, and covered with an even greater depth of oozy mud in winter. Of all the towns I saw at this season Tashkent was certainly the richest in mud. On one occasion when we were visiting two of the wealthiest families in the native town, who lived in the same street exactly

opposite each other, we had to get into the droshky to cross the road. Had we attempted it on foot the mud would have reached above our knees.

Meakin, *In Russian Turkestan*, 1903

During her year in Central Asia Miss Meakin was able to study the local women in the privacy of their own homes, and was even permitted to photograph them unveiled. The creatures who to male travellers seemed merely a shapeless mass of draperies, veiled in black horsehair and shod in clumsy boots, turned out often to be young and pretty. They all had glowing complexions, and indignantly denied that they ever used cosmetics, except on their eyebrows, which were frequently joined in a straight line over the nose:

> I was told by the ladies of Tashkent that it was the custom there for every woman to dye her eyebrows in summer with the juice of a particular plant that grows in the gardens. When the juice is fresh it dyes a dark green, but they do not mind that, as it is considered to impart brightness to the eyes, besides making the brows thicker.

She was amazed at the length of their hair, which hung to their ankles in numerous long plaits, finished off with a tassel of brightly coloured glass beads. 'One girl graciously allowed me to count her plaits,' wrote Miss Meakin. 'She had fifty-five long plaits, and all her own hair.' Those less well-endowed by nature extended their plaits with strands of black silk. Girls were always married very young, in line with the Sart proverb: 'Do not keep salt long or it will get damp. Do not keep a young girl or she will spoil.' Perhaps as a result, there was an appallingly high rate of infant mortality, for many mothers were little more than children themselves:

> Families are very numerous, sixteen children is not an unusual number for one mother, but she seldom rears more than half of them. Many young mothers die, and their babies too, for want of a skilled woman to attend to them ... A large proportion of children die because their girl-mothers have no notion how to look after them.

Miss Meakin made many Russian friends in Tashkent who showed her great kindness and hospitality, for by then it was no longer the 'punishment posting' it had been in the days of Schuyler and Curzon. Russian colonial rule, although paternalistic, had brought certain advantages to the ordinary people. The introduction of American long-staple cotton (thanks to Kaufmann's experimental farm) had increased their yields, and an impartial system of justice and a reasonable level of taxation had given them security from the extortions of the corrupt old khans, while the abolition of slavery had literally freed many of them from bondage. The early Russian colonists were often dedicated men who were on excellent terms with the local population. But the start of the new century had seen an influx of settlers of an entirely different stamp, who were resented by the early settlers and the natives alike.

Lured by grants of land, the impoverished, the unsuccessful and the plain greedy flocked to Turkestan from central Russia in search of a better life in an agreeable climate. 'They had no wish to work hard, were not interested in improved methods of husbandry, and looked down upon the hardworking and disciplined natives,' declared Count Pahlen. However, they served the government's purpose of ridding central Russia of its surplus rural population and simultaneously of Russifying an outlying region of the empire. Sadly, the proliferation of bureaucracy required to administer these new crown lands, not to mention the construction of the Orenburg-Tashkent rail link, led to a falling-off of the previous high standards, and by 1908 Turkestan was a byword for corruption.

So worried was Tsar Nicholas II that he dispatched Count Pahlen to the region in June 1908 with sweeping powers to investigate all aspects of the administration, and to prosecute offenders. A Baltic aristocrat of German extraction, Pahlen was enlightened, liberal, energetic and very thorough. This was a severe blow to the slack and venal officials of Turkestan, who tried in vain to pull the wool over his eyes. For a year he and a hand-picked group of assistants toured the province systematically, examining the books, interviewing both civil servants and native elders, and making exhaustive notes. His final report ran to nineteen volumes.

Pahlen sailed down the Volga to Samara (later renamed Kubyshev) and there transferred to the railway. As they travelled east the country grew ever more desolate, until at last it became a salty desert with an occasional camel on the horizon. At wayside stations they were gazed at – contemptuously, Pahlen felt – by slant-eyed Kalmyks in shaggy fur caps. 'I had my first glimpse', he wrote later, 'of that peculiar subtlety with which the Asian regards the European. What I believe to be genuine contempt is veiled by an appearance of outward submission that somehow suggests inner awareness of a culture and an outlook on life vastly older than our own.' (The Kalmyks are a Mongolian race, and therefore indirectly descended from Genghis Khan.)

Two days out of Orenburg, the Count was startled to see ships, apparently sailing over the steppe. They had reached the Aral Sea, at that time an immense expanse of water, though now sadly depleted by over-use for irrigation. 'After leaving the station called "The Sea of Aral" behind us,' wrote Pahlen, 'we were cheered by the view of the snow-covered summits of the Kara-Tau gradually rising on the horizon. From this time on I never once, during my entire sojourn in Turkestan, lost sight of mountains in the distance.'

The railway line between the Aral Sea and Tashkent had been built alongside the Syr-darya river, in spite of persistent warnings by local people. Now, to his annoyance, the Count discovered that a section of line had been washed away by a flash flood. He, his party and all their baggage had to be transported across the gap in 'a tiresome operation of trolleys and boats', and then had to wait while a new train was hastily sent to fetch them. There must have been some red faces in Tashkent, where officials were already awaiting him with considerable nervousness.

The Governor-General evidently decided that a sumptuous reception might mollify his powerful visitor, for Pahlen was greeted by an elaborate welcoming ceremony. Magnificent oriental carpets had been strewn on the railway platform, and a huge silken marquee erected over tables groaning with refreshments. Numerous delegations came to pay their respects and there were interminable speeches, all in a temperature of 130 degrees Fahrenheit. At the banquet given that evening in his honour at Government House, Pahlen was struck by the incongruity of this very European occasion in the middle of Central Asia:

> The women were in low-cut evening gowns with sparkling jewels and flowers in their hair. One would have found the same setting anywhere in St Petersburg, Berlin, Vienna or

Friday prayers in the Tilla Kari Medresseh, Samarkand

On the steps of the Shir Dar Mosque

The tomb of Tamerlane, Samarkand

The ruins of the Medresseh of Bibi Khanum

Looking towards the ruins of Bibi Khanum from Shah Zindeh

Stairs leading to the mausoleum of Shah Zindeh

The tiled facade of the mausoleum of Shah Zindeh

Colonade of wooden pillars in the Bokhara mosque

Paris. Even the flowers on the dining table – roses, white acacia, violets, lovely tulips and daffodils – were reminiscent of home. The fare we were offered, too, was anything but oriental. The menus, printed in French, informed us that we were to be served with a dinner of six or seven courses equal to anything we could have expected at home, while the champagne and other wines were all imported from Europe.

But when, after dinner, we moved into the garden where coffee was served, we were at once back in Asia, with its pitch-black night and the myriad stars of the Milky Way, with the all-pervading din of crickets, the murmuring water in the canals, the bitter taste of the scent-laden desert air which makes the heart beat faster, although it seems so light, since Tashkent lies 600 metres above sea level.

The enchanting garden of the Residence had been turned into a fairyland by candles and coloured lanterns. Noiselessly, the Sart servants glided among the guests, their white caftans, embroidered skull-caps and bright silk sashes catching the light. 'The formal black of European evening dress,' mused Pahlen, 'and even the pretty gowns of the ladies, seemed somehow out of place in this oriental setting.' He went on:

As I looked at the assembled guests I found myself wondering what we Europeans had brought this land, apart from perhaps a little ease and a few technical means of livelihood. Were the people happier before the Europeans stepped in? Was the advent of the soldier, the European engineer and technician to engender a ferment of disintegration destined eventually to destroy the souls of the people together with their ethical and moral standards?

Alas, Count Pahlen was a man ahead of his time. Although he succeeded in rooting out a good deal of corruption in the Turkestan administration – the Governor-General who had entertained him so lavishly at Tashkent was one of the first to resign – his broader recommendations were quietly ignored. This was not surprising since the Prime Minister, Stolypin, was a firm advocate of colonisation. Pahlen lost everything eight years later in the Bolshevik coup: his estates in Latvia and, worse, his library and all his notes and photographs from his year in Turkestan. He died, a poor refugee in Germany, in 1923, but not before dictating his memoirs to a member of his family. (*Mission to Turkestan, 1908–1909*, was published in English only in 1964, and it is from this work that the above extracts are taken.)

When the dust had settled after the Pahlen investigation, life resumed much as before in Tashkent. The allotment of land to Russian settlers – opposed by the Count because it deprived the local populace of their livelihood – proceeded amid growing resentment. Glittering balls continued to be given by the socially prestigious, to the mortification of the socially inferior, and in 1914, when the writer and anthropologist Ella Christie was there, 'European life was quite gay'. The Russians entertained lavishly, and there was a 'very fine' winter theatre, as well as an outdoor summer one, with regular visits by travelling dramatic companies. The roads in the Russian town had by now been macadamised, and were all bordered with acacia, poplar or elm trees, with rills of water running between them. Mrs Christie wrote:

> The chief streets have an imposing aspect, from the number of large and fine houses with which they are lined, many of them standing apart in their own walled-in gardens. The roofing of the houses generally consists of felt or painted iron. The interior both of the Russian and Sart houses is lighted by excellent petrol lamps of from five to twenty-six candle-power, and similar lamps also illuminate the streets, though after the electric station was installed for the tramway service electric light was gradually introduced, and a telephone service was in full working order.
>
> Christie, *Through Khiva to Golden Samarkand*, 1925

Although Stephen Graham, who visited Tashkent in the same year as Ella Christie, deplored the Russification of this Central Asian city, Mrs Christie pointed out that there were now hospitals and dispensaries where the Sarts could take their children to be vaccinated, and even X-rayed, and that lepers no longer lived in the midst of the healthy but had their own village and land. In the old town, however, there was still a weekly marriage market, where Kirghiz parents sold their little daughters of 9 to 12 years to the highest bidder. Mrs Christie was saddened at the spectacle, but noted that the girls seemed to feel 'no more concern than a puppy would on being transferred to a new master'. Girls were not highly regarded by the nomads.

Stephen Graham, who was there in May 1914, found the old city ablaze with colour. 'On the roofs of the mosques are thousands of red poppies in bloom,' he wrote, 'and occasionally the crane's nest is to be seen on the tops of the towers whence the muezzin calls to prayer.' He described the Sarts as 'an absolutely unambitious people, honest, quiet, sober. They are uninterested in everything except small deals in the wares they make or sell'. The underlying dissatisfaction of a subject people was evidently not apparent to the casual visitor. Neither did Graham or Ella Christie come into contact with the Russian working class, or suspect for one moment that within three years society would be torn apart. Graham went so far as to predict that 'the friendship of English and Russians in Central Asia must mean a larger, stronger life for both Empires'. But what they could not have known was that as early as 1905 an underground branch of the Social Revolutionary Party had been formed among the large contingent of railway workers based in Tashkent. The trickle of dangerous new ideas which arrived in Turkestan via the railway line from Russia gradually became a flood, and in October 1917 when the Bolsheviks seized power in the capital, the Tashkent revolutionaries were quick to follow suit.

A mob stormed the Residence, murdered the Governor-General and flung his corpse out of an upstairs window. It was only after several days that his widow was permitted to remove his remains for burial. In four days of rioting and bloodshed, most of the former Tsarist officials were either summarily executed or imprisoned by the newly formed Cheka, or secret police, and a witch-hunt of 'counter-revolutionary elements' was unleashed. The native population stood aside and waited to see whether the promised freedom and equality would apply to them. It soon became clear that they would not. The revolutionary government was composed entirely of Europeans, mainly railway navvies, and their attitude to the local people was as colonial as that of their predecessors. Resentment simmered in the old town, and things finally came to a head on Boxing Day, 1917. A Danish diplomat watched anxiously:

The long-expected and much-apprehended Sart revolution broke out at last – that is to say, it started as a general demonstration against the politics of the Government. The Sarts had gathered in large numbers, about 200,000, the whole of the street looking like a billowing sea of white turbans, many-coloured silk *talars*, green and light blue silk standards by the thousand. The whole procession, among which were a large number of mounted men, thronged and swarmed in the direction of the Government palace – fantastic and resplendent, like a scene from the *Arabian Nights* ... What would happen? As by a sudden flash of intuition, one glimpsed the terrible abyss between European and Asian culture, and the fundamental difference between European and Asiatic minds. Never before had the hatred against Russia been so livid as now.

A.H. Brun, *Troublous Times*, 1931

But despite their vastly superior numbers, the Sarts were disorganised and had no real leaders. When they stormed the jail and released the old Tsarist officers and other political prisoners, greeting many of them with affectionate cheers, the Tashkent Commissars decided that the natives must be crushed. Cannon and machine-gun fire soon dispersed the mob, with many casualties. As for the released Russians, most were recaptured and executed, on the grounds that they were the secret instigators of the riot. Similar revolts in other parts of Turkestan were also put down with great severity.

Captain Alfred Brun, as a representative of a neutral power, had the unenviable task of trying to persuade the Commissars now running Tashkent to look after the starving Austro-Hungarian prisoners-of-war who were held in camps in Turkestan. A Swedish colleague was trying to do the same for the German prisoners. Brun knew that in 1916 there had been 190,000 prisoners and that there were now thought to be around 40,000. Some had been moved to Siberia, but vast numbers had died of neglect and sickness. The Troitsky camp, just outside Tashkent, was known as 'the death camp'. Its cemetery contained over 8,000 graves. There was also a special 'punishment camp', mainly for officers, which Brun described as hell upon earth, where even the strongest minds could be toppled into insanity. 'I shall never forget', he wrote, 'the enthusiastic reception I got in this camp, simply because the prisoners realized that, after all, there was still somebody who would try to lighten the pressure of their ghastly circumstances.'

The Commissars took the view that the Great War had nothing to do with them, and if the prisoners cared to join the Red Army they would be fed, otherwise they could fend for themselves. This attitude was strenuously opposed by Brun and the other relief workers, but many prisoners did enlist, simply to better their lot. They proved very useful to the Bolsheviks in subduing the natives and fighting the White Russian resistance, and also in suppressing rival revolutionary groups when necessary (see ASHKHABAD). Some of the prisoners, like some of the revolutionaries, were simply freebooters, for both money and goods could be extorted at the point of a gun in these anarchic times. 'I regret to say', wrote Brun, 'that these marauding expeditions were a strong temptation to some of the lower natures among my charges.' Prisoners unwilling to join the Reds began to drift into Tashkent, hoping to find work. Some set up home with Sart women, and a few enterprising Hungarians formed a 'Gypsy Orchestra' and earned a precarious living playing in restaurants.

But the restaurants and shops began to close, for food was running out. The railway line to the north was in the hands of the Whites, while the Transcaspian line to the west was continually being fought over. By the summer of 1918, native parents were abandoning newborn babies to the wolves, cases of cannibalism were reported among the Kirghiz, and Brun's prisoners were dying at the rate of 500 a month. He did his utmost to help them, with no co-operation whatever from the Commissars, who were too busy denouncing each other and struggling for supremacy. There was a rapid turnover: Brun had to deal with ten different Commissars in his eighteen months in Tashkent. 'One of the most deplorable characteristics of the Bolshevist revolution', he later wrote, 'was the inherent distrust exhibited towards anyone who happened to possess a little more culture or knowledge than the rest.' Such men were speedily removed from the government, and usually shot. 'The special qualities at a premium during those times were hatred of the one-time upper classes, vindictiveness on the part of the working classes, coarseness and brutality.'

As Brun's difficulties multiplied daily, his only consolation was the company – in his rare moments of leisure – of a handful of fellow-

Scandinavians, mostly Red Cross workers, and some kind Russian families. The latter, although living in much reduced circumstances under the Bolshevik regime, were delighted to offer rooms to civilised foreigners rather than have their houses requisitioned. As well as welcoming them to their homes, they acted as interpreters and sometimes took considerable risks to help the foreigners if they got into difficulties with the unpredictable Commissars. In letters to his wife Brun referred to the 'charming, hospitable home' of Mr Korotsky, former President of the Supreme Court of Turkestan, and his family, with whom he celebrated Easter. In 1918 the Bolsheviks had not yet succeeded in abolishing religious practices, and all the services of Holy Week were enthusiastically attended:

> Palm Sunday heralded the approach of the Feast, the young people of the city streaming to the church in great numbers, all with a green branch or a cluster of lilacs in their hands. Service over, they returned to their homes in the dusk-hushed calm of the evening, only this time all the young girls carried a lighted taper, which made the whole length of the Pushkinsky appear like a procession of fireflies moving along. Locust flowers and lilac blossoms scented the air, but no breath of wind disturbed the little flame of light in the young girls' hands, and if they managed to reach home with the candle still burning they would find their true loves before Easter came round again.
>
> Then, in the midst of all this beauty and silence, a shot, then another, and then many of them – all coming from the same direction. But the young people on their way home from church did not greatly mind. Had they thought it over, they would have realized that these shots meant the plundering of a house, the destruction of a home. But human feelings are gradually blunted under conditions such as these: each man must look out for himself.

In August Captain Brun's circle was enlarged by the arrival of Colonel F.M. Bailey from British India. He had been sent to discover what the attitude of the Commissars was towards the war. Would they put up any resistance if the Germans and Turks tried to push through Transcaspia to India? Were they, on the contrary, co-operating with German agents around Ashkhabad and sending precious cotton to the Germans? Bailey received a distinctly frosty reception in Tashkent, which was by now dominated by Bolsheviks, for it seemed the British had been helping the Social Revolutionaries of Transcaspia (see ASHKHABAD). Although the Bolsheviks had been delighted to make use of revolutionaries of all descriptions when pushing through their October coup, they were now hell-bent on eradicating any rival factions, and the Tashkent Commissars were waging a ruthless war along the Transcaspian railway.

It soon became clear to Bailey that the Bolsheviks were not going to help the Allies win the war: indeed they became daily more hostile to all the Westerners in Tashkent. Brun's relief funds were soon seized at gunpoint, Bailey was for a while placed under house arrest and so was the young American Consul, Roger Tredwell. In October Bailey received a tip-off that his life was in imminent danger, and with Tredwell's help he managed to disappear. When he had first arrived in Tashkent he had been taken aback – as a British officer – at the sight of so many prisoners-of-war wandering freely around in the field-grey uniforms of the German army. Now he audaciously took on the persona of an Austrian prisoner, complete with false papers, and simply melted into the crowd. His own book, *Mission to Tashkent*, written with a very British understatement, gives an enthralling account of his adventures which are unfortunately beyond the scope of this book.

Early in January 1919, a counter-revolution took place, amid general jubilation and rejoicing, for conditions in Tashkent had reached a nadir. Alfred Brun heard a man reading a proclamation 'informing us all that the tyranny of the Bolsheviks had been broken, and would be succeeded by a new democratic government, bent on securing peace and orderly conditions for the inhabitants of the country'. He was amazed to recognise the man as the former chief of the Cheka. Church bells rang, prisoners were released, and 'joy and satisfaction reigned supreme'. But the celebrations were premature, for the coup had been bungled. 'Had all the different "Fronts" moved at the same time,' wrote Colonel Bailey later, 'there is in my mind no doubt that Bolshevism would have been crushed in Turkestan. But these forces never acted together; difficulties of communication and lack of unison were the causes.' Bailey himself was in no position to help, having broken his leg in the countryside outside Tashkent. As it was, the railway navvies proved the deciding factor. This considerable force of working men had at first supported the new democratic government, but they went over to the Bolsheviks *en masse* when they realised that many of the new leaders wanted to put the clock right back and restore the monarchy.

The triumphant Bolsheviks, back in control, unleashed a new reign of terror and wholesale slaughter. Brun was arrested and thrown into a foul-smelling prison with his Swedish colleague and a Red Cross worker called Johannes Kleberg. There were twenty-five prisoners in the cell when they arrived and others were being added all the time, including women. Night came, and they settled down as best they could. After some hours, Kleberg woke his friends to say goodbye: the guard had told him he was to be released. 'We shook hands and wished him good luck,' wrote Brun. 'That was the last we ever saw of Kleberg. He was shot that night, and his home was sacked, but we did not hear about it till some three days later. Nor did we know at that time that a promise of liberty always means that you will be the next to be shot.' The guards found it more convenient if the victims came quietly. Thanks to the efforts of his Russian friends, Brun and his other companion were released after ten nerve-racking days, during which many of their cell-mates were dragged out and summarily shot. Brun, the father of a teenage daughter, found it unutterably shocking that the self-appointed chief executioner was only a youth. 'It was horrible', he wrote, 'to see a man so young that his face had not yet lost the rounded contours of childhood, filling the part of a hardened executioner without flinching.'

Colonel Bailey meanwhile had slipped back into Tashkent, changing his papers so frequently that he sometimes had difficulty remembering his current name. He dared not sleep more than one night in the same place, and was entirely dependent on his gallant White Russian friends – who took enormous risks to hide him – and a spirited Irish girl, Rosanna Houston, who was governess to one of the Russian families. However, life had its lighter side, even in the revolutionary turmoil of Tashkent. One day an English showman turned up in the town with a troupe of performing elephants, *en route* for India. How on earth they had managed to get there during a world war and a revolution remains a mystery. An aged Serbian fortune-teller also passed through with an equally elderly parrot who would pick out a lucky envelope for you in return for a few coppers. He had spent his life making a meagre living in this way, and had travelled all over China and India. There was also an itinerant Chinese 'dentist' in the old town who, for a small fee, claimed to remove maggots from your teeth with a pair of chopsticks.

As Bailey racked his brains for a way of eluding the Bolsheviks and escaping to India, the end of winter raised his spirits:

> The spring now came on quickly and was very lovely in Tashkent. The streets for many days were scented by the flowers of the acacias which formed the avenues; this is, perhaps, the pleasantest memory I keep of my year in Tashkent. The scented air, deep shade and running water in the streets made one wish that men were not so unkind and that people had leisure and quiet to enjoy it all.

Brun also put his worries aside for a moment to enjoy the spring, despite having been bitten by a stray dog and dreading the possible onset of rabies. (Happily he was spared that horror.)

> How lovely the spring was here in Tashkent! The warm and delightful March winds spread a cloak of green all over the city when they opened the buds. The trees and bushes, especially the almond-trees and peach-trees, were in their glory, and each of the flat clay roofs of the houses in the Sart quarter shone like a purple carpet with wild crocuses, and over the wide streets and on the beautiful open squares, the scent of the locust-tree blossom lingered like incense.

For Brun, if not for Bailey, relief was in sight. The White Russian forces controlling the railway line to Orenburg were eventually beaten back, and Tashkent was once more in communication with the outside world. A special train was arranged by Moscow for the evacuation of foreigners and Brun, Tredwell and the remaining relief workers packed their bags. Rosanna Houston pluckily decided to stay on, feeling that her three young charges – not to mention Eric Bailey – still needed her. It was a courageous decision, for the situation for middle-class Russian families became increasingly unpleasant, and Miss Houston was soon forced to teach in a Soviet school. (In the end she managed to escape, by having herself transferred to Ashkhabad and then fleeing into the Kopet Dagh mountains, where bandits helped her to cross into Persia.)

For Bailey, of course, there was no question of evacuation, for he was still a wanted man. He felt the loss of his friends keenly, but at least both Brun and Tredwell were carrying well-concealed messages from him. One of these eventually found its way to England, to the great relief of Bailey's mother, who had feared the worst after so many months of silence. At Easter in 1919, he slipped into Kaufmann's ornate cathedral and at midnight joined in the joyful cry of 'Christ is risen!' The service, which unknown to the congregation would be the last public celebration of Easter for seventy years, was conducted by the Bishop of Tashkent, 'a very fine high-souled man with great influence for good'. Bailey discovered that he was later shot by the Bolsheviks. He himself was luckier, for he managed to escape in the end (see BOKHARA), disguised as, of all things, a Cheka agent.

It was many years before Tashkent saw another English visitor, but an Austrian prisoner who remained an unwilling resident of the city from 1916 to 1921 wrote this sad description of the run-down capital in a letter to Ella Christie:

> When I arrived in Tashkent it was a garden city of striking beauty, with modern shops, carriages, motor-cars, with the life of a small European capital. What has the October revolution made of Tashkent? Today it is a dead and filthy town, where nothing remains to remind us of her pristine beauty. The shops are all empty and closed, and they have generally been transformed into Soviet offices. The whole trade of the East has come to an end. One never sees those interminable caravans of camels, whose countless processions once filled the streets of Tashkent with their joyful bells. Hotels, restaurants and cafés are equally closed. The tram-cars have ceased to run. There is no more lighting in the streets. Everywhere we have the same picture of destruction and devastation.

At least the trams were running again when Fitzroy Maclean visited the city in 1937, even if they could only be boarded 'after a hand-to-hand fight', with fists, teeth and feet being used freely. Tashkent at this time had a very unsavoury reputation and Maclean, then a young diplomat serving in Moscow, was given a motherly talk by a ticket-collector on his train, warning him of the dangers and temptations to which he was about to be exposed. This was reinforced on arrival, when he tried to take a nap on a park bench:

> I had scarcely closed my eyes when I awoke to find my neighbours shaking me and asking me in agitated tones whether I realized that I had fallen asleep. On my replying that that was what I was trying to do, they seemed profoundly shocked and explained that if you were foolish enough to go to sleep out of doors in a city like Tashkent anything might happen to you.
>
> Maclean, Eastern Approaches, 1949

However, to Maclean the 'noise and strife' of Tashkent seemed quite a relief after the atmosphere of terror and suspicion in Moscow, where Stalin's purges were in full swing.

By now Kaufmann's graciously laid-out town had acquired a rash of 'the usual square white factories, Government offices and blocks of flats in the strictly utilitarian style of modern Soviet architecture', and many more were to spring up a few years later as heavy industry was relocated to Tashkent during the Second World War. Evacuees also poured in, and in three months the population doubled from 500,000 to a million. Among them, by chance, was Anna Akhmatova, one of Russia's great poets. Her husband had been shot by the Bolsheviks in 1921, her son disappeared in the purges, and she spent most of her life in penury and fear. But Tashkent's spectacular spring raised her spirits as it had done those of Brun and Bailey, and in 1944 she wrote 'Tashkent Breaks into Blossom':

> As if somebody ordered it,
>   the city suddenly became bright –
>   it came into every court
>   in a white, light apparition.
>   Their breathing is more understandable than words,
>   in the burning blue sky
>   their reflection is doomed
>   to lie at the bottom of the ditch.
>   I will remember the roof of stars
>   in the radiance of eternal glory,

> and the small rolls of bread
> in the young hands
> of dark-haired mothers.

Ten years later the Oncological Clinic of a Tashkent hospital received a rather special patient: the future Nobel prizewinner Alexander Solzhenitsyn. A victim of Stalin's paranoia, he had been arrested for making a light-hearted remark while serving at the front in the Second World War and consigned to a labour camp. There he developed a tumour and was operated on by a fellow inmate, but there was no opportunity for follow-up care, and the cancer recurred a few years later when he was living in exile in Kazakhstan. After a weary, 1,000-mile journey in 'hard-class' the sick man made his way to the hospital, only to be turned away. Patients could not be admitted without an identity card, snapped the receptionist, and as an exile he did not have one. But Solzhenitsyn could go no further and so he lay down on the floor, ignoring threats and curses. Fortunately for him a woman doctor took pity on him, he was treated and eventually cured. Ten years later the doctors, nurses and patients were immortalised in Solzhenitsyn's banned novel *Cancer Ward*.

His descriptions of Tashkent's old town, with its blind clay walls, sound very like those of Schuyler in 1873, but this air of timelessness would endure for only twelve more years. At 5.23 a.m. on 26 April 1966, a massive earthquake struck Tashkent and the factories, offices and blocks of shoddily built flats collapsed like a house of cards. Miraculously, only a handful of people are said to have lost their lives, but 300,000 were made homeless. Many former evacuees volunteered to help with the clearance and reconstruction of the city which had given them refuge during the dark days of the war.

THE TRANSCASPIAN RAILWAY

Is this railway the mere obligatory thread of connection by which Russia desires to hold together, and to place in easy inter-communication, her loosely scattered and heterogeneous possessions in Asia; or is it part of a great design that dreams of a wider dominion and aspires to a more splendid goal? Is it an evidence of concentration, possibly even of contraction, or is it a symbol of aggrandizement and an omen of advance?

George Curzon, *Russia in Central Asia*, 1889

CURZON SUMMED UP, in those words, the uneasy feelings of many Englishmen towards the Transcaspian desert railway, which was planned, built and run by the Russian Ministry of War. The railways of Britain, it must be remembered, were constructed and run by private companies, and the idea of a railway belonging to the government – let alone the Ministry of War – was a cause of grave suspicion in England. Both countries were superpowers by reason of their huge empires, but while Britain's rich possessions such as India were far from home, Russia's were contiguous. First Siberia had been colonised, then the Caucasus had been conquered, Kazakhstan and Turkestan had been quietly absorbed, and now Transcaspia was going the same way. With Central Asia in Russia's pocket, what was to stop her gobbling up Afghanistan, perhaps with the connivance of Persia, and finally relieving England of the jewel in her imperial crown, India itself?

Russia had built a fort at Krasnovodsk as early as 1869, but work on the railway did not begin until 1881. Its object was purely strategic: to carry military supplies across the waterless desert to the Akhal oasis, where Russia was struggling to subdue the Tekke Turcomans. In 1879 General Lomakin had lost 8,000 of his 12,000 baggage camels in the Kara Kum desert, and had suffered a humiliating defeat at the hands of the ferocious Turcomans. In the event his successor, General Skobelev, managed to destroy their resistance by his merciless conquest of the Tekke fortress at Geok-Tepe in January 1881, but he had only 350 camels left at the end of the campaign out of his original 12,500. Clearly, some sort of railway was called for if the region were to remain under Russian control.

At first a kind of tramway was envisaged, then an ultra-light railway running on narrow twenty-inch-gauge track. The wagons, it was suggested, could be drawn by horses, for fuel was a daunting problem in this treeless waste. Luckily for Russia, the Comptroller of the Army Transport Department at that time was General Mikhail Annenkov, an energetic and experienced man who had been in charge of transport arrangements in the Russo-Turkish War in 1877. He soon discarded the light railway and set about making plans for a proper system based on the broad five-foot gauge which was usual in Russia, and using locomotives which could run on naphtha. This by-product of crude oil refining was in plentiful supply at Baku, just across the Caspian in Russian Transcaucasia. His engineers would simply have to build plenty of storage tanks along the new line. Annenkov also knew that 100 miles of steel rails were lying around unused, ever since the Congress of Berlin had in 1878 put paid to Russia's plans to colonise the Balkans. He was off to a good start.

The railway which was destined to stretch for 1,000 miles across Central Asia, ultimately linking it with both Russia proper and Siberia, had modest beginnings. The 145 miles to Kyzyl Arvat, at the western end of the Akhal oasis, were completed in December 1881, using a newly recruited railway battalion of 1,500 skilled men. They lived on a special train, which moved forward with the line itself, comprising larder, kitchen, dining-room, ambulance, smithy and telegraph office, as well as sleeping accommodation in two-storeyed dormitory wagons. Another train brought up supplies from base twice a day, including water, for the nearest source of potable water was 110 miles from the Caspian at the tiny oasis of Kazanjik. Every single piece of timber, iron or steel had to be brought from central Russia, usually down the Volga and across the Caspian. Stone for the station buildings had to be quarried in the Persian mountains, but the necessary sun-baked bricks were often removed from old ruins in the vicinity.

The bit now firmly between his teeth, Annenkov began lobbying in St Petersburg for an extension to his line. He went so far as to publish a brochure enthusiastically advocating a line to Herat, in Afghanistan, and even suggesting a junction with the Indian railway system at Quetta. His reasons, admittedly, were commercial, but this was of little comfort to the British who in 1878 had been threatened with a Russian invasion of India from Tashkent during the Russo-Turkish War. A fort had by now been built at Ashkhabad, and Russian officers were making covert reconnaissances of Merv. Anxious British enquiries as to Russian intentions were brushed aside. Officially, there were no plans to extend the railway, or to annex any more of Transcaspia, and certainly none to attack India. Not everyone was reassured.

But for about three years Kyzyl Arvat remained the end of the line, for the railway had its opponents, even within Russia. From Tashkent it was ridiculed by Governor-General Cherniaev, who feared that Transcaspia might eclipse his own province of Turkestan in strategic importance. In St Petersburg many people felt that a new Russian province consisting mainly of sand would simply be a drain on the economy. As it was, Russia had crippling debts to repay to both Germany and France. The new Tsar, in any case, had other matters on his mind. His father had been assassinated in 1881, and he was determined not to suffer the same fate. New repressive legislation was being drawn up to subdue the discontent, sedition and outright terrorism now rife in Russia. However the Penjdeh Incident in April 1885, when Russia annexed a slice of northern Afghanistan and war with Britain seemed inevitable, offered Annenkov his chance. Alexander III gave permission for the railway to be extended towards the Afghan border, and the engineers got swiftly to work. Kyzyl Arvat became the Crewe of the Transcaspian, with foundries, forges and fitting shops filled with gleaming – mostly German – machinery. The first train steamed into Ashkhabad (136 miles from Kyzyl Arvat) on 11 December in the same year, and the line then ran parallel to the Persian frontier as far as Dushak, its most southerly point, before striking northeast to the Merv oasis. Merv, the former 'Queen of the World', had been surreptitiously annexed by Russia in February 1884, leading to anxiety in the British 'Forward School' (the hawks) and quips about Mervousness by the proponents of 'Masterly Inactivity' (the doves).

Annenkov had a bungalow built for himself at Merv – he already had one at Kyzyl Arvat – so there was no doubt where the railway was going next. Merv indeed saw its first train in July 1886, but as Curzon said, 'Merv could no more be a halting place than Ashkhabad', and the same year the line proceeded a further 150 miles to Charjui and the Oxus. There were now 650 miles of railway track, and a second railway battalion was recruited from the army. At this point a French engineer travelling in the Caucasus managed, through a lucky introduction, to obtain permission to travel on the new military railway as far as Merv. Edgar Boulangier soon discovered, however, that many people were highly sceptical about the railway's very existence. Even in Russia it was evidently suspected that it was actually just a piece of window-dressing, a sort of Potëmkin village on rails, intended to scare off the English. After a comfortless journey to Merv, where he was nonetheless charmed and impressed by General Annenkov, Boulangier returned to the Caucasus and the eager questions of his friends:

Nobody, as I have said, wanted to believe in the Transcaspian. The Russians themselves whom I had the honour to see before leaving the Caucasus, and these were by no means the first, always spoke of it with extreme circumspection. When I returned to Tiflis, I was interrogated at length, and I must say, I had to devote considerable eloquence in order to prove that this railway, regarded as impossible, was not made out of cardboard. If the Russians themselves did not believe, right up to the last minute, in the *tour de force* carried out in Central Asia, just imagine what foreign powers would have thought, and how the news that a railway had been opened in Merv, in a reputedly inaccessible Turcoman oasis, would have hit Europe like a thunderbolt!

Boulangier, *Voyage à Merv*, 1888

In 1888 George Curzon, then a young Member of Parliament, made a long trip to Russian Central Asia, gathering information as he went. There were now 900 miles of railway, terminating at Samarkand. The line was entirely single-track, except at stations, which often incorporated sidings and turning-triangles. The rails used were from nineteen to twenty-two feet long, and 2,000 wooden sleepers were laid per mile. The rails were simply spiked to the sleepers, without chairs or bolts. Native labour was employed for some of the manual work, Turcomans, Persians and Bokharans being used on different sections. Of these the Turcomans were the most highly regarded, for Russia's erstwhile enemies seemed to like the novel idea of regular work and good wages. According to Curzon the Persians were the least popular for, although physically strong, they were considered lazy and cowardly. Because the railway crossed the featureless Kara Kum desert, the engineers could often lay the track in a dead straight and level line. There was no need for tunnels, only the shallowest of cuttings were required, and there were very few rivers to be bridged. The main problem was the sand:

> Of the 650 miles which are covered by the railway between the Caspian and the Amu-darya, 200 at least are through a howling wilderness. The sand, of the most brilliant yellow hue, is piled in loose hillocks and mobile dunes, and is swept hither and thither by powerful winds. It has all the appearance of a sea of troubled waves, billow succeeding billow in melancholy succession, with the sand driving like spray from their summits, and great smooth-swept troughs lying between, on which the winds leave the imprints of their fingers in wavy indentations, just like an ebb-tide on the sea-shore.
>
> Curzon, *Russia in Central Asia*, 1889

Annenkov used various methods to consolidate the sand. Near the Caspian the permanent way was soaked with sea-water or covered with a layer of clay. In the more desolate regions, fences were built next to the line and the sand-hills planted with tamarisk, wild oats and a long-rooted local shrub called saxaoul (*Haloxylon ammodendron*). Nurseries for desert shrubs were even set up in the Persian mountains. But after a sandstorm there was nothing for it but to send out relief parties with spades and shovels. An even worse hazard, though less frequent, was the flash flood. After the melting of the snows in spring, a sudden torrent could pour down from the Kopet Dagh mountains, tearing up the rails and temporarily turning the desert into a lake. One of these floods occurred at a most inopportune moment. In May 1888, when the Transcaspian railway was officially inaugurated, Annenkov's big moment was marred – and the opening ceremony delayed several hours – when the line was flooded east of Kyzyl Arvat.

By the time the railway battalions reached the Amu-darya, or Oxus, they had developed into highly expert teams who prided themselves on laying at least a mile of track a day, if not a mile and a half. Even Curzon, who was by no means pro-Russian, had to admit that the Transcaspian was probably laid in the shortest time and at the least expense of any railway in the world. However, when the Tsar gave permission in February 1887 for the line to be extended to Samarkand, the engineers were presented with their biggest problem to date: how to bridge the Amu-darya. Only two other rivers had crossed the path of the railway so far – the Tejend and the Murghab – and it had been relatively easy to span these with wooden structures on piles. For neither was very wide, and the banks were high enough to ensure that the bridges were well above the highest water level.

But the width of the Amu-darya varied from half a mile to five miles according to the season, with four different stream-beds at Charjui, separated by three islands. At first a steam ferry was considered, worked by cable, but in the end a wooden bridge in four sections was decided upon. It took seven months to build, under the supervision of a Polish engineer named Bielinsky, and measured 2,000 yards in all. It rested on 3,300 piles, driven very close together into the stream-bed, and appeared to be startlingly high. But although the rails were thirty feet above the water in the dry season, they were only five feet clear of the highest flood level. All the wood required for this mammoth undertaking had to be brought from central Russia. Curzon called the bridge 'an inelegant structure', but remarked that the engineers looked on it fondly with 'parental pride'. Trains had to crawl across at low speed – it took Curzon fifteen minutes – and passengers were not allowed to smoke, for fear of the whole structure being burnt to the ground. There were also six fire stations with pumps and hoses set up at intervals along the bridge.

The Russians regarded the Amu-darya as a potential trade route to Afghanistan, so a central section of the railway bridge was designed to swing open to allow steamboats through. Unfortunately someone got his sums wrong, and just before the opening ceremony it was discovered that the special boat laid on to take VIPs on a little excursion up-river was an inch or two too wide. The boat had been brought from St Petersburg in pieces and put together on the spot, but for some reason the spot chosen to assemble it was downstream of the bridge. As no one dared tell the Governor-General of Turkestan and his fellow-bigwigs of this débâcle, there was nothing for it but to chop a bit of the bridge down. It must have broken the engineers' hearts, but they proceeded to cut a different section of the bridge in two, pulling up two batteries of piles. The guests thus got their excursion, but the bridge very nearly collapsed and it took many weeks to repair it again. Bielinsky's creation survived, however, for nearly twenty years, when it was replaced by a steel lattice-girder structure laid over thirty-foot-high granite piers.

Someone who travelled over both bridges was Catherine Macartney, wife of the British Consul in Kashgar. Her first journey was as a young bride in the autumn of 1898, her second in 1902 when she and her husband travelled back for their first home leave:

> On coming nearer, we saw a rickety wooden bridge ahead of us, and wondered whether we were expected to trust ourselves and the train to it. Evidently we were, for the train stopped, and the guard got out. Then we started on to the bridge at a slow crawl, with the guard walking ahead waving a red flag, and looking to see how much more had fallen away since the last train crossed. What the red flag could do to help us, I have never quite understood, for we did not need to be told that there was danger.
>
> Slowly we went on with the whole structure swaying, and creaking, as though it was strained to its utmost limit of endurance. In places great beams had gone and we looked down the holes to the chocolate-coloured river rushing beneath us.
>
> It took us over half an hour to reach solid ground on the other side, and until we felt we could breathe freely again. Still, in spite of its unsafe appearance, the bridge was used for some time after we crossed it, without accident. Four years later, when we travelled home, we found that a fine iron bridge had been built for the railway, though the old wooden one, or some of it at least, was standing to remind us of an anxious half-hour.

Lady Macartney, *An English Lady in Chinese Turkestan*, 1931

Curzon had found travel on the Transcaspian railway excruciatingly slow. His journey from the Caspian to Samarkand averaged twelve miles per hour. Admittedly, as there had been no restaurant car on his train, this had included leisurely stops for refreshments *en route*. But he reckoned that the shifting sub-structure would always restrict top speeds to about 30 m.p.h., and much less if trains were heavily laden. (He seems to have been right, for the writer Stephen Graham reported an average speed of only 17 m.p.h. as late as 1914. 'Russia,' he commented philosophically, 'is not excited about loss of time.') By the time of Catherine Macartney's first journey there were daily trains from Krasnovodsk, which in 1896 had become the western terminus. The railway had originally started lower down the Caspian coast, first at Mikhailovsk and then at the island of Uzun Ada, but the water there was shallow and sometimes froze in winter, making it difficult for the Caspian steamers to dock.

No one had a good word to say about Krasnovodsk, and it can still be truly said that its only building of any distinction is the railway station. Mr J.T. Woolrych Perowne, who began a Cook's Tour of Transcaspia there in 1898, has left us this description:

Krasnovodsk lies in an amphitheatre of picturesque hills, evidently of volcanic origin and absolutely bare. The town itself is a mere collection of mean little one-storeyed, flat-roofed houses ... here as elsewhere all along the line the railway station is *the* architectural feature of the place.

Francis Skrine, of the Indian Civil Service, agreed:

The Government offices, substantially built of a warm brown freestone, surround a central square, where a patch of grass and a few scraggy trees strive in vain to relieve the desolation which recalls the surroundings of Aden to the Eastern traveller ... But the chief ornament of Krasnovodsk is, strange to say, the railway terminus. Unlike those which disgrace so many English towns, it is a highly successful effort to blend the ornamental with the useful.

Stephen Graham, writing of his journey in 1914, was even more dismissive:

Krasnovodsk is one of the hottest, most desert, and miserable places in the world. The mountains are dead; there is no water in them. Rain scarcely ever falls, and the earth is only sand and salt.

Little seems to have changed by 1935 when another writer, Ethel Mannin, passed through on her way to Samarkand. 'Krasnovodsk by daylight revealed itself as a desolate dust-heap of a town,' she wrote, adding:

As a town, Krasnovodsk scarcely exists. Outside the station there is a square planted with dusty tamarisks, but the place appears to be used more as a public latrine than as a public garden. In the streets behind there are a few small cafés and eating-houses, very dirty and full of flies, and a few equally squalid shops.

In defence of this much-maligned little town, I must say that in March 1991 when I was there, it actually rained a bit, and its inhabitants were the kindest and most helpful of any I came across in the Soviet Union. The central square is now a garden of remembrance to the soldiers who fell in the Second World War.

As the terminus of the Transcaspian railway, Krasnovodsk was naturally entitled to a rather splendid station, made of stone and embellished with crenellations, but many of the smaller halts along the line were, in Curzon's words, simply 'dingy wooden shanties half buried in the sand'. The French explorer Gabriel Bonvalot once remarked that he would be 'sorry to accept the post of station-master at the well of Uch-Haji, even with the salary of a prime minister'. The middle-sized stations, however, were generally made of brick. Annenkov had conducted some interesting experiments on temperatures inside structures made of kiln-baked bricks and those made of bricks dried in the sun. The latter proved far superior in terms of insulation, and were 10–12 degrees centigrade cooler in the height of summer. This led Annenkov to use sun-dried bricks for his station buildings whenever possible, though to the detriment of any old ruins in the vicinity.

There were in all four classes of station, and a fully equipped one like Ashkhabad would comprise a guest-house, telegraph office, station-master's house and staff accommodation as well as the actual station buildings. The single-storey structures were made either of stone or of bricks plastered over with lime and finished with stone copings and mouldings, with flat roofs smeared with asphalt from the Baku oil-wells. The practical but harmonious standard design was provided by a German engineer named Urlaub. The bigger stations had excellent buffets before the Bolshevik Revolution, and at the smallest the local entrepreneurs would provide tea, melons and grapes for next to nothing. Ella Christie, a Scotswoman travelling to Khiva in 1913, reported having 'quite a good meal of roast meat and stewed dried apricots' at Krasnovodsk station, while Stephen Graham a year later noticed that whenever a patch of irrigated land was to be seen, people would begin to appear at the stations:

> Many women stood at the stations with hot, just-boiled eggs, with roast chickens, milk or *koumiss* in bottles, even with pats of butter, with samovars. And there were native boys with baskets heaped full of *lepeshki* (cakes of bread). Each station was provided with a long barrier, and the women, in lines of twenty or thirty, stood behind their wares and cried to the passengers. The many steaming samovars were a welcome sight, and at the charge of a halfpenny I made myself tea at one of them.
>
> Graham, *Through Russian Central Asia*, 1916

Even in July 1918, at the height of the civil war in Central Asia, a British intelligence officer obtained some 'excellent soup' at the small station of Kaahka, near the Persian border. Captain Reginald Teague-Jones was amused when the daily train from Tashkent came panting and hissing into the station with crowds of people of both sexes clinging to the roofs of the carriages. 'Next moment,' he wrote in his diary, 'the buffet was raided.' He continued:

> Never have I seen such a sight. It might well have been a scene from one of the London musical comedies. There were Russian peasants in red shirts, Armenians and Persians, Cossacks and Red soldiers, Sart traders and Bokhariotes, Turkmans in their gigantic *papakhas*, while among the crowd were a number of pretty young girls and women in the latest Paris summer fashions. All this medley came crushing into the buffet and

clamoured for glasses of tea, hunks of black bread and platters of soup. Somehow or other they all seemed to get served and Asiatic and European, Mongol and Muscovite, sat down literally cheek by jowl, and satisfied their hunger.

Teague-Jones, *The Spy Who Disappeared*, 1990

By 1935, when Ethel Mannin was travelling on the Transcaspian, station buffets were reserved for Red Army or Communist Party officials, and food became a serious problem for humbler passengers. Supplies on the train began to run out on her second day from Krasnovodsk, and she was grateful for the few scraps obtainable from (now illicit) private enterprise. The crowds at the stations are noticeably poorer in her descriptions than those encountered by earlier travellers:

On every station there are the same tatterdemalion crowds with dressing-gown-like coats, some of them so patched or in such shreds that it is difficult to determine their original colouring, and verminous-looking sheepskin or fur hats. Many of the men wear turbans. They are on the whole a wild, dirty, cheerful, poverty-stricken looking lot, these Turkistan crowds ...

These station crowds remind me of the railway stations in remote villages in the west of Ireland, where the villagers troop down to the station to see the train come in, for something to do, and because the train is an event in the day – almost the only event of social consequence. Here, too, are crowds of people who are obviously not travellers, but who have merely come to wave to the train and enjoy the spectacle of strange faces crowded at its windows. At every station and halt, peasant women and children run alongside the train, holding up jugs of sour milk, plates of hard-looking little scones, yellow-fleshed roast chickens.

Mannin, *South to Samarkand*, 1936

And yet when Annenkov and his successors first built the railways of Central Asia, they had been regarded with fear and suspicion by the native population. The Emir of Bokhara, for instance, had insisted on the railway bypassing his capital. As Curzon wrote in his book:

It was regarded as foreign, subversive, anti-national, and even Satanic. Shaitan's Arba, or the Devil's Wagon, was what they called it. Accordingly it was stipulated that the line should as far as possible avoid the cultivated land, and should pass at a distance of ten miles from the native city ... Now, however, the Bokhariots are victims to much the same regrets as the wealthy English landowners who, when the railway was first introduced in this country, opposed at any cost its passage through their property. Already when the first working train steamed into Bokhara with rolling stock and material for the continuation of the line, the natives crowded down to see it, and half in fear, half in surprise, jumped into the empty wagons. Presently apprehension gave way to ecstasy.

The first engines were foreign-built, some American and some German. John Bookwalter, an American who spent three months in Russia in 1898 assessing its potential for US exports, noted with satisfaction that the locomotive pulling his train out of Krasnovodsk had been made in Philadelphia. (Later they were manufactured at the Kolomna Works in Moscow, 0–6–0 for freight and 2–4–0 for passenger trains. Today all engines are diesels.) Bookwalter was greatly excited by the new railways spanning Siberia and Central Asia, and looked forward to the day when enterprising Americans would sell their goods at the great annual fair at Nizhny-Novgorod. Alas, his long-term forecasts were overturned by the revolution and the invention of the aeroplane and there is no longer a trade-fair at Nizhny. Re-named Gorky, it was for long a closed city used for the internal exile of political dissidents such as the late Dr Andrei Sakharov. But Bookwalter left some excellent photographs and descriptions of the Transcaspian at the turn of the century:

> There are trains leaving daily for the East on the Transcaspian railway, but as they are mixed freight and passenger trains, designed to carry soldiers, emigrants, merchandise, and material for new railways under construction farther on, they offer no facilities or comforts for the traveller. There is, however, a train that leaves here [Krasnovodsk] three times a week, consisting wholly of second, third and fourth class passenger cars, for the purpose of accommodating the better

class of travel, which is rapidly on the increase. This train, usually composed of twelve or fifteen cars, presents a neat and pleasing appearance, all the cars being painted snow white, even to the locomotive. They are plain in the interior, with uncovered seats, and but little comfort. Those who design travelling at night are obliged to provide themselves, before starting, with bedding, linen, towels, etc.

Bookwalter, *Siberia and Central Asia*, 1899

Mr Bookwalter was an optimist and saw the best in everything, but others were less polite. Francis Skrine, with a very English fastidiousness, described the trains thus:

The trains which leave Krasnovodsk for the heart of Central Asia are made up of second and third class carriages on the corridor system. They are warmed in the abominable fashion peculiar to Russia, by air heated in a roaring stove, and their lavatories are on the most primitive model. The stuffy compartments contain narrow wooden benches; and the upper berths, which let down at night, form very indifferent beds. In one of these little purgatories the traveller bound for Samarkand ensconces himself at 4.30 p.m., after a substantial meal at the railway buffet.

Skrine and Ross, *The Heart of Asia*, 1899

One English traveller who managed to avoid all this discomfort was Mr J.T. Woolrych Perowne, for on his Cook's Tour his group had a special train to themselves. There was no first class on the Transcaspian, so General Annenkov's personal train was taken out of mothballs and put at their disposal. (His Energy, as Annenkov was affectionately known, had died a couple of years before.) There were three ordinary first-class carriages, three saloon coaches, a kitchen car, dining-car, baggage car, servants' car, hospital car and finally an observation car at the rear. Mr and Mrs Perowne had one of the saloon coaches:

For the information of those who do not know Russian railways, I must say that the gauge is much wider than ours, and that therefore the carriages are more roomy. Nearly one-third of the saloon is taken up with a sitting-room, upholstered in morocco. Leading from this is a two-foot passage at the side, in which is a door opening into the bedroom. This is a cabin six foot by seven and contains a bed, a large writing table with drawers, a mirror, and a ship's washing arrangement – a very snug little room, though we found the bed somewhat narrow.

Perowne, *Russian Hosts and English Guests in Central Asia*, 1898

There was even a bathroom with hot and cold water, and electric bells for summoning one's servants. 'Some of us, especially the ladies of the party,' confessed Perowne, 'had been anticipating all sorts of hardships and inconveniences, and we were all not only relieved but delighted when we saw how relatively comfortable we were to be.'

Two charming Russian officers accompanied the group on their tour of Transcaspia, and they whiled away the journey in discussion of such congenial topics as the servant problem. Unlike the Indians of the British empire, Turcomans did not make ideal servants, it appeared. If not treated with the utmost tact, confided the Russians, they were quite likely to storm out in the middle of a dinner party leaving the hostess to fend for herself. And life was difficult enough for the Russian ladies, in all conscience, what with the lack of fresh meat and vegetables ... The English party sympathised with their new friends, and stoically endured the wearisome diet of sturgeon and caviar.

But despite this solitary tourist excursion, the Transcaspian was still firmly in military hands, and no foreigner could travel on it without the express permission of the Minister of War in St Petersburg. John Bookwalter had noted that 'all the officials of the train, the engineer, the fireman, and even the workmen on the track, are drawn from the army'. (Once the Transcaspian was fully integrated into the other Central Asian railway system in Turkestan, however, its running and maintenance were handed over to civilians.) In 1895 the line had been extended from Samarkand to Tashkent, and a few years later it went on further to Andijan. But more worrying to the British was the construction in 1897 of a branch line up the Murghab valley, from Merv to the small town of Kushka on the Afghan frontier. Curzon had noticed that whenever the Russian illustrated papers published pictures of the

Transcaspian railway at various stages of its construction, they were invariably headed 'On the Road to India'! In the event, the southern branch line was never extended across the frontier, and it was not until 1992, after the break-up of the Soviet empire, that work began on a branch line from Shatlik, west of Merv, to Tehran.

Meanwhile other Russian engineers had started work in 1891 on the great Trans-Siberian line, destined one day to be the longest railway in the world. Russia had come relatively late to railway building and was now making up for lost time. Another line struck southeast across the steppe from Orenburg, past the Aral Sea, alongside the course of the Syr-darya river to Turkestan. This Trans-Aral line, which had to cross the Kyzyl Kum desert, was prone to the same disasters as the Transcaspian line in the Kara Kum. An important government official from St Petersburg, who travelled to Turkestan in 1908 to investigate a corruption scandal (see TASHKENT), found part of the railway line to Tashkent had been washed away by a flash flood:

> The Syr-darya, which we first saw as a silvery streak in the distance, had just then played a nasty trick on the engineers who, against the persistent advice of the natives, had laid the railway line at a distance varying from eight to twenty kilometres from its course. Like all other rivers in Turkestan, the Syr-darya is apt to change its course with very little notice. Large quantities of rubble and loose stones are brought down from the glaciers every year, and gradually a solid dam is built up which forces the water out of the original channel and sets the river meandering over the sands, sometimes miles from its original course.
>
> Some distance from the Russian township of Perovsk the embankment along the Syr-darya had been partly washed away and we were delayed while a tiresome operation of trolleys and boats was mounted to get us over to the other side, where we were met by a train sent out to take us to the end of our journey. A chocolate-coloured tide of muddy water filled with swirling debris spread over a scene of utter desolation, watched derisively by the native Kirghiz mounted on their shaggy little ponies.
>
> Count Pahlen, *Mission to Turkestan*, 1964

The Trans-Aral was not a military railway, but the construction and maintenance workers were a tightly knit group, organised on quasi-military lines, and shunned by the rest of the population. They had their own barracks and their own arms, for the nomads encountered along the more desolate stretches of track were not always friendly. This was the region where, not long before, slave raiders had snatched their victims and sold them in the markets of Bokhara and Khiva. Most of the railwaymen had been recruited in central Russia and brought with them anti-establishment grievances and a ragbag of the new socialist ideas. This was to be an important factor at the time of the Bolshevik takeover, and the power of the railway workers was certainly instrumental in sealing the fate of Russian Central Asia (see TASHKENT and ASHKHABAD).

The Trans-Aral and Transcaspian railways, which met at Tashkent, were in due course extended eastwards to Vierney (now Alma Ata), and later linked to the Trans-Siberian network via the 'Turk-Sib' line to Novosibirsk which was completed in 1930. Russian Central Asia, for so long the back-of-beyond, was now within easy reach of Moscow. But how much long-term benefit the railway brought to the native inhabitants is debatable. For the Tsarists it was undoubtedly an instrument of colonisation, and for their Communist successors it enabled the centralised authorities to remove local resources on a gigantic scale. But as a feat of engineering the Transcaspian, the greatest of the Central Asian railways, must remain an enduring monument to the vision, energy and devotion of General Annenkov and his indefatigable railway battalions.

TUNHUANG
The Secret Cave

A Tartar horn tugs at the north wind,
Thistle Gate shines whiter than the stream,
The sky swallows the road to Kokonor.
On the Great Wall, a thousand miles of moonlight.

Li Ho, On the Frontier, 9th century

There is one art gallery in the Gobi which has become world-famous. Not many travellers have seen the Caves of the Thousand Buddhas, for they lie far from any main track, hidden behind wide-spreading dunes. The nearest oasis is Tunhuang (Blazing Beacon) for at a short distance there are several of the desert landmarks called *tun* by the Chinese. These old erections were used to convey messages by fire-signal across desert spaces, hence the name Blazing Beacon for the town and tower placed at this strategic point.

Mildred Cable, The Gobi Desert, 1942

TUNHUANG WAS A very important staging-post on the old Silk Road, for it was the last haven of safety for westbound caravans before they launched into the treacherous Lop desert. There was no avoiding this perilous stage for merchants heading for the southern arm of the trade route, which led ultimately to Gandhara and India, or who were returning that way, but it was always dreaded. There were no landmarks and no discernible track in the moving sands, and before settling down for the night the caravan leader would set up an arrow pointing in the direction they needed to follow next day, for fear of losing his bearings. Even so, many caravans disappeared entirely, and the legend grew up that the deserts of Central Asia were inhabited by demons whose evil pleasure was to lure men to their doom.

The other side of Tunhuang, to the east, lay Anhsi, where the Silk Road divided into its northern and southern arms, and the Kansu corridor leading to China proper. Here the road passed between mountain ranges and was clearly delineated, as the missionary traveller Mildred Cable describes:

> At the foot of the mountain range lay the old travel road, wide and deeply marked, literally cut to bits by the sharp nail-studded wheels of countless caravan carts. The ruts parted and merged, then spread again, as the eddies of a current mark the face of a river. Over this road myriads of travellers had journeyed for thousands of years, making of it a ceaselessly flowing stream of life, for it was the great highway of Asia, which connected the Far East with distant European lands.

As early as the first century BC Tunhuang was inhabited by Chinese settlers, for it was their westernmost outpost against the Huns. The Great Wall ended further east, at Jiayukuan (Barrier of the Pleasant Valley), but extensions were built to Tunhuang with watch-towers which were manned night and day. An impending attack was signalled by smoke during daylight and flames by night, and it was said that a message which would take three months to arrive at Peking by horse-courier took only a day and a night to arrive by beacon. Despite the pleasant situation of the Tunhuang oasis, the constant threat of attack by barbarian Huns, Tibetans and Mongols made it a punishment posting for Chinese officials and soldiers. In fact, anywhere west of the wall was regarded with dread, and Mildred Cable noticed that the gateway facing the Gobi at Jiayukuan was covered with ancient graffiti by the exiles, disgraced officials, criminals and others who had been forced to take the road to the west:

> The long archway was covered with writings, and anyone with sufficient knowledge to appreciate Chinese penmanship could see at once that these were the work of men of scholarship, who had fallen on an hour of deep distress. There were lines quoted from the Book of Odes, poems composed in the

pure tradition of classic literature, and verses inspired by sorrow too heavy for the careful balance of literary values, yet unbearable unless expressed in words.

As well as being used by merchants and soldiers, parts of the Silk Road soon became well-trodden by Buddhist pilgrims. The gentle religion of Buddhism, born in India in the fifth century BC, seems to have reached China by the first century AD, after which a steady stream of pilgrims travelled to India to visit the sacred bo tree in Buddh Gaya beneath which Gautama had meditated for six years before receiving enlightenment. The best route to India was generally the southern trail, passing through Tunhuang, Miran, Cherchen and Khotan, and then either through the Karakoram mountains to Kashmir or over the Pamirs into Gandhara. Over the years shrines and temples sprang up along the route and themselves became places of pilgrimage.

Legend has it that the Thousand Buddha caves at Mogao, about twelve miles south-west of Tunhuang, were inspired by a vision. A devout monk travelling to India in the fourth century AD halted at Tunhuang to rest. Wandering into a little valley he came upon a cliff, and there he saw a thousand figures of the Buddha, surrounded by a golden haze. He at once told his fellow-pilgrims of this glorious revelation, and they vowed to hallow the spot by carving shrines in the rock-face and decorating them with holy pictures. After that every rich merchant or pilgrim would donate something towards the adornment of the site, either as a supplication for safe passage or to give thanks for a happy arrival.

As well as being on the trade and pilgrim route between China and the west, Tunhuang was crossed by a road leading from Lhasa towards Mongolia and southern Siberia. Many who travelled this road were peaceable Buddhist pilgrims, but not all. In the second half of the seventh century AD Tunhuang was captured by the Tibetans, although after a century it was reclaimed by the Tang rulers of China, who endowed and decorated many cave temples. In the tenth century a Uighur kingdom was established there, and Turkic influences can be detected in some of the wall-paintings. The Uighurs were displaced by the Tanguts, or Hsi Hsia, a Buddhist people of Tibetan origin, who were in turn displaced by the Mongols in 1227. The region then became Muslim and the cave temples seem to have been abandoned.

Eventually the area was pacified once more by the Chinese, and the oasis of Tunhuang was repopulated in the eighteenth century.

Towards the end of the nineteenth century Tunhuang was visited by a Chinese monk from Hupeh province who had devoted most of his young life to tramping the pilgrim tracks of China and visiting shrines. When he came upon the Caves of the Thousand Buddhas and found them sadly neglected, he decided to make their care and preservation his responsibility, and set about collecting alms. Buddhism had virtually disappeared from China and Central Asia, remaining only in Tibet and Mongolia in a somewhat debased form, and Abbot Wang (as he came to be known) was himself a Taoist. But the Chinese had a great reverence for the past and a respect for religion, and Wang was soon able to carry out basic repairs to the more accessible shrines. He also built a small guest-house for visiting pilgrims, and constructed an irrigation channel which enabled him to plant a row of poplar trees at the foot of the cliff.

There are at least 500 caves at Mogao, and it took Wang many years to explore them all. In 1900 he came upon a cave which had been walled up, and when he broke away some of the bricks he found a hidden cache of early manuscripts, scrolls and crumbling silken banners. Some were written in Chinese but many were indecipherable, and he decided to leave them undisturbed, fitting a door with a lock to the aperture. But he was so excited by his discovery that he mentioned it to some of his wealthy patrons, and word gradually got round in the locality. In fact, five years later the German archaeologist Albert von Le Coq heard about a secret hoard of ancient manuscripts when he was at the oasis of Hami, 200 miles to the north. He considered crossing the desert to Tunhuang and investigating the rumour, but time was short and he had often been misled by native 'tall stories' in the past. He decided to spin a coin. He never went to Tunhuang, and thus deprived himself of perhaps the greatest prize to be carried away from Chinese Turkestan.

Sir Aurel Stein from British India was the first Westerner to see the now-famous Cave 17, closely followed by the Frenchman Professor Paul Pelliot. The Hungarian-born Stein (who took British nationality in 1904) had since 1900 been systematically excavating old Buddhist ruins which had been submerged by the wind-blown sands of the Taklamakan desert. Starting at the south-western end of the Tarim Basin, around Khotan, he had painstakingly uncovered manuscripts, sculptures, wall-paintings and everyday objects such as furniture at a number of long-forgotten sites, now buried in the desert but which had clearly once been situated along the southern arm of the Silk Road. The increasing desiccation of Central Asia, as well as the destruction wrought by the waves of barbarians who repeatedly swept through this area, had led many once prosperous townships to be abandoned in antiquity. But the swiftly encroaching sand had not only buried them, it had also preserved them, and Stein had been amazed to see the brightness of the paintings and the freshness of the stucco-work once they were rescued from the bone-dry desert.

The Christmas of 1906 found Stein at the remote site of Lou-lan, near the salt-marshes of Lop-nor. In the ruins of this ancient garrison town he discovered documents of the third and fourth centuries AD chronicling the losing battle fought between this far-flung outpost of China and the Huns. Ironically, Lou-lan was to acquire a military significance once more in the twentieth century, for it was here in the Lop desert that Communist China tested its nuclear weapons. Stein did not linger there, for icy winds made work doubly arduous and he feared his native workers might die of exposure. Retreating south to Miran, he stopped to uncover some magnificent Graeco-Roman frescoes, which 'curiously suggest an affinity to the angels of some Early Christian church', before striking north-east across the desert towards Tunhuang. Stein knew there were decorated caves there, and as soon as he arrived in March 1907 he hastened to the site to see for himself:

> They are carved into the precipitous conglomerate cliffs overlooking from the west the mouth of a barren valley some twelve miles to the south-east of the oasis. A small stream descending from the westernmost portion of the Nan-shan range has cut its way here through the foothills overlain by huge ridges of drift sand, but now loses itself a short distance below the caves. On the cliffs above the broad waste of rubble and sand on which the streamlet debouches, there were first seen a multitude of dark cavities, mostly small, like troglodyte dwellings of anchorites. From the small size of most of these recesses and the absence of wall paintings in almost all of them, it seemed safe to conclude that they had served largely as quarters for Buddhist monks.

Farther up there were to be seen hundreds of grottoes, large and small, honeycombing in irregular tiers the sombre rock faces, from the foot of the cliff to the top of the precipice, and extending in close array for over half a mile. This bewildering multitude of grottoes all showed paintings on their walls or on as much as was visible of them from outside. Among them two shrines containing colossal Buddha statues could at once be recognized; for in order to secure adequate space for the giant stucco images of the Buddhas, close on ninety feet high, a number of halls had been excavated one above the other, each providing light and access for a portion of the colossus.

In front of most of the shrines there had been originally antechapels or porches of oblong shape carved out of the rock. Owing to the fall of the outer wall the tempera paintings with which the inside wall surfaces had always been decorated were now often fully exposed to view. Many of the shrines high up on the rocks had become inaccessible.

Stein, *On Central Asian Tracks*, 1964

Stein soon familiarised himself with the ground-plan of the shrines, which all followed the same general pattern:

From the oblong antechapel the cave-temple proper was entered through a high and rather wide passage, which alone admitted light and air to the interior. This consisted everywhere of a single rectangular cella, usually almost square, hewn out of the solid rock and provided with a high conical roof. Within the cella I found generally a big rectangular platform decorated with painted stucco. Its centre was usually occupied by the colossal stucco image of a seated Buddha, with groups of Bodhisattvas, saintly disciples and divine attendants on either side. It was only too easy to see how much of all this statuary in stucco had suffered in the course of centuries through the natural decay of its material, and even more from the hands of iconoclasts and pious restorers.

Abbot Wang, the self-appointed guardian of the shrines, was away on a begging tour of the neighbouring oasis when Stein arrived, but his young assistant showed the archaeologist round and mentioned the 'great mass of ancient manuscripts' which had been unearthed a few years previously. He pointed out to Stein the locked door, and estimated the hoard to contain 'several cartloads' of old books. There was nothing to be done until Wang returned so, mastering his excitement as best he could, Stein went off to investigate the ancient extensions to the Great Wall in the meantime. When he returned he found Wang had taken fright and had actually walled up the secret chamber. It took Stein some time to gain his confidence and convince him of his serious and scholarly interest in the hoard. A shared admiration for the early Buddhist traveller Hsuan-tsang helped to tip the balance.

The story of how Stein gradually persuaded Abbot Wang to show him the priceless manuscripts and finally to sell him a large number of them is too well-known to need repeating here in any detail. For the sum of £130, which of course was an enormous amount to Wang, Stein obtained twenty-four cases of manuscripts and five more of painted banners and other works of art.

In retrospect the Chinese regard this transaction as no better than robbery, for among the treasures was the world's oldest known printed book – a block-printed version of a famous Buddhist text, the Diamond Sutra, dated 11 May 868. The sixteen-foot-long scroll is currently on display in the British Museum – a fact which, according to a modern history of printing published in Peking, causes the Chinese to 'gnash their teeth in bitter hatred'. In fairness to Stein it must be said that Wang had reported his find to the Provincial Governor of Kansu and had even sent samples to Lanchou for examination, but the authorities had shown little interest.

Tunhuang was not the final destination of Sir Aurel Stein's expedition and it was many months before he returned to England and publicised his finds. Meanwhile the French scholar Paul Pelliot, who had been excavating sites along the northern arm of the Silk Road, heard a rumour in Urumchi about the hidden manuscripts. For a professor of Chinese this was particularly exciting news, and he hurried to the oasis quite unaware that Stein had already been there. Arriving in March 1908, he seems to have charmed Wang for, unlike Stein, he was allowed to enter the secret chamber himself and examine whatever he chose. Pelliot quickly realised that it would take at least six months to do the job properly, for there were probably 20,000 scrolls crammed into the little cave. But he was determined to look at every single one, however briefly, in order not to miss any gems, for he knew it would be impossible to persuade Wang to part with the whole collection. Finally, after three weeks spent crouched in the chamber, he made Wang a donation of 500 *taels* (about £90) and departed with the cream of this ancient hoard packed discreetly into small boxes.

Returning home via Peking, Pelliot showed some samples to Chinese scholars there and pointed out their importance. As a result an urgent message was sent to Tunhuang forbidding the sale of any further manuscripts and instructing Wang to send the residue to the capital. Many, needless to say, failed to reach their destination, for it was now common knowledge that these crumbling bits of paper could command a good price. Many years later an American art historian was offered manuscripts from Tunhuang on the black market in China, and they still appear very occasionally in the catalogues of rare-book dealers in Europe. Abbot Wang, clearly reluctant to lose this useful source of income entirely, kept back a secret supply which he discreetly sold in the ensuing years to the Japanese, the Russians and even to Sir Aurel Stein when he made a second visit in 1914.

After the Russian Revolution and civil war, streams of White Russians fled into China, and the Caves of the Thousand Buddhas were sadly defaced when 400 former soldiers were interned for six months there while the Chinese decided what to do with them. Part of the damage was caused by smoke from their cooking fires, but some was deliberate. 'Across some of these lovely faces are scribbled the numbers of a Russian regiment', wrote the American archaeologist Langdon Warner to his wife in 1923, 'and from the mouth of a Buddha where he sits to deliver the Lotus Law flows some Slav obscenity.' The missionary Mildred Cable who was there a few years later also deplored the Russian graffiti:

> The Russians left evidence of their visit in long lists of their names written on any available wall-space which they could find. This passion for recording the trivial was in striking contrast with the dignified reticence of the unnamed artists who, having made of these caves a unique reliquary of art, asked for no personal recognition or that any man should remember them by name. The scrawled hieroglyphics of the Russian script seemed rather pitiful alongside the master-touch of those great anonymous artists.

Happily, Chinese art restorers were able to remove much of this damage during the 1960s and '70s.

Mildred Cable and her fellow missionaries Francesca and Eva French spent many years in the 1920s and 1930s tramping the highways and byways of Kansu spreading the Gospel, tending the sick and teaching the children. As well as being dedicated Christians, they were perceptive and sympathetic observers, and all Miss Cable's books are valuable social records of China at a time of turmoil. For the collapse of the Manchu dynasty in 1911 had been followed by a series of revolutions and uprisings, and in the ensuing anarchy much of northern China fell into the hands of local warlords. One of these was Ma Chung-yin, or Big Horse, whom the missionaries came to know rather better than they might have wished after he came to power in 1930. In her book *The Gobi Desert* Mildred Cable describes his brutal methods:

> He was a fierce fighter, and terrified north-west Kansu by the violence of his methods of warfare. The only alternative to unconditional surrender was death by the sword, and in one resisting town after another every male over fourteen years of age was slaughtered, boys under fourteen were taken over by the army to be trained as little orderlies, and the young women were left to the pleasure of the soldiers. In Chen-fan alone he left three thousand corpses lying in the streets. At last no city dared to answer that terrible challenge save by throwing its gates open and by placing its arsenal, food-supply, horses and all else at the disposal of young Ma Chung-yin and his brigand band, until the suffering peasants surnamed him 'General Thunderbolt'.
>
> Ma Chung-yin's strategy was based on the assumption of the paralysing effect of frightfulness in action, and as a method of temporary invasion it answered his purpose well, but it never served him as a basis of true conquest, nor did he ever establish rule over one single acre of the land which he invaded. His was the method of the locust and the Hun, and his army was always viewed as a plague. It came, it devoured, and when it had passed over, the patient, constructively minded peasants instantly began to repair the damage done to their fields, and to beget sons to replace those who had been swept away in his train.

In the course of all this upheaval the three women found themselves trapped at Tunhuang for eight months when the oasis was surrounded by Ma:

> The town was robbed of everything in the nature of food, goods and money on which the men could lay hands. Silver, however, is easily hidden beneath floors of stamped earth, and the dryness of the land was such that wheat also could be buried for one season without fear of the grain sprouting. Thus the farmer's greatest treasure, seed for the next sowing, was hidden under the sand-hills and kept from the looter. Next to food the most coveted possession of the oases were the young, vigorous, hardy men, such as the heat, the cold, the sand-storms and the blizzards, the fatigue and the constant hardships of desert life, have trained. From generation to generation these rough, enduring youths have been produced by the natural elimination of the weak, until only the toughest specimens have emerged, able to accept as natural conditions a standard of life which would spell death to any who were not inured to it.
>
> These were the men whom Ma Chung-yin wanted for gunfodder, and orders were issued to the press-gang to fetch them in from every farm of the neighbourhood, and collect them in Tunhuang city. Every day we saw them being rounded up. The ropes which they themselves had twisted from desert grass were used to tie their hands behind their backs, and to noose their necks in a running-knot …
>
> Carts, horses, fuel and fodder, all was commandeered, and the luxuriant oasis of Tunhuang became a city of beggars. There was nothing to be bought in the open market and we, as others, were dependent upon the kindness of some farmer who smuggled a few pounds of flour into our house after nightfall. Then typhus began to take its toll of victims and the temple entrances were full of men and women muttering in delirium and calling on passers-by for a drink of water to slake their intolerable thirst. Dogs and wolves had a good time outside the north gate, for by ancient custom the bodies of all who died in the roadways were wrapped in matting and buried there in shallow graves.

One freezing morning in November 1932 the missionaries received a peremptory summons from General Ma himself: they were to be taken, by force if necessary, to his camp at Anhsi. It transpired that Ma had been wounded while besieging Hami and had heard of Miss Cable's skill as a doctor. The desperate citizens of Hami – north of Tunhuang on the road to Urumchi – had, when they ran out of conventional ammunition, resorted to an old store of 'fire-arrows' tucked away in the depths of their arsenal. Miss Cable found that these primitive weapons caused wounds which were difficult to heal:

> Among the soldiers who were brought to me for treatment were many with wounds caused by the 'fire-arrows'. These wounds were septic and the flesh was charred as though burned by a chemical. It is known that as early as AD 75 a certain Chinese envoy, when in a desperate plight, used phosphorus for poisoning arrows, and by this means overcame his besiegers, and it is not improbable that the old fire-arrows of Hami had been treated in the same way.

While treating Ma's wounds Mildred Cable was able to observe at close quarters this 'callous, flippant youth who enjoyed his exercise of power', and who flew into uncontrollable rages if anyone dared to argue with him. Aitchen Wu, an educated Chinese official who was cut off in Urumchi at this time, and who tried to negotiate with Ma, felt there was a certain amount of good in the hot-headed young warlord (see URUMCHI), but to the three missionaries he seemed an unmitigated disaster. Their sympathies, not surprisingly, lay with the hard-working and uncomplaining peasants among whom they lived and worked. Once his wounds had healed Ma allowed the women to return to Tunhuang, and they eventually escaped from there to the relative safety of Sinkiang. Ma himself was overthrown in 1934 and managed to escape to Kashgar and then to the Soviet Union.

Today the visitor to the Tunhuang oasis would have no reason to suspect the dramatic events of sixty years ago. There is a bustling bazaar in the town, and organised tours to the Caves of the Thousand Buddhas, now much restored and festooned with unlovely walkways. They are as dark as ever, though, and visitors are well-advised to take a powerful torch. If you have time, pause and spare a thought for Abbot Wang who died in 1931 and is buried on the stone glacis outside the caves, having devoted over thirty years to their care. And perhaps reflect like Mildred Cable on the long succession of simple monks and artists who decorated them over the centuries:

> It must have been the unbroken quiet of this place, the remoteness of the oasis and its great solitude, which produced an eerie sense that the caves were guarded by the presence of those who once worked here so busily. Generation after generation, century after century, they had lived the absorbed life of creative artists, handing on, when their own time came to die, that great tradition of a production in which no individual artist is glorified, but in which an unnumbered crowd of craftsmen make their humble contribution toward the whole.

TURFAN
Cockroaches, Scorpions and Spiders

There is no more interesting oasis on the Asian highways than Turfan, which lies on the trade-route between Hami and Kashgar. The town lies in a hollow the lowest part of which is claimed to be the deepest dry depression on the face of the earth.

Mildred Cable, *The Gobi Desert*, 1942

Without a doubt, the women of Turfan are the most beautiful in all of Sinkiang.

Gunnar Jarring, *Return to Kashgar*, 1986

THE TURFAN DEPRESSION, 260 feet below sea-level and once the bottom of a huge Central Asian sea, still has salt marshes on its southern fringes and a lake in its centre called Moon Lake, the surface of which is completely covered in a crust of salt, rather like a layer of ice. The depression – roughly 100 miles long and 50 wide – is ringed by 'bare, red hills, strangely rent and torn', in the words of the archaeologist Albert von Le Coq, who found when he was working there that the hills absorbed the pitiless sun of Central Asia by day and radiated it out again at sundown. To add to the discomfort the depression, though happily not the town of Turfan, is home to a host of unpleasant creatures, including jumping spiders, giant cockroaches, scorpions and several varieties of poisonous snakes. Vegetation in the gritty semi-desert beyond the edges of the oasis is confined to scrubby clumps of tamarisk and other shrubs able to withstand scorching summer heat. 'In the centre of these uncompromising surroundings,' wrote the missionary and traveller Mildred Cable,

Turfan lies like a green island in a sandy wilderness, its shores lapped by grit and gravel instead of ocean water, for the division between arid desert and fertile land is as definite as that between shore and ocean. Its fertility is amazing, and the effect on the traveller, when he steps from sterility and desiccation into the luxuriance of Turfan, is overwhelming.

The mystery of Turfan's fertility, like that of Ashkhabad in Turkmenistan, derives from an ancient system of irrigation invented in Persia. To the north of the Turfan depression lie the Tien-shan mountains, with the magnificent peak of Bogdo Ula covered in eternal snow. Water is brought southwards along underground channels from wells dug at the foot of the mountains to catch the melting snow, the depth of the channels diminishing as they reach the plain and finally emerge into the open. There are 1,000 miles of these tunnels in the Turfan district, the longest measuring about 25 miles. The fresh cool water can then be tapped by the farmer, who produces a rich crop of grain, cotton and fruit, especially grapes, of which there are at least a dozen different varieties. Shafts have to be dug at intervals into the water tunnels, or *kariz*, to enable silt to be removed. These are easily visible by day, because of the heaps of mud beside them, but von Le Coq found them a death-trap at night. The official in charge of water distribution – a most responsible position – used to be known as the 'Water King'.

The Turfan area took on a strategic importance around the beginning of our era, for once the Han dynasty in China had managed to subdue the marauding Huns in 52 BC, the trade route which came to be known as the Silk Road was gradually established. One of its branches travelled westwards through the Turfan oasis on its way to Korla, Kucha, Aksu and Kashgar, while another went north-west to Urumchi and along the northern foothills of the Tien-shan to Tashkent. On the return journey the road led to Hami, Anhsi and through the Jade Gate into China proper. The old town of Karakhoja (or Khocho, or Gaochang) was the junction of these trade routes, and thus whoever ruled Karakhoja, to the east of the present-day town of Turfan, controlled the caravan trade. Usually China was in charge, but whenever the Chinese grip slackened the Huns would be waiting to raid the rich oasis and plunder passing caravans. In these times of trouble the local peasants and the Chinese soldiers of the garrison would take refuge in the fortress town of Yarkhoto (Jiaohe), the ruins of which can still be seen on a cliff to the west of Turfan.

Excavations at the old cities of the oasis have revealed traces of many civilisations, cultures and religions which put down roots here during their gradual passage along the caravan trails which ultimately linked China with India and the eastern Mediterranean. The classical influence brought to Afghanistan and the western end of Central Asia by Alexander the Great in the fourth century BC found its way to the Tarim Basin and the western confines of China via the Graeco-Buddhist kingdom of Gandhara, visited by many pilgrims once a Chinese emperor became a Buddhist convert in the first century AD. But Buddhism was not solely a court religion and was aimed at the ordinary people: the peasants, merchants and soldiers. Buddhist wall-paintings found at Turfan show a wide variety of types, including some with blue eyes and Western features. The austere creed of Manichaeism also found a home here, its art displaying the Persian imagery of its origins, and there is Christian art brought by the Nestorians, and the Turkic art of the Uighurs, a steppe people from the north.

The seventh century, when a strong Tang dynasty ruled both China and the Tarim Basin, was perhaps the heyday of Turfan. At that time the kingdom of Turfan included twenty-one towns, a large number of religious establishments and an impressive burial ground at Astana, just north of the principal city of Karakhoja. Further north, carefully hidden in the Flaming Hills, was the large Buddhist monastery complex of Bezeklik. The Chinese pilgrim Hsuan-tsang visited Karakhoja in the middle of the seventh century on his way to India to search for sacred Buddhist texts, and his preaching was esteemed so highly by the King of Turfan that he had to resort to a hunger strike before being allowed to leave. Taking the northern arm of the Silk Road, he travelled on to Kucha, Tashkent and Samarkand before striking south into India, where he spent fourteen years studying. When he returned, via Kashgar, Yarkand and Khotan, he brought with him so many manuscripts, relics and statues that a special monastery was built in the Chinese capital of Chang-an to house them all.

Along with religion and art some less elevated benefits travelled east to the sumptuous Tang court from Central Asia, including musicians and dancing girls. Turfan played its part by sending choice grapes, packed in ice, and a newly discovered product which was much appreciated by the Chinese: wine. After the fall of the Tang dynasty in AD 790 Turfan was ruled for a while by the Tibetans, but by the middle of the ninth century the great Turkic tribe of the Uighurs had taken control, after being ousted from their grazing grounds in the Altai mountains by another Turkic group, the Kirghiz. Previously a nomadic people, the Uighurs now began to settle, taking their flocks and herds north of the Tien-shan in summer, but making Karakhoja their capital in winter. A talented and adaptable people, they adopted both Buddhism and Manichaeism and became adept at trading. They managed to survive the Mongol terror of the thirteenth century by co-operating with the conquerors and helping to educate them. For though Genghis Khan was a brilliant soldier, his people had no written language until the Uighurs taught them to write, using their own Turkic script.

The enforced pacification of most of Asia by the Mongols allowed Western visitors to travel to the previously rather dangerous region of Central Asia for the first time. Some were missionaries and others were merchants, among them Marco Polo. To his Christian eyes the inhabitants of Turfan were, of course, unfortunate infidels, but he was forced to admit that they were quite civilised:

> The idolaters are very well versed in their own laws and
> traditions, and are keen students of the liberal arts. The land
> produces grain and excellent wine. But in winter the cold here
> is more intense than is known in any other part of the world.

The climate is certainly extreme, the thermometer plunging to minus 15 degrees centigrade (5°F) in winter and soaring to 40 degrees centigrade (104°F) in summer.

By the end of the fourteenth century the Uighurs (like their Mongol masters) had been converted to Islam, and the militancy of the new religion prompted the inhabitants of Turfan to attack neighbouring oases like Hami which were still Buddhist. In the end the entire region became Muslim and has remained so to this day. All the Buddhist, Manichaean and Nestorian temples and monasteries were destroyed or abandoned, and most of their inmates slaughtered. Over the years the buildings gradually crumbled or were dismantled by villagers who needed the bricks. Anything of obvious value was carried off, and even the paint from the wall-paintings was often scraped off and sprinkled on the fields, in the belief that it would enrich the soil. Earth tremors did further damage and sand blew into the ruins, filling and covering them. Thanks to the extreme dryness of the climate, what remained lay hidden, but perfectly preserved, for the next five centuries.

In the meantime the militant Uighurs of Turfan had suffered a reversal of fortune. While the Mongols ruled China the Uighurs did very well, for the Chinese ruling classes hated and despised the Yuan dynasty who only a generation ago had been unlettered nomads, and the new rulers depended heavily on Uighur support in matters of both trade and administration, and for internal security. Many Uighurs moved into western China at this period, where they prospered but were not popular. Having hitched themselves so firmly to the Mongol bandwagon, they found themselves in an equivocal position when the Yuan dynasty fell in 1368, to be replaced by the Chinese house of Ming. Towards the end of the fifteenth century the Ming rulers felt strong enough to expel all Uighur merchants from the western province of Kansu, and no further caravans from 'Uighuristan' were permitted to enter China. This, technically, was the end of the Silk Road, though China took care to keep in touch with the oasis of Turfan, for a dye was produced there which was needed for the decoration of blue-and-white porcelain.

The conquest of China by the Manchus in 1644 led to a revival of trade and other contact with the outside world, and the petty kingdoms of the Tarim Basin became again vassal states of China. Chinese garrisons were re-established in the old Silk Road oases by the new Ching dynasty, and inevitably there grew in time a certain resentment and hostility among the Muslims of Central Asia towards their overlords. Strong, impartial leaders could always command respect, but these became few and far between as the Ching lost their original vigour. As the centre became weak, the far-flung outposts of the empire became increasingly corrupt. Indeed, the only consolation for Chinese officials serving in such uncivilised posts as Turfan, Urumchi or Kashgar was the prospect of lining their own pockets. By the nineteenth century this rapacity towards the native population had reached such a degree that revolts flared up all over the region. In 1865 a Uighur chief called Yakub Beg proclaimed Kashgar and its surrounding area to be an independent kingdom, with himself as monarch, and embarked on tentative relations with both Imperial Russia and British India. This proved too much for even the lackadaisical Ching Emperor, and in 1873 he sent an army to defeat the upstart 'king'. Eastern Turkestan was declared to be part of China proper and was renamed Sinkiang – the New Frontier province. Turfan, which had risen against its Chinese garrison in sympathy with Yakub Beg, was severely punished.

When the British explorer and soldier Francis Younghusband passed through Turfan in July 1887, life had returned to normal. He found two separate towns at Turfan, the Chinese and the Turki, each surrounded by a wall. Arriving from Peking, the first thing he saw on approaching the town from the east was 'a mosque with a curious tower, which looked as much like a very fat factory chimney as anything else. It was about eighty feet high, circular, and built of mud bricks, and it was ornamented by placing the bricks at different angles, forming patterns'. This somewhat irreverent description by the 24-year-old subaltern was of the eighteenth-century Emin minaret. Younghusband put up at an inn in the Chinese town, which was smaller – and he hoped quieter – than the bustling Turki quarter. It was extremely hot, but the locals had found one way of coping with this:

> I had read in some book that at Turfan it was so hot that people lived in holes underground. I never quite believed it, but today I found it was a real fact. Here in the inn yard is a narrow flight of steps leading underground. I went down them and found a room with a *kang*, and a Chinaman lying on it smoking opium. It was perfectly cool below there, and there was no musty smell, for the soil is extremely dry. The room was well ventilated by means of a hole leading up through the roof.
>
> Younghusband, *The Heart of a Continent*, 1896

Younghusband had been greeted on his arrival in Turfan by cries of 'Ooroos', meaning 'Russian', for this was the only European nationality the locals were at all familiar with. Merchants from Andijan had always brought their goods to the caravanserais of Turfan, and their new colonial masters in St Petersburg had begun to send explorers and scientists in their wake. Dr Albert Regel had stumbled upon the ancient walled city of Karakhoja in 1879, but was suspected of spying by the Chinese, who had watched nervously as the Tsar had clawed more and more of western Turkestan into his vast empire. Regel was swiftly sent back to Russia, and the unfortunate natives who had helped him were put to death by slow torture. His report, however, and those of other travellers prompted the Imperial Russian Geographical Society to send an expedition to Turfan in 1898 under the leadership of Dmitri Klemenz. They explored a number of ancient cities, including Karakhoja, Astana and Yarkhoto, making plans of buildings, copying inscriptions and taking photographs of the sites. Klemenz counted 130 cave temples, many of them containing wall-paintings. Some of these he removed and took back to St Petersburg, together with antiquities and manuscripts unearthed at the sites.

The finds of the Klemenz expedition caused a sensation among Central Asian scholars, for they confirmed that an advanced culture – predominantly Buddhist – had existed in Eastern Turkestan long before the Islamic era. The Germans were the quickest to react, and the Ethnological Museum of Berlin sent its first archaeological expedition to Turfan in 1902. Even this preliminary foray yielded forty-six crates of antiquities, but this was as nothing compared to the awe-inspiring total which the three subsequent German expeditions carried back to Berlin. Thirty-four tons of antiquities – many of them huge wall-paintings – were sent back to Germany in a total of 387 crates, between 1905 and 1914. The Germans were not the only ones, however. In 1908 a party of Japanese excavators spent two months digging at the Turfan sites, and in 1915 Sir Aurel Stein sent 141 crates of antiquities from the area to British India.

Today this might seem like looting, but no one objected at the time. To the local Muslims, Buddhist culture – especially the wall-paintings – was anathema and many paintings and sculptures representing the human form had already been mutilated. As for the Chinese, those who took an interest in the matter tended to sympathise with the desire of Western archaeologists to rescue these works of art from oblivion. For apart from the ravages of wind, sand and local iconoclasm, this was an earthquake zone. Later, of course, once China had its own archaeologists, they began to feel that they had been robbed of their heritage.

Albert von Le Coq, the moving spirit behind most of the German expeditions, wrote a most entertaining account of his work and travels entitled *Buried Treasures of Chinese Turkestan*, which was first published in English in 1928. Here is his description of some of the repulsive insects of the Turfan Depression:

> Insect pests are very much in evidence here. There are scorpions whose sting is a very serious matter and, in addition, a kind of great spider that, in spite of a hairy body the size of a pigeon's egg, can take mighty jumps with its long, hairy legs. It makes a crunching noise with its jaws and is said to be poisonous, although I have never known any bitten by it.
>
> Another spider, very much smaller and black but hairy too, lives in holes in the ground. It is very greatly feared and its bite is said to be, if not deadly, at any rate extremely weakening and dangerous. The cockroaches too are a repulsive pest, in size quite as long as a man's thumb, with big red eyes and formidable feelers. It was enough to make a man uncontrollably sick to wake in the morning with such a creature sitting on his nose, its big eyes staring down at him and its long feelers trying to attack its victim's eyes. We used to seize the creature in terror and crush it, when it gave off an extremely disagreeable smell. Fortunately there were no bugs, although fleas abounded everywhere, but were not very obtrusive. The louse, on the contrary, is *the* domestic animal of all Turkestan and Tibet.

The ruined town of Karakhoja, lying in the desert to the east of Turfan, covered an area of about one square kilometre and was still enclosed by the remains of its massive mud-brick walls. Here the Germans quickly made an exciting discovery:

> Some peasants led me into the centre of the town, where they had torn down a thin wall of more recent erection in a great hall-like building. Behind this wall, on the more ancient wall, appeared the remains of a great mural painting, representing a man over life-size in the dress of a Manichaean priest, surrounded by Manichaean monks and nuns also dressed in the white garb of their order. We have reason to think that we

had there a traditional representation of Manes, the founder of the Manichaean religion. The picture forms one of the principal objects of our collection.

This fresco probably dated from the eighth century AD and was the earliest known depiction of Manes, who had founded this fanatical faith – based on the opposition of Light and Dark or spiritual versus carnal – five centuries earlier in Persia. Manes, who outlawed sex, meat and all forms of pleasure, was regarded with fear and loathing by the adherents of other faiths, and was finally burnt at the stake as a heretic, but his religion survived until the ninth century, and was at one time adopted by the Uighurs. Von Le Coq was saddened to see how much damage had been done at Karakhoja by the natives, with 'their constant digging'. Apart from straightforward treasure-seeking, they had levelled many areas in order to plant crops, scraping off paint from frescoes to use as fertiliser. The water they channelled into the site for irrigation had also caused untold destruction:

> I had the grief of discovering in the Manichaean shrine K a library which was utterly destroyed by water. When I had unearthed the door from the heaped-up loess dust and sand we found on the threshold the dried-up corpse of a murdered Buddhist monk, his ritual robe all stained with blood. The whole room, into which this door led, was covered to a depth of about two feet with a mass of what, on closer inspection, proved to be remains of Manichaean manuscripts. The loess water had penetrated the papers, stuck everything together, and in the terrible heat of the usual summer there all these valuable books had turned into loess. I took specimens of them and dried them carefully in the hope of saving some of these manuscripts; but the separate pages crumbled off and dropped into small fragments, on which the remains of beautifully written lines, intermingled with traces of miniatures executed in gold, blue, red, green and yellow were still to be seen. An enormous treasure has been lost here.

After working for several weeks at Karakhoja, von Le Coq and his cheerful handyman Theodor Bartus moved north up the Sangim gorge to investigate some cave temples hewn out of the rock. Here they unearthed quantities of early manuscripts but also found, to their chagrin, that native treasure-hunters were at work and causing a good deal of random destruction. At least it was much more pleasant working in the mountains, where the air was fresher. Down in the depression it was already stifling by the end of February. Moving thirty-five miles north-east of Turfan, the Germans found a hidden monastery complex tucked away on a mountainside:

> To get there the traveller follows the Sangim ravine in a northerly direction as far as the point where the Murtuk water-course flows, between steep cliffs, into the stream rushing down the Sangim valley. Then he must climb the high cliffs on the right bank to follow a narrow road winding on the top of these cliffs to the great monastery settlement of Bezeklik, which lies a little to the south of the great village of Murtuk. A visitor to the monastery reaches its immediate neighbourhood without once catching sight of the great settlement. Only in one spot is it possible to get a glimpse of the temple, but there the old monks put up a wall – parts of which are still standing – which protected their settlement from the eyes of passing travellers. Evidence is everywhere forthcoming of the endeavours made by monastery dwellers to secure the greatest possible isolation from the busy world and its doings.
>
> The road suddenly widens and ends on a broad, sandy plain, behind which rise high, curiously shaped hills. Even from here the monastery is not to be seen, for it is situated on a terrace, about ten yards above the bed of the stream and the same distance below the precipitous edge of the level expanse, lying in a horse-shoe curve of the high river bank. It is only when the traveller gets quite close to this edge that he sees the building on its terrace.

Von Le Coq found that there were about seventy temples altogether, almost all decorated with wall-paintings. All those at the southern end of the site had been used as dwellings by goat-herds, and the smoke from their fires had spoiled the delicate paintings. Others were full of sand which had blown in over the centuries from the barren mountains. Clambering up a heap of sand in one of these cave temples, von Le Coq started a miniature landslide and 'suddenly, as if by magic, I saw on the walls bared in this way, to my right and left, splendid paintings in colours as fresh as if the artist had only just finished them'. He and Bartus began to clear out the sand, uncovering more and more frescoes of astonishing freshness and beauty. The paintings depicted monks of the ninth century from various places along the Silk Road: Indians, with their names written in an Indian script, and eastern Asiatics whose names were written in both Chinese and Uighur. Others had Persian features, and a curious group showed men with red hair, blue eyes and faces 'of a pronounced European type'. Von Le Coq was excited by the fact that the paintings were genuine portraits and not, as was often the case, produced from stencils. 'By dint of long and arduous work,' he wrote later, 'we succeeded in cutting away all these pictures. After twenty months of travelling they arrived safely at Berlin, where they fill an entire room of the museum.'

Tragically, these particular paintings – which had to be cemented into the museum walls because of their weight – could not be removed to safety during the Second World War and were destroyed when the building was hit by Allied bombs. The temples at Bezeklik can still be seen with their ravaged walls, and are pointed out reproachfully to tourists. Basil Davidson, whose left-wing sympathies allowed him to visit this remote site in 1956, said in his book *Turkestan Alive* that he found it 'sad and sickening' to see the gaps where the murals had been. His guide repeated the word 'stolen' as they passed each 'large and painful excision', and Davidson made it plain that he felt the Chinese had every right to feel aggrieved. To von Le Coq, however, it was a rescue operation for, quite apart from local vandalism and official indifference, he had seen other temple complexes where everything had been destroyed by earthquakes. He would certainly be amazed to learn that Turfan and its archaeological sites are now on the tourist circuit.

In 1905 Bezeklik seemed to the Germans like the back of beyond, magnificent but somehow sinister:

The mountain, rising behind the monastery settlement, is snow-white in colour, but regularly flooded with crimson under the rays of the rising and setting sun. In front of this mountain there lies a sharply outlined accumulation of black mountain sand; below this stretches the plain, covered like the ruins themselves with the golden hue of the yellow loess.

But when we saw the moon rise enormous in the heavens, the colour of [the] mountains and the loess changed in a surprising manner. The mountain peak became a violet blue, the heap of black sand green with golden shadows, but the loess assumed the most marvellous and magical colours that varied with the brightness or shadow in which it lay; here crimson, there violet, now blue, then deepest black – in short, I have never seen such a fantastic and wondrous colour symphony as we enjoyed on every bright moonlit night. And on such nights, when we went to bed, sleep would not come at first in spite of all fatigue; the impressions and experiences of the day were too strong to let our minds find rest at once.

In the death-like silence that always reigns there, the splashing of the rushing stream, as it fell over the rocks at the foot of the gorge in the mountain-side, sounded like scornful laughter. Even though the landscape was one of incredible, indescribable beauty, it did not lack with this note of demoniacal laughter a certain suggestion of something weird and uncanny, and one understood why, in all these temples, the ugly demons appeared on the walls.

Occasionally the silence was shattered, and this was even more unnerving:

On such a night, when all was still as death, ghastly noises suddenly resounded as though a hundred devils had been let loose. We sprang up in terror, seized our rifles, and rushed out on to the terrace. There, to our horror, we saw the whole horse-shoe gorge filled with wolves that, head in air, were baying the moon with long-drawn-out howls.

Our servants hurried up to reassure us with: 'Sir, sir, you needn't be afraid, they'll not hurt you.' And that was true, too. After a few shots, one of which hit one of the visitors, the animals left us after they had eaten their dead comrade. The wolf, like the tiger in the northerly and westerly inhabited regions, especially near Maralbashi and also in Lop-nor, is in this country a relatively harmless creature.

I only heard of one case where a human being had been killed by wolves. This was the tragic history of a pretty twelve-year-old little girl of Karakhoja – we knew the child – who was to be married, against her will, to an old man of sixty. She ran away to Lukchun across the desert, but only got half-way to a spot where an enormous elm tree on the banks of a spring provided a resting-place amid the sandy wastes. Here she lay down to rest, and was attacked by wolves in her sleep. All that was found later were blood-stained fragments of her clothing and her long top-boots with her legs still inside.

Von Le Coq and Bartus departed from Turfan well-pleased with their finds, but when Sir Aurel Stein, the Hungarian-born British archaeologist, visited the sites a few years later he described the Germans privately as little better than treasure-hunters, with no scientific method. Indeed, some sites looked like the scene of a hit-and-run accident, but perhaps these were the places where the unskilled but enthusiastic Bartus had been allowed to do a spot of unsupervised digging. Stein himself found plenty which the Germans had missed, even at Bezeklik, although he concentrated mainly on the seventh-century city of the dead at Astana. The tombs had all been stripped of their obvious valuables by native diggers, but to Stein the ancient silk in which the corpses had been wrapped and which had been miraculously preserved by the extreme dryness of the atmosphere, was of far more interest anyway. The fact that each body had been buried with a baked funerary brick inscribed with biographical details and dates enabled textile historians to trace the progress of various decorative motifs as they passed along the Silk Road between China and the Middle East. The art of Central Asia, which resulted from this intermingling of influences from China and India, with a dash of the classical thrown in, was described by Stein as 'Serindian'.

The collapse of the Ching dynasty in 1911 led to a long period of unrest and uncertainty in China, with a succession of republican governments which were unable to unite the whole country. The north in particular became the battleground of rival warlords who cared nothing for any government, and who imposed their rule by fear and violence. Sinkiang was soon too chaotic and dangerous for archaeological digs, and the militant republicanism of some Chinese officials made foreign excavators unwelcome anyway. But during the 1920s and 1930s the region was still visited by Christian missionaries, many of whom suffered great danger and privation. In the interludes of peace, however, they trundled around the desert in their mule-carts, dispensing medicines, kindness and religious tracts to the villages and towns. In her book *The Gobi Desert* Mildred Cable, who worked for the China Inland Mission, gives an affectionate description of life in Turfan:

The natives of Turfan are strict Moslems and builders of handsome mosques, of which there are several in the town. The most striking of these buildings stands to the south-east of the Chinese quarter. It was built by the royal family of Lukchun, and though in its present form it dates only from 1760, yet it was probably erected on the site of a much more ancient building, possibly of Nestorian origin. During the fast of *Ramazan* the whole life of the town is altered, as for this one month of the year no Moslem may touch food or drink between sunrise and sunset. During short, cold winter days this restriction merely amounts to a severe discipline, but if it falls in the great heat, when days are long and nights are short, the necessity for drink is urgent and the suffering imposed by abstinence is intense. Wealthy people sleep away the hours of daylight, but labourers, who must do their task in spite of everything, long for the fast to be over.

In more sophisticated countries the close of the fast is fixed by the calendar, but in Central Asia it is marked by the first sight of the new moon in the sunset sky. Everyone watches for the first streak of silver, and roofs are covered with people peering into space, each hoping to be the first to give the great news that the faint crescent is visible. As soon as she appears the fast is over, but her presence must be vouched for by at least three witnesses. When this is done the young men run helter-skelter down the roof ladders and back to the homes, where feasts are spread of special dishes; these they eat and enjoy in complete satisfaction, feeling that one more *Ramazan* is over.

She goes on to describe the bazaar, where the 'Turki shop-keepers, in high leather boots stitched with many colours, and wearing embroidered skull-caps, sit tailor-fashion on long wooden counters, with their goods spread around and a teapot and cup beside them from which they sip pale-green tea'. The bazaar had its separate quarters for different goods, ranging from luscious dried fruits to medicinal herbs, and including silk-merchants, leather vendors, young boys weaving the traditional Turki carpets, and the sellers of tie-dyed cotton. 'Rolls of bright chintz fill the shelves at the back of the stall,' wrote Miss Cable. 'Some of this material is very cleverly dyed, for the women know how to knot little bunches in the length of stuff before it goes to the dyer, so that when it comes back they open it out and find a pattern of flowers or butterflies scattered at regular intervals over the material.'

Turkis and Chinese appeared to mingle in the throng, but in reality, she noticed, the two communities led quite separate lives:

> The bazaar is always crowded and always noisy. The little city carts which ply between different quarters of the town move quickly, and their drivers shout '*Huish, Huish!*' as they go, a cry which commands right of way. The stream of Turki and Chinese people in the bazaar only mingles superficially for, in fact, each keeps separate from the other and follows his own way of life. The Chinese buys at Chinese stalls, the Turki shops among his own people, and the food vendors serve men of their own race. The pleasures and entertainments of Turkis and Chinese are of a different order, for the mentality and outlook of each nation are profoundly different and neither trusts the other.

In spite of all the variegated din of the market-place, another strange sound could often be heard:

> Above all the noise and shouting there can be sometimes heard a strange, weird, lilting chorus of men's voices. It comes from a band of *kalandars*, a group of strange, dishevelled men with long, uncombed hair, dressed in fantastic costumes. One will have iron chains hanging to his arms which he shakes rhythmically as he moves, another will have a frame of

hanging discs on which he plays a primitive accompaniment, another will knock pieces of bone together, marking time for the chant. They have sonorous voices, and though many are deformed and some blind in one or both eyes, they are strong creatures and greatly feared, no-one daring to refuse their demand for money lest they call a curse down on him. These *kalandars* are a guild of professional beggars, and as they walk they sing old religious songs, always ending with the refrain 'Allah, Allah-hu'.

You are unlikely to be confronted by a band of *kalandars* in present-day Turfan, but it is a colourful place, especially on Sundays, the main market day. The bazaar is still heaped with succulent fruit and vegetables, and the sellers of carpets and embroidered caps still sip green tea among their wares. Private enterprise is tolerated on a small scale, and there are always customers around the little food-stalls, still selling – as in Mildred Cable's day – 'snippets of meat and kidney grilled over a portable charcoal fire'. The meat, she noted, was 'very tasty, though generally tough'. The Turki, said Miss Cable, 'is a burly man and a voracious eater, and there is always a crowd in that part of the bazaar where food is sold'. Some things do not change.

URUMCHI
Most Sinister Town in Asia

The town has no beauty, no style, no dignity and no architectural interest. The climate is violent, exaggerated, and no season pleasant.

Mildred Cable and Francesca French, *The Gobi Desert*, 1942

Dinners are a particularly convenient occasion for packing off any unwanted person to the other world by means of poison. For this reason guests who have any grounds for expecting a dish specially prepared for them by their host always take the precaution of changing the dish served to them, either with that of the host himself if they can manage it, or with their next-door neighbour.

Paul Nazaroff, *Moved On! From Kashgar to Kashmir*, 1935

N O ONE HAS a good word to say for Urumchi. Its name, which means in Uighur 'Beautiful Grassland', proves that it had a certain appeal to nomads with flocks and herds to feed, situated as it is between the Tien-shan mountains and the sandy steppe of Dzungaria to the north. For it lay on a route which was in times of peace a branch of the Silk Road, and in times of trouble a funnel for the successive waves of nomadic tribes driven westwards by the population explosions of Manchuria and Mongolia. It came to prominence only in 1873 when China defeated the rebel chief of Kashgaria, Yakub Beg, and declared eastern Turkestan its 'New Frontier' province of Sinkiang, with Urumchi as the capital. Standing 3,000 feet above sea-level, the town suffers deep snow in winter, with temperatures often plunging to minus 10 degrees centigrade. A newly arrived missionary was startled to find his courtyard filled with an eight-foot snowdrift one December morning, but he soon discovered that this was nothing unusual. In summer, on the other hand, Urumchi is unbearably hot and dusty, while spring used to be, in the days of unmade roads, a nightmare of glutinous mud.

Peking paid the Governor of Sinkiang a small annual subsidy, but he was expected to raise his own revenue by means of taxes and customs dues. It went without saying that he and all his officials would enrich themselves in the process, for basic wages for officials were very low. Everyone 'squeezed' a little out of those below them in the pecking order, those at the bottom of the heap suffering most, as there was no one for them to squeeze. This was the time-honoured system in China, and provided order was kept and there were not too many complaints, Peking usually left Provincial Governors in peace. Sinkiang's Governor had the added advantage of being a very long way indeed from the central government, and Urumchi soon acquired an evil reputation for extortion, intrigue and sudden death.

When the German archaeologist Albert von Le Coq passed through Urumchi in 1904, a sizeable Chinese town had grown up around the Red Hill, the town's main landmark on which there were pagodas and lookout posts. Next to it was the old native town, the whole being surrounded by mud walls pierced by narrow gates. The commercial life of the town had spilled outside the gates, however, particularly the Great West Gate where a prosperous suburb had established itself, and to the south where the Russian merchants lived around the Imperial Consulate. Von Le Coq found some of the sights of Urumchi repugnant:

> The fortifications are those usual in China, and the streets, on the whole, are representative of a Chinese town. The sight of a Chinese execution apparatus, set up in the principal street, made a very unpleasant impression on me. It was a cage in which a condemned man was standing on a movable footboard. His head was firmly fixed between planks and every day the foot-board was moved down a little so that the unhappy man's neck was slowly dragged out more and more until in the end – eight days it was said to last – death occurred. The traffic went on as usual past this barbaric apparatus, and a melon-dealer was selling his juicy fruit with no concern for his neighbour's misery.
>
> Von Le Coq, *Buried Treasures of Chinese Turkestan*, 1928

Despite being liberally entertained by the Chinese Governor to a banquet of no fewer than eighty-six courses von Le Coq found Urumchi's atmosphere decidedly sinister, and left as soon as possible. Two years later, a Scottish missionary named George Hunter began a lonely ministry there which was to last for nearly forty years, only ending when he was forcibly dragged off to a Communist jail. Hunter became something of a legend in his own lifetime, translating the Scriptures into slightly dubious Uighur, trundling around the province in a converted ammunition cart, and very occasionally visiting Kashgar, where he shared some highly dramatic experiences with the Macartney family (see KASHGAR).

A succession of grasping Governors, willingly abetted by their cohorts of embezzling officials, brought Sinkiang to the verge of bankruptcy by the turn of the century. Soldiers were discharged through lack of funds to pay their wages, and the makeshift solution of running off vast quantities of paper money only added inflation to the province's problems. By 1910 a secret society, the Ko-Lao-Hui, dedicated to the overthrow of the decadent Manchu dynasty, had spread its tentacles throughout China, and in Sinkiang it was whispered that many army commanders were members. In 1911 uprisings began to break out all over the empire, and the dynasty which had ruled China since the middle of the seventeenth century tottered into oblivion. Sun Yat-sen became President of a provisional republican government in December 1911, although he stood down after a few months in favour of the wily and ambitious Yuan Shih-kai. In Sinkiang a series of violent revolts spread westwards along the old Silk Road, stirred up by the Ko-Lao-Hui, and the province was plunged into panic and terror. For few of the rebels were genuine revolutionaries with political aims. Many were disgruntled ex-soldiers, others belonged to the underclass of criminals, gamblers and opium-smokers, while some were simply out to settle old scores.

Urumchi itself had a close shave at the end of December 1911 when a mob of riff-raff, led by four members of the Ko-Lao-Hui from far-off Honan, tried to rush the armoury, the Governor's residence and the police headquarters. As it happened, the troops remained loyal and the attack was repulsed. The authorities reacted swiftly, beheading the four ringleaders forthwith and gradually rounding up local members of the Ko-Lao-Hui. These they put to death by slow torture as a warning to anyone else who might be tempted to join the secret society. The weak and terrified Governor of the day was quickly replaced by his formidable Chief Justice, Yang Tseng-hsin, who was to rule the province with an iron hand for the next seventeen years.

Yang was always a shadowy figure to the British, whose nearest representative was 800 miles away in Kashgar, but he had a reputation for being a just man and he certainly managed to give Sinkiang stability, while nearby Kansu and Shensi were torn apart by feuding warlords. The political future of China was very uncertain during Yang's lifetime: President Yuan soon suppressed Sun Yat-sen's Nationalist Party and even had himself declared Emperor, but after his death in 1916 the country relapsed into anarchy. Yang made no attempt to bend with the wind. He ran Sinkiang on the same autocratic lines regardless of what happened in Peking, and always behaved as though there was an emperor on the throne. Indeed, in remote Sinkiang it made little difference who claimed to be in control of the country. As a result he had many enemies among those Chinese with republican sympathies, as well as those whose extortions he curbed, but he had one great advantage: the loyalty of the Tungans, or Chinese Muslims.

Not to be confused with the Turkic Muslims of Central Asia, the Tungans were descended from Chinese merchants who had intermarried with the Mongols in the thirteenth and fourteenth centuries when China was ruled by a Mongol dynasty, the Yuan. During the course of their dealings with Arab and Persian traders they had been converted to Islam, and there were large numbers of them still in Kansu where Yang had spent much of his career. Described by a British diplomat as a 'formidable and unpleasant race', the modern Tungans were more interested in fighting than trading, and the Governor had 2,000 fierce Tungan soldiers at his disposal.

But China's internal problems, grave as they were, were not Yang's only worry: there was also the ever-present threat from Russia. During the nineteenth century the armies of the Tsar had steadily annexed enormous tracts of what came to be known as Russian Turkestan, and which had formerly been ruled by a number of Turkic khans. The whole of Transcaspia had then been wrested from the Turcomans, and there was no reason to suppose that the predations of the Russians had ended. They already had a strong foothold in Chinese Turkestan, with Consulates at Kashgar, Urumchi, Kuldja and Chuguchak. George Hunter had been amazed to find an entire Russian suburb outside the gates of Urumchi, with an imposing Consulate guarded by Cossacks, and von Le Coq had remarked on the arrogant behaviour of the Russian Consul there, natives being driven from his path with horsewhips when he entered the town.

One of the Russian strategies was to create as many Russian citizens as possible among native traders now settled in Chinese Turkestan who had originally come from across the border. Some of these individuals had very dubious claims indeed, but as possession of a Russian passport meant exemption from local taxes, there was no lack of eager applicants for citizenship. They were all Turkic Muslims, and whenever there was an outbreak of violence between Muslims and Chinese – and this was frequent in these troubled times – Russia would send in some more Cossacks 'to protect its citizens'. One way and another, Governor Yang had his hands full. He was nearly toppled in 1916, after the province of Yunnan rebelled against Peking and looked to Yang, himself a Yunnanese, for support. The canny Governor refused to drag Sinkiang into the turmoil, but a number of Yunnanese officers in his province secretly plotted to outflank him by declaring Sinkiang independent too, supposedly on his behalf. Needless to say, Yang got to hear of the plot, and his remedy was to invite the rebels to a banquet. While he calmly replenished the glasses of his other guests, the plotters were beheaded one by one, their blood spattering the tablecloth and the robes of their neighbours. Yang himself ate a hearty meal, though most of his guests found they had lost their appetites.

After the Russian Revolution and civil war Urumchi, like Kashgar, became a place of refuge for many White Russians. Some were soldiers, including the Cossack leader Ataman Annenkov, who had fought desperately against the Bolsheviks but had finally been driven across the border. Yang realised at once that if he harboured a large body of armed men the Bolsheviks would have a good excuse to pursue them into China, and probably to annex Sinkiang for good measure. Another banquet was arranged, at which the unsuspecting Annenkov was seized and thrown into prison. There he was kept in chains, but liberally supplied with opium, which gradually sapped his will. Later he was quietly handed over to the Bolsheviks who executed him. Demoralised, his followers laid down their arms and lived in destitution, sometimes reduced to eating rats and tortoises. White women, perhaps for the first time in Asia, were forced to beg from natives or even to sell themselves in order to feed their children. However, once Yang felt confident that they were no threat to security, he allowed them to settle in Urumchi's Russian suburb and become traders – uneasily close to their Communist compatriots at the Consulate.

While Yang preserved law and order in Sinkiang by sheer force of will, the rest of China now began to fall apart. Civil war raged, and the northern provinces fell into the hands of a number of unpredictable and brutal warlords. Amazingly, in the middle of all this strife, the Swedish explorer Sven Hedin decided to embark on a scientific expedition to the Gobi desert in the winter of 1927–8. He had some difficulty persuading Yang to allow his team into Sinkiang, but the Governor eventually relented:

So now we were in Urumchi, the Tihua of the Chinese, the capital of the powerful Yang Tseng-hsin, and the two whole months that I and some of the members of the staff spent here became of great importance for the further development of the expedition.

After we had fulfilled the usual obligations of travelling guests, had given notice of our arrival and presented our visiting-cards, I was requested to present myself at 12 o'clock on the 29th February [1928] at the house of the Governor-General.

Through the bottomless mud of the streets, in which during our stay two horses were drowned and even children are said to have perished, we travelled in a line of little blue carts, the *droshkies* of China, through the main street of the White Russian settlement, through Turkish quarters and the great gates in the wall of the Chinese town, to the *yamen*, a group of red houses with intervening courtyards, from whose holy of holies the enormous province is governed. We had two rectangular courtyards to cross before we reached the audience hall. At the porch sentries were standing and presented arms. In the vestibule we were received by the ruler of Sinkiang, surrounded by officers and ministers as well as the soldiers of his bodyguard.

Here we now stood face to face with the autocratic ruler who had set himself against us with such icy coldness on the eastern frontier of his province, and who could, if it had occurred to him, have frustrated our plans and forced us to turn back. Without moving a feature of his stern face, he inspected us one after the other with penetrating glances, and greeted each one separately with a soft warm shake of the hand and a scarcely perceptible bow.

Hedin, *Across the Gobi Desert*, 1931

After this somewhat unnerving silent inspection, Yang bade them welcome and glasses were filled. He made a speech thanking them for the valuable investigations they would be making in his province, and promised to facilitate their work. Hedin saw the Governor frequently over the next few weeks, and grew fond of the old man:

We who came into close contact with him during the last period of his life treasure a deep, enduring impression of his great personality and his powerful form. He was, perhaps, the last representative of an age gone by, and possessed in high degree the great virtues of Old China: pride, and love of fatherland. His only dream was of a united China, and he once declared to me that on the day when the southern troops marched into Peking, he would not hesitate to recognize the new order. To us he was a benefactor; he helped our expedition across a gulf which could have become dangerous for us. For that reason we remember him with veneration and gratitude.

At the beginning of May 1928 Hedin planned to leave for Sweden and then return to do some further work in Sinkiang after an interval. Yang asked him to bring back some motor vehicles from Europe, suitable for the local roads, and some mechanics to look after them. Hedin promised to do so. 'The old governor was tired and I took leave after a quarter of an hour. He accompanied me across the courtyards right up to my cart and once again wished me a safe journey. Finally he said: "Come back soon". Now the driver cracked his whip, and we rolled away. I had seen Yang Tseng-hsin for the last time.'

For in that same momentous year, when the southern troops did indeed march into Peking under Chiang Kai-shek, and most of China was uneasily unified, Governor Yang was murdered. Predictably the deed was done at a banquet, masterminded by an ambitious colleague. A Chinese official who went to Urumchi a few years later heard what happened from an eyewitness:

> Fan [the Commissioner for Foreign Affairs and chief conspirator] then raised his cup towards the Soviet Consul-General to drink his health, and as their cups met, shots rang out simultaneously, all aimed at the Governor. Seven bullets in all were fired and all reached their mark. Yang, mortally wounded, but superb in death, glared an angry defiance at his foes. 'Who dares do this?' he questioned in the loud voice which had commanded instant obedience for so many years. Then he fell slowly forward, his last glance resting upon the face of the trusted Yen [the eyewitness, and one of Yang's loyal ministers] as though to ask forgiveness that he had not listened to the advice so often given to him.
>
> The seven bullets soon took effect. A faithful aide-de-camp rushed forward to help his master, but a further shot rang out and the young officer collapsed, mortally wounded, while Yang, whom he had been in the act of raising, sank down upon him.
>
> When they saw what had happened the high officials stampeded for the door. The Russian Consul and his wife took refuge in the lavatory. Lieutenant Tu was shot and Yen, who was wounded in the shoulder, only escaped by feigning death. As he lay beneath the overturned tables Yen saw Fan standing over the sorely wounded but still breathing Governor, revolver in hand. Two further shots completed the crime.
>
> Aitchen Wu, *Turkistan Tumult*, 1940

The treacherous Fan was himself slain in the ensuing bloodbath – by torture, it was said – and the other conspirators were all rounded up by the faithful Tungan troops and either deported or executed. But there was no one of stature to step into Yang's shoes, and the next Governor, Chin, proved quite unequal to the task. Muslim revolts flared up throughout the province from 1930 onwards, and Urumchi itself was threatened by a young Tungan warlord called Ma Chung-yin – nicknamed Big Horse – who aimed to unite both Turki and Tungan Muslims under his banner.

Aitchen Wu, a scholar and poet by inclination but a government official by profession, was sent to Urumchi at the end of 1932 to advise the Governor. Although Chiang Kai-shek's government theoretically ruled the whole of China, in practice the northern warlords were a law unto themselves, and travel through their regions could be extremely dangerous. Wu and his companions took a cautious route via Vladivostock and the Siberian railway, entering Sinkiang through the frontier town of Chuguchak, or Tacheng. After four more days of travelling, when there were never less than thirty degrees of frost, Wu was cheered to see the outlines of Urumchi appear on the southern horizon:

> The road was now excellent and we could see on a hill in the distance the twin pagodas which are the famous landmark of the city. Soon the low walls were in sight and we could see the people crowding out to meet us. After 36 days of travel I was now in the heart of Sinkiang, my journey was now at an end. Here before me lay the mysterious city of Urumchi. It had, I was aware, a dark history, but I was full of hope for its future.

Wu's imagination was clearly stirred by this exotic Central Asian city, though he little suspected then what horrifying scenes he would witness in the year to come. In his memoirs he gives one of the best descriptions of Urumchi as it used to be, calling it by its Chinese name of Tihwa, which means 'Return to civilisation':

> The walls of Tihwa make a circuit of eleven *li*, that is, rather less than four miles. There are seven gates in all, two facing each point of the compass except the north, on which side there is only one. These gates are narrow and rounded, admitting only one stream of traffic. The wall is about fifteen feet in height and is of baked clay, reinforced by stone. In colour it is a dull ochre, a drabness which blends with the surroundings. Nevertheless, the provincial capital is far from drab; the Urumchi river gives fertility to the soil, and in summer the green of the trees delights the eye. From the pagoda of the Red Temple, situated upon a windy eminence to the north of the city, the course of the river can be seen, bridged at this point by the rough highway to Tacheng along which we entered. To the south-west lie the Tien-shan or

Celestial Mountains, whose peaks when I first beheld them were white with snow. Through a pass to the south runs the road to Turfan; eastwards the great range continues, rising in height, to culminate in Bogdo Ula, the Holy Mountain, black crags surmounted by three sharp summits, frowning upon the peaceful city. Northward lie the great plains, where the meandering river loses itself first in marshland and then in barren sands. This region is the vast Dzungarian steppe, where between marsh and desert are herded the huge flocks which supply the wants of the capital.

Fully one third of Tihwa lies outside the walls. Entering from the north the traveller first passes into the Chinese city; then comes the Moslem city, still within the walls; lastly, on the far side, lies the Nan Kuan, the 'southern suburb', where the Russian merchants dwell. On my first crossing of the city I was struck by the contrast between one quarter and the next. In the Chinese quarter all was familiar to me, the walled *yamens*, the neat wooden houses, the seething bazaars. This was China as I knew it; but within a distance of a few yards I was plunged into an alien atmosphere. Here was the vigorous life of a city of the southern steppes, where Turk and Tartar meet – the mosque, the market, the endless rows of stalls. And passing beyond the fortifications I came into another world, the bare spaciousness of a Russian market town, the walled compound of the Soviet Consulate serving as its focus, from which it straggled to the south.

Wu Ai-chen means in Chinese 'the gentle Wu', and Mr Wu's book is indeed written gently, philosophically even, in stark contrast to the events it records. One feels he was always looking for the best in everything. Mildred Cable, a tireless missionary who spent most of her life in western China, was another gentle soul but a very practical one, and she viewed Urumchi with more acerbity:

Urumchi's shopkeeping class lives to make money, and its official class lives for promotion. Nothing draws men to the place but the prospect of good business or of political advancement, and the sordid streets are typical of its sordid civic life. In government circles friendly social intercourse has become impossible, as any visitor might be an informer. A secret report can always command a price, and promotion often depends upon supplying it, therefore no man trusts his neighbour. For such reasons as these no one enjoys life in Urumchi, no one leaves the town with regret, and it is full of people who are only there because they cannot get permission to leave and may not leave without permission.

No one has troubled to develop the natural resources of the locality. On one side of the town a wide river flows, but the water it supplies has to be laboriously carried in pails to the houses of the people and there paid for. There are coal-mines in the vicinity, but they are worked so casually, and transport is so badly organized, that delivery is uncertain and it is not unusual, in the coldest weather, for fuel to be unobtainable.

Cable and French, *The Gobi Desert*, 1942

Miss Cable and her companions Eva and Francesca French were based in Kansu, the other side of the Gobi desert, but in 1928 they wrote to George Hunter to ask if they could stay in Urumchi for a while on their way home on leave. Hunter's assistant, Percy Mather, had not left China for sixteen years and it was arranged that he would accompany the three women to England for a short furlough, bringing back copies of the Bible in Russian for the many White refugees who had lost theirs along with their other possessions. Hunter himself had for many years declined home leave. He had not seen his native Scotland since 1900 when, after praying at his fiancée's grave, he had turned his face resolutely away from home and had dedicated the rest of his life to Chinese Central Asia.

Hunter and Mather had not seen a fellow-countrywoman for at least twelve years, and the two men were afraid that their simple and austere establishment might not be suitable. They each had a tiny house, too small for guests, so they quickly built another one in their compound, which was thereafter always known as 'The Ladies' House'. George even discarded his tattered Chinese robe and cut off his pigtail in their honour, and 'in a most courtly manner he welcomed his guests to his home'. They stayed with him until 1929, concentrating their evangelical efforts on the women of the town. Bidding farewell to his friends and his young assistant was almost too much for George, who rode out with them on the first stage of their journey. When the moment of parting came, he was quite unable to speak. A strict Calvinist who even refused to celebrate Christmas because it smacked of 'popery', he cannot have been an easy colleague, but no one who knew him could deny his goodness of heart or his unwavering faith.

Soon after their departure the first of the Muslim revolts erupted, and by the end of 1932 the citizens of Urumchi realised they were in danger of being cut off by Big Horse and his rebels. More and more people began to take refuge inside the city walls and this led to friction between the different ethnic communities and to a shortage of basic supplies. Traders no longer dared venture forth with caravans, even from nearby villages. Aitchen Wu describes the worsening situation:

> The tension within the walls was becoming acute, for refugees were of all faiths, and as they were crowded together there was every possibility that fighting might break out among them. Moreover, every Moslem was a possible spy, which fact increased our anxiety. Mr Hunter, the benign and elderly representative of the China Inland Mission, who for forty years had worked unceasingly in Tihwa (not with much success so far as converts were concerned, but always for the general good), was very anxious when I called upon him, and confessed himself more apprehensive concerning racial hatreds within our walls than hostile armies without.

Wu struggled 'to preserve detachment of outlook', and forced himself to copy out useful extracts from the *Illustrated Encyclopedia of Sinkiang*. But at dawn on 21 February 1933 he was awoken by the sound of heavy shell-fire:

> The enemy had advanced towards the city under cover of night and had attacked the Great West Bridge which, after strong resistance, the Government troops had been forced to abandon to them. General Pai, who was directing the defence, had only seven hundred troops, but just as things had appeared desperate, a body of some three hundred White Russians, newly arrived in Tihwa and hastily armed, had flung into the fray ...

The White Russians were splendid fighters, but they suffered from moods of savage melancholy in which they drank recklessly and would then tolerate no discipline. They were thus a source of anxiety at times, but it cannot be denied that without them Tihwa might have fallen. Their counter-attack which won back the slopes of Red Mountain was a triumph of disciplined fury. Opposed to them were fierce Moslems and Tungans, aflame with religious zeal and intent upon winning the paradise of true believers; yet the White Russians outdid them in boldness and wild endurance. On foot no less than on horseback they carried all before them, and on the second night of the fighting they were retaining the ground that they had won.

For those refugees who had not found a place inside the city walls, however, the situation was 'indescribably awful', for according to Wu thousands had been caught between the opposing forces. Outside the west gate ran a street which was normally one of Urumchi's most prosperous but was now 'crowded with innocent fugitives, whose plight was terrible indeed'.

There was worse to come, however, for now the advancing rebels came to this quarter and seizing the houses made loop-holes in the walls. On the flat roofs they set up machine-gun posts which could enfilade Government positions on either side of them. I could see for myself that the situation was desperate and that our troops would be penned against the walls. General Pai did not hesitate. He gave the order that the street should be set on fire.

Then followed a scene so frightful that to describe it is not possible. As the flames swept down the long lane of wooden structures they became an inferno of horror, for the roar of the conflagration was added to the rattle of gun-fire, and the hideous shrieks of those who were trapped. The rebels sought safety in flight, and as they crossed the open were machine-gunned from the Red Mountain. But the fugitives had nowhere to fly to and perished to the last man, woman and child. Nevertheless the city was saved, and when at last the flames died down the approach to the West Bridge was strewn with the bodies of our assailants.

But the lull that followed was accompanied by cold and near starvation, for still the caravans were not getting through, and the nomads had fled with their flocks to the hills. Aitchen Wu and his colleagues from the Chinese capital, who had come simply as advisers, began to organise the burying of the dead. Putrefying corpses were heaped up everywhere, and they realised that it would only need a few days of mild weather for epidemics to break out.

> We worked long hours in frost and mud, thrusting into the last embrace of earth Moslem and Buddhist, Tungan and Mongol, their savage hatreds now blotted out by death. I found myself wondering as we worked, why had all these human creatures died? Not for a cause, not even in the winning of their desires. In attacking Tihwa the Moslems had probably slain more of their own faith than of unbelievers, as the mounting totals in my diary showed.

Wu was greatly helped in his relief activities by George Hunter and the other European missionaries in Urumchi, including of course Percy Mather – now returned – who helped to run an emergency hospital for the wounded. Before long the wounded were outnumbered by the sick, for the battered city was struck by what Wu had feared most, a typhoid epidemic. The missionaries worked night and day to nurse the victims and two of them died of the disease themselves. One was a young doctor and the other was Mather, Hunter's cheerful companion and assistant since 1914. The grateful government donated a small plot of land for the Christian burial of the two men, and Mildred Cable recounts how 'the first anguished period of George Hunter's loneliness was spent in building with his own hands the wall which kept the ravening wolves from prowling round the graves'. Hunter had loved the much younger Mather like a son, although even after eighteen years together they had still addressed each other as 'Mr Mather' and 'Mr Hunter'.

The horrors of the Muslim rebellion were blamed by many people on the corrupt and incompetent Governor Chin, whose misrule had allowed Sinkiang to slide into chaos. In a coup masterminded by the White Russians – whose arms he had tried to confiscate – he was replaced early in 1933 by a Manchurian soldier, General Sheng, who had fought the rebels ruthlessly in other parts of the province. Sheng knew that Urumchi was still in grave danger for young Ma Chung-yin had simply withdrew his forces while he recovered from a gunshot wound, and it was only a matter of time before he returned to attack the capital. Because of the enormous distances involved, it was well-nigh impossible for the government troops in one Central Asian town to come to the aid of another – if indeed they even knew what was happening. Not far from Urumchi entire villages had been put to the sword, and this was only discovered by chance when a German engineer building airstrips in Sinkiang came across some grisly remains one moonlit night:

> As we advanced farther we were dazzled by the mirror-like expanse of a salt lake of seemingly limitless length and about twenty miles broad. The spell which the magnificent panorama unfolding before my eyes cast over me was rudely broken by a cry of horror from Kranich. Following the direction of his gaze I saw that both sides of the road were densely strewn with corpses – the aftermath of the battles which had raged in this region. That majestic valley in which the great silvery lake was embedded, one of the most wonderful sights in Central Asia, was one vast necropolis. Wherever I looked, to the right or to the left, before me or behind me, I saw piles of mummified bodies. There they lay scattered about in the most gruesome and fantastic postures, some huddled together in indistinguishable heaps, some leaning towards one another as though they were chatting, some lying like scarecrows athwart the stunted bushes, their tattered garments billowing in the wind.
>
> Georg Vasel, *My Russian Jailers in China*, 1937

Deeply shocked, the young German and his White Russian driver returned to their lorry and continued their journey, only to find the same ghastly sights at the next village.

It was not long before Big Horse again turned his attention to the capital, and in June 1933 General Sheng was sufficiently worried to consider negotiating with the enemy. Aitchen Wu was unanimously chosen as envoy, being a scholar and man of peace, although he admits in his memoirs that he was most reluctant to take on this dangerous mission, fearing that he would simply be taken hostage. The leading Turki merchant of Urumchi, a much-respected elder, volunteered to accompany him:

'It is your duty,' he said, 'to go.' I protested that I had no official status whatever. 'My friend,' he said, 'our highest duties are appointed by God.' I knew that he was right, and I felt ashamed that I had so long sought to evade this dangerous task. 'Very well,' I said, 'I will go.' 'I will go with you,' said Hussein. 'Never will I leave your side, and my life shall be a pledge for your safety.' I knew that I could trust his word.

They set out for Kucheng, hearing on the way that Ma had just ordered the massacre of scores of Russian and Mongolian prisoners. Daunted but undeterred by this chilling news, they continued 'into the tiger's lair', as Wu put it, only too aware that summary execution might lie ahead. In the event the 23-year-old warlord received them courteously, and Wu felt that 'there was good in this man', although his grandiose dreams of a great Muslim empire had undoubtedly led him into folly. The negotiations, however, proved inconclusive and although they were able to glean some useful military intelligence they returned to Urumchi without any sort of guarantee of its safety. An uneasy truce ensued, but when Ma moved his forces nearer to the capital Governor Sheng felt obliged to turn for help to the one source which was only too willing and able to assist him: Soviet Russia. The price was a high one, for Sinkiang became for a while a virtual province of the Soviet Union, but Big Horse was put to flight.

The Red regime brought its own reign of terror, with waves of arbitrary arrests and imprisonments, and psychological as well as physical torture. Georg Vasel was an early victim, arrested in 1934 in spite of his Herculean efforts to build airstrips, for as a German he was regarded as a Fascist by the Bolsheviks. George Hunter, the missionary, now old and frail, spent thirteen nightmarish months in jail in the early 1940s while every conceivable effort was made to break him. He survived, but was never again to see his beloved adoptive home in Urumchi, and died in Kanchow at the end of 1946. The plight of the White Russians was perhaps the saddest of all. Some in desperation joined the Reds, others hung on in anxious penury, many simply disappeared. Diana Shipton, wife of the British Consul-General in Kashgar, visited Urumchi in 1947:

As we drove into the outskirts of the capital on a blustering October day, I thought it a miserable place. The three weeks I stayed there, in early winter, did nothing to alter my first impression. It had all the depressing characteristics of a semi-westernized town, none of the charm of a frankly native one. The main street was flanked by solid, two-storeyed buildings. There were shops with counters; there were pavements, and policemen on point duty. But all this seemed an uncertain, pathetic facade. The essential primitiveness showed through the veneer all the time. Poor Chinese struck me as much more dirty and dilapidated than poor Turkis. The sight of White Russians, reduced to a humble misery, was startling. The tragedy behind the exile of these people haunted me. Immediately outside the main gates of the town an ugly, tumbledown, haphazard bazaar broke out like a rash. The main impression was one of dirt; an impression I never had of Kashgar, in spite of its mud houses, poky little shops and dust. Perhaps knowledge of evil things done in this town, of political intrigue and murder, coloured my feelings. People said it was easier to get into Urumchi than to get out of it. No sooner had we arrived than I began planning to leave.

Diana Shipton, *The Antique Land*, 1950

By the time Basil Davidson, the left-wing writer, visited Urumchi in 1956 the town had shed even more of its 'native' character. Most of the old city walls had been pulled down, there were asphalt roads to replace the mud and mire described by Sven Hedin, and sixteen Skoda buses had taken the place of camels and droshkies. Since then the march of 'progress' has been unrelenting, and today Urumchi is simply a vast modern sprawl. But the visitor who is interested will still find a few traces of the earlier city. Most of the mosques are very modern, but the one in Nanmen Square – in the elaborate Chinese style – dates back to 1906, when George Hunter was just beginning his ministry. There are still Turki markets in the south of the city, and from the pagodas and viewing platforms of the Red Hill you can see the town spread out below you, as Aitchen Wu did in the New Year of 1933 when he arrived in Urumchi so full of hope for its future.

THREE MODERN CAPITALS
Alma Ata, Bishkek and Dushanbe

A fine thing in Alma Ata was the snow, white, clean and dry.
As there was very little walking or driving, it kept its freshness
all winter long. In the spring, it yielded to red poppies. Such
a lot of them – like gigantic carpets! The steppes glowed red
for miles around.

Natalya Trotsky, 1927

ALMA ATA, CAPITAL of Kazakhstan, is now a large modern city
in a beautiful situation. Standing 2,600 feet above sea-level
in the northern foothills of the Zailisky Alatau mountains, facing
the vast Kazakh Steppe, it has an extreme climate ranging from
40 degrees centigrade (104°F) in summer to minus 34 degrees
centigrade (–28°F) in winter. Mount Kok-Tyubeh, which can
be ascended by cable-car, gives a panoramic view over the city.
However, Alma Ata began as a small trading post, the Kazakh
settlement of Almaty.

During the nineteenth century Imperial Russia expanded
steadily south-eastwards, ostensibly as a 'civilising mission' to the
Kazakh nomads but also as a means of easing the pressure for land
in central Russia. (The emancipation of the serfs in 1861 led to
agricultural chaos, with most peasants working uneconomic plots
for which they were heavily mortgaged.) A Russian fortress was
built at Almaty in 1854, around which Cossack colonists erected
homes and planted their crops. The surrounding region, between
the mountains and Lake Balkash, was known by the number of
rivers which flowed north into the long thin lake: Semirechia, or

Seven Rivers Land. Over the next ten years or so, a regular Russian town grew up and in 1867 it was given the new name of Vierney.

Much of Vierney was destroyed by a severe earthquake in 1887, and after that only small wooden buildings were erected and the town declined. In fact by the end of the century Vierney was mainly used as a place of exile for political prisoners. The writer Stephen Graham passed through in 1914 and left the following description:

> It is not necessary to say much about Vierney, the capital of Seven Rivers Land. It is so subject to earthquakes that it is difficult to see in it a permanent capital. No houses of two storeys can with safety be built, so it is more suited to remain a military centre and fortress than to be a great city. In order to look imposing, shops and stores have fixed up sham upper storeys; that is, they have window-fronts up above, but no rooms behind the fronts ... Vierney has its bazaar, its inns and doubtful houses, its baths, dance halls, clubs, restaurants. It has no Bond Street or West End. One may say, however, that it has its Covent Garden. Vierney is a great market for fruit and vegetables ... Carts heaped high with giant red radishes are driven through the town, and the strawberry hawkers make many cries. Many horses are adorned with fancy garments, and I noticed donkeys with trousers on.
>
> Graham, *Through Russian Central Asia*, 1916

After the Bolshevik Revolution Vierney was renamed Alma Ata (City of Apples) and in 1929 became the capital of the new Soviet Socialist Republic of Kazakhstan. Leon Trotsky was banished to Alma Ata in 1927, having lost his battle for the leadership with Stalin, and lived there for a year with his wife. Although it was an anxious and unhappy time for them, increasingly cut off from all links with the outside world, Natalya Trotsky left some vivid descriptions:

> The town had no central waterworks, no lights, and no paved roads. In the bazaar in the centre of the town, the Kazakhs sat in the mud at the doorsteps of their shops, warming themselves in the sun and searching their bodies for lice. Malaria was rampant. There was also plague, and during the summer months an extraordinary number of

mad dogs. The newspapers reported many cases of leprosy in this region. In spite of all this, we spent a good summer. We rented a peasant house from a fruit-grower up on the hills with an open view of the snow-capped mountains, a spur of the Tien-shan range. With the owner and his family, we watched the fruit ripen and took an active part in gathering it. The orchard was a picture of change. First the white blossom, then the trees grew heavy, with bending branches help up by props. Then the fruit lay in a motley carpet under the trees on straw mats, and the trees, rid of their burden, straightened their branches again. The orchard was fragrant with the ripe apples and pears.

In 1929 Trotsky was deported from the Soviet Union, and lived a haunted existence in a number of countries before being dispatched by an ice-pick through the skull in Mexico in 1940.

Towards the end of the 1920s modern buildings began to be erected in Alma Ata, in the Constructivist style then favoured in the Soviet Union. The most ambitious was the massive complex of government buildings designed by the architect M. Ginzburg, who was clearly influenced by Le Corbusier. The style did not find favour with Stalin, however, and was suppressed during the 1930s as politically incorrect.

The completion of the Turksib railway in 1930 connected Alma Ata with the main rail networks of the Soviet Union, greatly aiding the town's development. By the 1940s the streets had been paved and a sewage system installed, and a number of hydro-electric schemes provided the town with light and power. Trams, buses and lorries had replaced the peasant carts which were the only form of transport in Stephen Graham's day, and despite his prediction Alma Ata has become not only a permanent capital but also a heavily industrialised city. Because of its situation it has, in addition, become a centre for mountaineering expeditions.

BISHKEK, the capital of Kirghizstan, was until recently called Frunze, after the well-known Bolshevik general who was born there, but it originated as the native fortress of Pishpek. This had been built by the Khan of Khokhand in 1852, but was captured by the Russians in 1862 in the course of their expansion into Central Asia, and transformed into a military settlement. In 1878 Pishpek was declared a town, but being of little economic or political importance it hardly developed at all. Caravanserais, tea-houses and native dwellings clustered around the old fortress, which soon fell into disrepair. By 1913 it was still a conglomeration of mud-brick houses, roofed with cane-rushes and having a population of only 18,000. Its sole claim to fame was as the market town for the surrounding region. Most Kirghiz were still nomadic and lived in circular yurts, only riding into town to visit the large bazaar or the tea-houses.

But after the Bolshevik Revolution all this changed. Pishpek, by now renamed Frunze, became the capital of the Kirghiz Soviet Republic in 1928 and was connected to the Turksib railway. Asphalt streets were laid out in a neat grid, and water mains and electricity were introduced. The Kirghiz began to be collectivised, and by 1939 the population had risen to 93,000. During and after the Second World War the town became steadily more industrialised, and by 1992 the population had leaped to 670,000.

Like Alma Ata, 180 miles to the east, Bishkek is dominated by snow-capped peaks to the south (the Kirghiz Alatau) and endless steppe to the north. Its altitude is about 2,500 feet and its climate extreme. The Trotsky family, on their way to exile in Alma Ata, climbed down from the train at Frunze (then the end of the line) on a freezing January morning in 1927. 'There was a biting frost,' wrote Natalya Trotsky. 'The sun's rays pouring on the clean white snow blinded us. We were given felt boots and sheepskins. I could hardly breathe for the weight of my clothes, and yet it was cold on the road. The autobus moved slowly over the creaking snow packed down by vehicles; the wind lashed our faces.'

About 100 miles east of Bishkek is Lake Issyk-Kul – 2,230 square miles of salt lake which, despite its altitude of 5,000 feet, never freezes. Volcanic activity beneath the surface heats the water all the year round, and one of the translations of the name is 'Warm Lake'. On the south-east shore stands a huge memorial, surmounted by an eagle, to the great explorer Nikolai Prejevalsky. He died of typhoid there in 1888 during his last expedition to the Tien-shan mountains, aged only 49.

DUSHANBE, the mountain-ringed capital of Tajikistan, stands 2,700 feet above sea-level, on the banks of the river Dyushambinka. It is a modern city, built on the site of three villages, one of which was called Dyushambe – 'Monday' in Tajik – after its weekly market. In 1929 it was linked by rail with Termez, on the Afghan frontier, and thus by a roundabout route with the old Transcaspian railway, a dramatic improvement for a town whose previous communications with the outside world had been largely by camel. That same year it was renamed Stalinabad and declared the capital of the newly formed Tajik Soviet Socialist Republic. After Stalin's death, the gradual revelation of his atrocities led to a flurry of name-changing, and the city reverted to a version of its earlier name.

Dushanbe was a temporary refuge for the last Emir of Bokhara, who fled there in 1920 after being overthrown by the Bolsheviks. In his haste he had left behind his harem, but he tried to delay his pursuers by dropping off comely dancing-boys from time to time. What the Bolsheviks made of these symbols of decadence is not recorded, but a Communist writer has described the shocked disillusion of the Emir's former subjects as he travelled through their villages on his way to Dushanbe:

> The first day, peasants by the thousands milled around the house where the Emir was lodged, anxious to get at least one glimpse at the divine being they so often blessed in their Friday prayers. By the end of the second day, however, there was not a peasant left. They had all sought refuge in the villages, hiding their young wives and daughters, smearing dung over the faces of the prettiest youngsters.
>
> Joshua Kunitz, *Dawn Over Samarkand*, 1936

The infamous Emir conceded defeat in 1921 and retired to Afghanistan.

In 1922 Dushanbe experienced high drama, for it was briefly captured by Enver Pasha and the *basmachi*. The latter were Muslim freedom-fighters who looked to Turkey for their salvation, in the face of first Russian and then Bolshevik oppression. During the First World War, Muslim peasants from Central Asia were conscripted into the Russian army, leaving no one to till the land or harvest the crops, and this caused resentment and uprisings in 1916. Things were no better under the Bolsheviks, who requisitioned the farmers' stores of food and cotton, precipitating a famine in which 100,000 people are believed to have perished. The brutal Tashkent Soviet alienated the entire Muslim population of Central Asia in 1918 when they sacked the ancient town of Khokhand, and ruthlessly suppressed an uprising in Tashkent itself. More and more flocked to the *basmachi* banner – probably 20,000 all told – though they were disorganised and had no single leader. For several years they harassed the Bolsheviks with sabotage, ambushes and assassinations, but once the Communists had disposed of not only the White Russians but all their socialist opponents as well, they were able to devote more attention to crushing the *basmachi* movement. Capable generals like Mikhail Frunze were drafted into the area in 1920 and began to close in on the partisans.

By 1921 the movement seemed doomed. But then Enver Pasha, Turkey's former military supremo who had been disgraced after dragging his country into the First World War, turned up unexpectedly in Central Asia. Lenin, the arch-manipulator, planned to use this charismatic figure who was still revered by many Muslims to steer the natives away from dangerous ideas of nationalism and into the Communist fold. What Lenin did not realise was that Enver, although a military man, was also a dreamer, easily fired by heady ideas. So moved was he at being in the ancient cradle of Turkish civilisation that he soon slipped away from his Bolshevik minders and joined the rebels as their leader.

This gave a tremendous boost to the *basmachi* movement, and the neighbouring King Amanullah of Afghanistan began covertly supplying them with arms and trained soldiers. Both Enver and Amanullah had visions of a vast pan-Islamic empire encompassing both Turkey and Afghanistan, and most of the Central Asian states of Russia and China, though both privately planned to be its emperor. Few of the rank-and-file *basmachi* shared this grandiose dream, of course, simply wanting freedom from oppression and exploitation.

At first Enver was wildly successful and the Bolsheviks were seriously worried. In February 1922 he captured Dushanbe, and by the spring he controlled much of the old Emirate of Bokhara. The Bolsheviks even sent a 'peace delegation' to try and arrange a settlement, but Enver refused and 100,000 more troops were sent by

Moscow to crush the movement for good. As the tide turned against Enver, Amanullah withdrew his aid and his soldiers – a cruel blow – and many of the *basmachi* themselves began to drift back to their villages. But Enver and his core of loyal supporters refused either to surrender or to flee. They made their last stand in August near the Tajik village of Abiderya, dying in a hail of machine-gun bullets. The local mullah retrieved Enver's body and buried him beside the river in an unmarked grave. The Bolsheviks quickly reasserted their authority in Dushanbe and the Bokhara region, and the *basmachi* again became guerrilla bands, uncoordinated and leaderless, easily dismissed by the Bolsheviks as mere bandits.

Dushanbe was developed and industrialised during the Soviet period, and like other Central Asian cities it saw a great influx of industry from western parts of the Soviet Union during the Second World War. As a result its population increased by leaps and bounds: 5,600 in 1927, 42,000 in 1933 and over 100,000 in 1945. (It is now in the region of 600,000.)

Few Westerners had the chance to visit Dushanbe in the post-war period, but an exception was made for Mr and Mrs W. Coates, an elderly London couple sympathetic to the regime, who were taken on a VIP tour of Central Asia in 1949. It was a seven-day rail journey from Moscow to Dushanbe in those days, but they were rewarded by seeing the city from afar, rising in terraces from the river bank to the foothills of the Ghissar mountains, and overlooked by massive snow-capped peaks. Their favourable impression continued when they arrived:

> The visitor cannot but be delighted at his first acquaintance with Stalinabad, as he alights at the large station, built in Eastern style. On the square he sees the usual modern means of conveyance – buses and cabs – inviting Eastern tea-rooms, pleasant and airy restaurants, and the shady boulevard bordered by the murmuring *aryks* (canals). The first pleasant impression is heightened as the visitor proceeds through the city. The streets are wide, straight and lined with greenery – many of them are, in fact, delightful shady boulevards, with rows of trees and *aryks* running the entire length.
>
> W.P. and Zelda K. Coates, *Soviets in Central Asia*, 1951

Today foreigners are brought in by air, but the proximity of the mountains makes the descent into Dushanbe a spectacular one. The Tajiks are a beautiful race, of Persian origin and speaking a Persian language. In the big covered market north of the Hotel Tajikistan they can still be seen wearing their national dress and in something like their traditional surroundings. Unhappily, at the time of writing, Dushanbe – like Tajikistan as a whole – is racked by political conflict, with this new nation facing an uncertain future.

Principal Sources

Literally hundreds of books on the various aspects of Central Asia have been published over the last two centuries. The following are simply those I found the most useful in compiling this book, and certainly do not constitute a comprehensive bibliography. Many are long out of print and prohibitively expensive when occasionally they turn up in the catalogues of specialist book-dealers, but they can sometimes be borrowed through the public library system. Happily a number have been reprinted in paperback, while of course the more recent ones can still be found in good bookshops. I have marked with an asterisk those which I particularly recommend as a starting-point for the general reader. Except where otherwise indicated they were published in London.

Abbott, Major James, *Narrative of a Journey from Heraut to Khiva, Moscow & St Petersburg, during the late Russian Invasion of Khiva*, 1843.
* Bailey, Colonel F.M., *Mission to Tashkent*, 1946.
Barthold, W., *Turkestan down to the Mongol Invasion*, 1928.
Blunt, Wilfrid, *The Golden Road to Samarkand*, 1973.
Bookwalter, John W., *Siberia and Central Asia*, Ohio, 1899.
Boulangier, Edgar, *Voyage à Merv*, Paris, 1888.
* Boulnois, L., *The Silk Road*, 1966.
Brun, Captain A.H., *Troublous Times*, 1931.
* Burnaby, Captain Frederick, *A Ride to Khiva. Travels and Adventures in Central Asia*, 1876.
Burnes, Sir Alexander, *Travels into Bokhara*, 1834.
* Cable, Mildred, and Francesca French, *The Gobi Desert*, 1942.
—— *George Hunter, Apostle of Turkestan*, 1948.
Carruthers, Douglas, *Beyond the Caspian*, 1949.
* Christie, Ella, *Through Khiva to Golden Samarkand*, 1925.
Clavijo, Don Ruy Gonzales de, *Narrative of the Embassy of Don Clavijo to the Court of Timur at Samarkand 1403–6*, Hakluyt Society, 1859.

Craig-McKerrow, Margaret, *The Iron Road to Samarkand*, 1932.

* Curzon, George, *Russia in Central Asia*, 1889.

Czaplicka, M.A., *The Turks of Central Asia*, 1918.

Davidson, Basil, *Turkestan Alive*, 1957.

Durand, Colonel Algernon, *The Making of a Frontier. Five Years' Experience and Adventures in Gilgit, Hunza, Nagar, Chitral and the Eastern Hindu Kush*, 1899.

Ellis, Colonel C.H., *The Transcaspian Episode*, 1963.

Etherton, Colonel P.T., *In the Heart of Asia*, 1925.

Fa-hsien, *The Travels of Fa-hsien*, trans. H.A. Giles, 1923.

* Fleming, Peter, *News from Tartary*, 1936.

Forbes, Rosita, *Forbidden Road – Kabul to Samarkand*, 1937.

Graham, Stephen, *Through Russian Central Asia*, 1916.

Hedin, Sven, *Through Asia*, 1898.

—— *Across the Gobi Desert*, 1931.

—— *Big Horse's Flight. The Trail of War in Central Asia*, 1936.

* Hopkirk, Peter, *Foreign Devils on the Silk Road*, 1980.

* —— *Setting the East Ablaze*, 1984.

* —— *The Great Game*, 1990.

—— *On Secret Service East of Constantinople*, in preparation.

Hsuan-tsang, *Buddhist Records of the Western World*, trans. Samuel Beal, from the Chinese of Hiuen-tsiang AD 629, 1884.

Ignatiev, N.P., *Mission to Khiva and Bokhara in 1858*, ed. and trans. Prof. John L. Evans, Oriental Research Partners, Newtonville, Ma., 1984.

Jarring, Gunnar, *Return to Kashgar*, 1986.

Jefferson, Robert, *A New Ride to Khiva*, 1899.

* Keay, John, *The Gilgit Game*, 1979.

Ker, David, *On the Road to Khiva*, 1874.

Khanikoff, Nikolai, *Bokhara: Its Amir and Its People*, 1845.

* Knight, E.F., *Where Three Empires Meet*, 1895.

Kunitz, Joshua, *Dawn over Samarkand*, 1936.

Lansdell, Revd Henry, *Russian Central Asia*, 1885.

Lattimore, Owen, *High Tartary*, Boston, 1930.

Le Coq, Albert von, *Buried Treasures of Chinese Turkestan*, 1928.

Le Messurier, Colonel A., *From London to Bokhara*, 1889.

* Macartney, Lady, *An English Lady in Chinese Turkestan*, 1931.

MacGahan, J.A., *Campaigning on the Oxus and the Fall of Khiva*, 1874.

* Maclean, Fitzroy, *Eastern Approaches*, 1949.

* —— *A Person from England*, 1958.
* Maillart, Ella, *Turkestan Solo*, 1934.
—— *Forbidden Journey*, 1937.
Mannin, Ethel, *South to Samarkand*, 1936.
Marvin, Charles, *The Russian Campaign against the Turcomans*, 1880.
—— *Merv, the Queen of the World, and the Scourge of the Man-Stealing Turcomans*, 1881.
Meakin, Annette, *In Russian Turkestan*, 1903.
Nazaroff, Paul, *Hunted through Central Asia*, 1932.
—— *Moved On! From Kashgar to Kashmir*, 1935.
O'Donovan, Edmond, *The Merv Oasis*, 1882.
Olufsen, Professor O., *The Emir of Bokhara and his Country*, 1911.
Pahlen, Count K.K., *Mission to Turkestan 1908–9*, 1964.
Perowne, J.T. Woolrych, *Russian Hosts and English Guests in Central Asia*, 1898.
Polo, Marco, *The Book of Ser Marco Polo*, trans. and ed., with notes, Sir Henry Yule, 1903.
Polovtsoff, Alexander, *The Land of Timur*, 1932.
Roy, M.N., *Memoirs*, 1964.
Schuyler, Eugene, *Turkistan*, 1876.
Shakespear, Captain Sir Richmond, 'A Personal Narrative of a Journey from Herat to Orenburg, on the Caspian, in 1840', *Blackwood's Magazine*, June 1842.
* Shipton, Diana, *The Antique Land*, 1950.
Shoemaker, M.M., *Trans-Caspia, The Sealed Provinces of the Czar*, Cincinnati, 1895.
—— *The Heart of the Orient*, New York, 1904.
Skobelev, General M.D., *Official Report on the Siege and Assault of Denghil-Tepe*, trans. Lt. J.J. Leverson RE, 1881.
Skrine, C.P., *Chinese Central Asia*, 1926.
—— and Pamela Nightingale, *Macartney at Kashgar*, 1973.
Skrine, Francis, and E. Denison Ross, *The Heart of Asia*, 1899.
Staley, John, *Words for My Brother*, 1982.
Stein, Sir Aurel, *Sand-Buried Ruins of Khotan*, 1903.
—— *Ruins of Desert Cathay*, 1912.
* —— *On Central Asian Tracks*, 1964.
Sykes, Miss Ella and Sir Percy, *Through Deserts and Oasis of Central Asia*, 1920.

* Teague-Jones, Reginald, *The Spy Who Disappeared*, Prologue by Peter Hopkirk, 1990.

Teichman, Sir Eric, *Journey to Turkistan*, 1937.

* Trevelyan, Raleigh, *The Golden Oriole: Childhood, Family and Friends in India*, 1987.

Vambery, Arminius, *Travels in Central Asia*, 1864.

—— *Sketches of Central Asia*, 1868.

—— *History of Bokhara*, 1873.

Vasel, Georg, *My Russian Jailers in China*, 1937.

Vincent, Irene, *The Sacred Oasis*, 1953.

Warner, Langdon, *The Long Old Road in China*, Arrowsmith, 1927.

Wolff, Revd Joseph, *Narrative of a Mission to Bokhara*, 1889.

Wu, Aitchen K., *Turkistan Tumult*, 1940.

* Younghusband, Captain Francis, *The Heart of a Continent*, 1896.

Index

ELAND

61 Exmouth Market, London EC1R 4QL
Email: info@travelbooks.co.uk

Eland was started thirty years ago to revive great travel books which had fallen out of print. Although the list soon diversified into biography and fiction, all the titles are chosen for their interest in spirit of place. One of our readers explained that for him reading an Eland is like listening to an experienced anthropologist at the bar – she's let her hair down and is telling all the stories that were just too good to go into the textbook.

Eland books are for travellers, and for those who are content to travel in their own minds. They open out our understanding of other cultures, interpret the unknown and reveal different environments, as well as celebrating the humour and occasional horrors of travel. We take immense trouble to select only the most readable books and many readers collect the entire series of one hundred titles.

Extracts from each and every one of our books can be read on our website, at www.travelbooks.co.uk. If you would like a free copy of our catalogue, please order it from the website, email us or send a postcard.